Landing Page Optimization

FOR

DUMMIES®

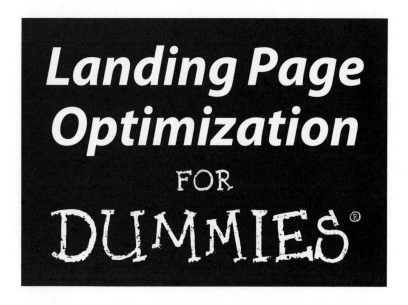

Landing Page Optimization FOR DUMMIES®

by Martin Harwood and Mike Harwood

WILEY

Wiley Publishing, Inc.

Landing Page Optimization For Dummies®

Published by
Wiley Publishing, Inc.
111 River Street
Hoboken, NJ 07030-5774
www.wiley.com

WILEY

About the Authors

Martin Harwood has 15 years experience in Web development and design. In that time, he has managed Wavefire Technologies, a publicly traded company that specializes in Internet marketing technologies. From this experience, he's worked as a consultant in e-commerce, landing page design, and development.

For more information on Martin Harwood's background and experience, visit www.anthillpress.com.

Mike Harwood (MCSE, A+, Network+, Server+, Linux+) has more than ten years experience working in information technology and related fields. In that time, he's held a number of roles within IT, including network administrator, instructor, technical writer, Web site designer, consultant, and online marketing strategist. He's been a regular on-air technology contributor for CBC Radio and has authored numerous computer books.

Dedication

Martin Harwood: I dedicate this book to the entrepreneurs who have had to learn it the hard way and their families that have to put up with their eccentricities, including my own family: Jolene, Lee, Justin and, of course, my parents.

Mike Harwood: As always, I dedicate this book to my three amazing daughters, Breanna, Paige, and Delaney, who fill me with pride each day; and to my adorable and loving wife, Linda, who keeps me structured, supported, and always amused.

Authors' Acknowledgments

Rarely an easy process, the creation of a book requires the talents and dedication of a number of people. With that in mind, we thank the folks at Wiley for their work on this project.

Specifically, we thank Kyle Looper for overseeing the project and keeping the ball rolling, Paul Levesque for his patient editing, and our editors — Jen Riggs, copy editor, and Paul Chaney, technical editor — for their gentle corrections that helped to make the text flow smoothly. If we are fortunate enough to write another *For Dummies* title, we'd love to work with these folks again.

A special thanks to Selkirk College's English Professor Linda Harwood (who's also Mike's wife) for her content contributions. She's been teaching college composition, literature, and business communications for the last 16 years, so when it comes to the writing process, we knew she was the one to bug.

Finally, we're thankful to our friends and family who once again had to put up with the late hours and book-related ramblings.

Publisher's Acknowledgments

We're proud of this book; please send us your comments at http://dummies.custhelp.com. For other comments, please contact our Customer Care Department within the U.S. at 877-762-2974, outside the U.S. at 317-572-3993, or fax 317-572-4002. Some of the people who helped bring this book to market include the following:

Acquisitions and Editorial

Senior Project Editor: Paul Levesque

Acquisitions Editor: Kyle Looper

Copy Editor: Jen Riggs

Technical Editor: Paul Chaney

Editorial Manager: Leah Cameron

Editorial Assistant: Amanda Graham

Sr. Editorial Assistant: Cherie Case

Cartoons: Rich Tennant
(www.the5thwave.com)

Composition Services

Project Coordinator: Katherine Crocker

Layout and Graphics: Joyce Haughey, Mark Pinto, Christin Swinford, Ronald G. Terry

Proofreader: Linda Seifert

Indexer: Potomac Indexing, LLC

Publishing and Editorial for Technology Dummies

 Richard Swadley, Vice President and Executive Group Publisher

 Andy Cummings, Vice President and Publisher

 Mary Bednarek, Executive Acquisitions Director

 Mary C. Corder, Editorial Director

Publishing for Consumer Dummies

 Diane Graves Steele, Vice President and Publisher

Composition Services

 Debbie Stailey, Director of Composition Services

Contents at a Glance

Table of Contents

Introduction

$\bullet\,\bullet$

Sounds simple; come up with a product, create your landing page, relax, and count the money. If only real life was that easy! Alas, with billions of Web sites competing for attention, marketing online is not simple at all.

On the other hand, marketing online isn't rocket science. This book charts a practical course of action to put your *landing page* — that first page visitors see when they click an online ad or search engine result link — to work for you. Whether you're just beginning to develop an online presence or you've been online for years and are anxious to build traffic, this book helps you drive prospects to your site and convert them into customers.

Landing Page Optimization For Dummies leverages and enhances your knowledge of marketing to the point that you can establish and build a successful, income-generating online business. Because we've written this book specifically for those who want to enhance their landing page presence, you're going to find a boatload of strategies you need to get those all important conversions.

No simple formula says that shoe companies should use this Web marketing method and architects should use that one. We urge you to keep a picture of your customers or clients in mind while you read this book. If you always ask whether a particular method would appeal to your target audience, you'll make the right decisions. Answer your customers' question, "What's in it for me?" and your Web marketing plan will work magic for you.

About This Book

This book is a reference guide to landing page optimization. We wrote it how we write good Web copy: short sentences, short paragraphs, short chapters, with lots of bullets and tables so you can find information quickly.

Please look at the pretty pictures. Not only do they save you thousands worth of words to read, but they're good examples of what you want to accomplish.

Dip in to a chapter when you confront a particular problem with landing page marketing to find the information you need right then and there. The rest can wait.

This book is intended for business people, not techies. Whenever we present technical information, we do so in a friendly manner, making it easy to understand and directly applicable.

Conventions Used in This Book

Doing something the same way over and over again can be boring, but consistency makes stuff easier to understand. In this book, those consistent elements are *conventions*. Here are the main ones:

- ✔ When *URLs* (Web addresses) appear within a paragraph, caption, or table, they look like this: `www.dummies.com`.
- ✔ New terms appear in *italics* the first time they're used, courtesy of the copy editor (see *URLs* in the preceding bullet if you don't believe us).
- ✔ Anything you have to type is in **bold**, but frankly, you don't have to type much. Mostly, you just have to think.

Fortunately, landing page optimization is platform- and operating-system independent. Whether you're on a Mac with OS X or a PC running Windows Vista doesn't matter, but we do recommend a high-speed Internet connection. You can no longer realistically monitor your landing page, upload content, review statistics, or research your market at turtle speed (also known as *dialup*).

What You Don't Have to Read

You don't have to read anything that seems irrelevant to your business! You can scoot past any content that isn't applicable directly to your landing page goals. Be careful not to skip too much, however, because you'll find helpful tips and tricks spread throughout the book. A few of these tips can have a real impact on your overall conversion rate.

The book is designed as *modular;* that is, you can pick it up, flip to any page, and start reading. However, you can also read this book from cover to cover because we made it flow sequentially as well. As much as you may be tempted to skip some of the more seemingly mundane elements, such as creating a landing page business plan, all the content you find between this book's covers is in some way, part of your landing optimization strategy.

Foolish Assumptions

In our heads, we constructed a picture of you, the reader. We assume you (or your designated staff member) already

- ✔ Have a computer with high-speed Internet access.

- ✔ Are (or soon will be) an owner or a department manager in a small-to-mid-size business.

- ✔ Have (or plan to write) a business plan.

- ✔ Frequently use standard applications, such as Word and Excel, e-mail, and browsers.

- ✔ Are comfortable searching the Web by using keywords and search engines.

- ✔ Can write and do basic arithmetic, especially when dollar signs are involved.

- ✔ Have a passion for your business and a commitment to providing excellent customer service.

If our assumptions are incorrect, you'll probably find this book either too easy or too hard to read. On the other hand, if our description is accurate, this book is just right for you.

How This Book Is Organized

We divided this book into parts that follow a systematic development process, from business planning and market research, through the design of a marketing-effective landing page, and to online promotion that pushes qualified traffic.

For information on a specific topic, check the headings in the Table of Contents or look at the index.

By design, this book enables you to get as much (or as little) information as you need at any particular moment. If you're starting from scratch, you might want to start with Part I. If you already have a successful landing page and want to increase traffic, start with Part II or Part III.

Part I: Landing Page Basics

Unless you have endless wealth and infinite time, you need some idea of what you're trying to accomplish online before you start. This section introduces landing page basics and stresses the importance of landing page planning as it intersects with all aspects of your business, including the financial outcomes. Stocked with useful planning forms and checklists, this part shows how to plan for success from the beginning.

Part II: Building Landing Pages

Profitable business Web sites don't happen by accident. From a marketing perspective, a successful site attracts visitors, keeps them on the site, and brings them back for repeat visits. This section addresses building a marketing-effective landing page and implementing marketing ideas right on your site. This section includes information on writing for landing pages, using trust elements on your site, working on landing page aesthetics, and working within the *fold* — the area a visitor first sees on your landing page before he scrolls.

Part III: Getting to Know Your Customers

Want to know one of the secrets for creating successful landing pages? Get to know your customers well. The better you know exactly who your customers are — their likes, dislikes, age, and so on — the more conversions you'll make. This section is all about getting to know your customers and meeting their expectations, which is a critical part of your online success.

Part IV: Increasing Your Sales

Selling well online doesn't happen by accident. Rather, developing a strategic approach to your sales provides the best results. This section looks at the techniques for increasing your online sales, including fine-tuning your landing page and closing online sales.

Part V: Driving More Visitors to Your Site

Landing page success is closely linked with driving *qualified* traffic to your site — traffic that is specifically looking for what you have to offer and is ready to buy. A book about landing page optimization would be incomplete without discussing the strategies used to drive traffic to your site. These strategies include pay per click (PPC) campaigns, keywords, search engine marketing, and more.

Part VI: The Part of Tens

Like all *For Dummies* books, this one has a Part of Tens. These chapters list a ten-point inspection list for your landing page as well as ten surefire ways to increase conversion rates. Turn to the Part of Tens for good ideas again and again.

Icons Used in This Book

To make your experience easier, we use various icons in the margins to indicate particular points of interest.

Whenever we provide a hint that makes an aspect of Web marketing easier, we mark it with the Tip icon — just our way of sharing what we've figured out the hard way — so that you don't have to. Of course, if you prefer to get your education through the school of hard knocks, be our guest.

Ouch! This icon is the equivalent of an exclamation point. Heed these warnings to avoid potential pitfalls.

This icon is simply a friendly reminder. More details are in this book than any normal person can remember. Use this icon to help you remember basic principles of Web marketing. Look up all the rest when you need it!

Sometimes we feel obligated to give developers some technical information; they don't always know as much as they think they do. We mark that stuff with this geeky guy so you know it's information to share, not necessarily to understand.

Where to Go from Here

You'll find helpful features on the companion Web site for this book at www.justmakeiteasy.com.

From the site, you can download workshops, various articles on landing page optimization, and other business-related content. Use the information on this site to help develop your own landing page optimization marketing plans. For convenience, you can use the live links to key resource sites to stay up-to-date, subscribe to blogs or newsletters, or simply find out more than fits between any two covers.

If you find errors in the book or have suggestions for future editions, please e-mail Mike at mikej.harwood@gmail.com.

Part I
Landing Page Basics

The 5th Wave · By Rich Tennant

"You know, I've asked you a dozen times <u>not</u> to animate the torches on our Web page!"

In this part . . .

In this part, you get a full-scale introduction to landing pages — what they are, what their function is, and what types you can choose from. You discover not only what a landing page is, but also what a landing page is not.

We also review online marketing and debunk some of the more common online marketing myths. We also look at the customer lifecycle management — specifically the relationship among acquisition, conversion, and retention.

Finally, we look at developing a business plan for your landing page business. A comprehensive plan is a great place to start when you create your online business.

Chapter 1

Introducing Landing Page Optimization

In This Chapter

▶ Understanding what makes up a landing page

▶ Determining the focus of your landing page

▶ Understanding your audience

*I*n the past few years, the popularity of online marketing has exploded. Advertising opportunities from Google, Yahoo!, and social networking sites (such as Facebook) have all brought with them new online marketing avenues. For many individuals and companies, these online opportunities are simply too good to pass up. Just imagine being able to take a product or a service, mix in some creativity, add a little bit of hard work, and from that, create an income-generating online business? This sounds too good to be true — and it often is. The brutal fact is that few people can even augment their salaries, much less earn a living from the results of their online marketing efforts.

Face it: Moving from a concept to a successful online marketing campaign can be a difficult, hard road to travel with many wrong turns, roadblocks, and the occasional pothole. But knowing the lay of the land may help you avoid some of the bigger potholes.

The one key feature of the online marketing landscape is the *landing page* — that (hopefully welcoming) doorway to your online storefront, which you present to your Web site visitors. You may not be too familiar with the concept or aren't quite sure what's all wrapped up in the idea of a landing page, but don't let that bother you now. With this book in your hands, you'll be okay because it acts as your landing page GPS, steering you in the right direction.

In this chapter, we introduce what landing pages are, what you use them for, and who they're designed for.

Introducing the Landing Page

Perhaps the most logical place to start a book on landing page optimization is to come up with a clear, concise definition of landing page. We believe that creating a successful landing page starts with a good understanding of its intended purpose, so here's our attempt at crystalline clarity:

> A *landing page* is the Web page your visitors arrive at after they click an online ad or an e-mail link, or follow a search engine result or any form of offline advertising campaigns, such as radio ads. The landing page is an extension of these ads and is designed specifically to generate interest and persuade the visitor to take a desired action.

For a real-world landing page example, follow these steps:

1. **Go to** www.google.com **to open a Google search box.**

2. **In the Google search box, type** running shoes.

   In the new Web page that appears, you see search results displayed on the left side of the screen as well as a list of Google ads running down the right, as shown in Figure 1-1.

3. **Click any of these Google ads to view an honest-to-goodness, bona fide landing page.**

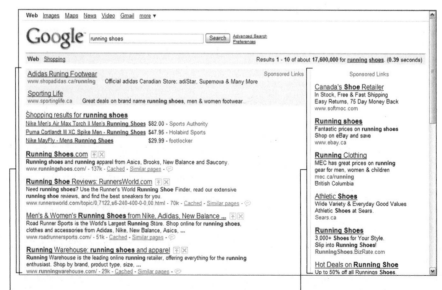

Figure 1-1: The Google search results for running shoes.

Search results   Google Ads

Click through several Google ads that you find when you search for running shoes to get an idea of the types of landing pages used. Some of the landing pages you click through are pretty darn good, and some of them, quite honestly, aren't very good at all. When you browse these landing pages, see whether the content of the landing page and the ad actually match. Recall (from the definition we gave earlier) that the landing page is an *extension* of the ad; it's *not* a bait-and-switch, in other words. (For example, a *bait-and-switch* is when you click an ad for running shoes and are taken to a landing page for clothes, hammocks, or travel packages.) If, in your quest to get running shoes, some landing page owner takes you on a wild goose chase, that someone could probably use a copy of *Landing Page Optimization For Dummies*.

People new to developing a landing page often ask, "How can you tell the difference between a good landing page and a great landing page?" The answer is straightforward: A *good* landing page is well-designed, professional, and easy to read; but a *great* landing page makes you buy. With that in mind, in the earlier running-shoes example, were you tempted to buy anything? Did any of the sites entice you to read more? If so, bookmark that landing page to refer to it later. Those landing pages that carry you through to the checkout are typically great landing pages.

Understanding what a landing page is not

Folks sometimes confuse a landing page with other types of Web pages, such as splash pages, home pages, gateway pages, and microsites. Although you may find some overlap among some of these pages, they all tend to serve quite distinct purposes, which the following list makes clear:

- **Splash pages:** Often used as an introductory page to a Web site, splash pages capture the visitor's attention for a short time and can introduce a promotion or a lead-in to the site home page. Splash pages are often fancy, full of color, and sport Flash animation or other eye-catching features. Although splash pages can be pretty, they're typically bad to use with landing pages — essentially, they're just one more click to get in the way of a sale! You want your visitors to go directly to a landing page and not be annoyed by a flashing advertisement.

- **Home pages:** A home page is the introductory page to an entire Web site. A home page typically has many elements to it and many pages from which you can navigate. A landing page doesn't have to be (and shouldn't be) all things to all people. A landing page is much more focused than a home page and is designed specifically for converting visitors to customers.

- ✔ **Gateway pages:** In the Web developers' world, gateway pages have been optimized, so they rank high in search engine results. A gateway page attracts visitors from searches with keywords and phrases. As such, gateway page design is geared toward search engines and not visitors per se.

- ✔ **Microsites:** As auxiliary supplements to a primary Web site, microsites provide more specific information and easier-to-find content than their parent site. A microsite often has its own Web address but links to a parent site. A microsite sits somewhere in between a landing page and a regular site. A landing page may have linked pages, whereas the microsite typically has more navigation options.

The function of landing pages

The function of your landing page is straightforward: Convert an online visitor to a customer or a client by persuading her to complete a specific transaction. End of story. Now, this persuasion often encourages the visitor to buy a product or a service, but not always. Landing pages may persuade visitors to find out more about a particular theme, issue, topic, or organization. Such *informational* landing pages recruit visitors through ad links or other means. These landing pages may take visitors to a page of content to increase exposure to a company, a church, or a particular group (such as a political party), as well as to an organization looking for donations and so on.

Persuading a visitor to complete some transaction on your landing page may not sound all that hard. Reality check: Here's just a taste of what you're up against:

- ✔ **Most visitors don't like reading lots of text.** Brevity and precision are absolutely necessary.

- ✔ **Most visitors hate revealing contact info.** Such resistance to giving up e-mail addresses and phone numbers is going to make any follow-up with a potential customer difficult.

- ✔ **Most people don't take the time to fill out information onscreen, including forms, surveys, and so on.** This makes any customer follow-up difficult.

- ✔ **Many people are very concerned about using their credit cards online.** They need to feel completely secure before even considering doing so.

- ✔ **Visitors choose from a billion Web sites.** How do you get them to hang out, for even a few seconds, on yours?

The list is almost endless. These factors make landing page *conversions* — that moment when a visitor becomes a client — difficult, but successful landing pages take such factors into account and address all these concerns. You can put specific and proven strategies to use to manage each of these areas. In a nutshell, landing pages are all about dealing with these concerns, which is the purpose of this book.

Choosing Your Landing Page Focus

The overall landing page function is to persuade and convert a visitor to a customer or a client. Within this framework, you can use your landing page to promote a variety of different products and services. Also true, though, is that you have a variety of different landing page options to choose from, with each one organizing and presenting information in a slightly different way, often depending on the specific product being promoted. For instance, a landing page that promotes a running shoe would present itself differently from one that recruits volunteers for a political rally. Despite the differences, each landing page still contains the same key components to make it successful. The following list identifies some of the landing page types you may be using. Selecting one type is important in terms of helping you focus on a specific area:

- **Selling physical products:** Many landing pages are designed to sell a specific physical product. This includes everything from shoes to books, tires, mousetraps, kitchen gadgets, and so on. Physical products, and their associated landing pages, have additional considerations, such as shipping issues, transportation costs, storage costs, return policies, and so on. Landing pages for physical products must overcome the fact that your customer can't pick up the product and look it over the way they can in a regular store.

- **Offering virtual products:** Virtual products can be a gold mine because they don't have shipping costs, storage costs, and other hard costs. Such products include e-books, downloadable software applications, and any product that can be delivered digitally. Virtual offerings are often the holy grail of landing page products because of less overhead. They can be configured to automatically download to paying customers, and all you have to do as a product provider is log on and check sales. Figure 1-2 shows a typical virtual product landing page.

- **Specializing in educational products:** Many landing pages are used to promote educational material, such as books, textbooks, and online courses. Educational landing pages may include both virtual and physical products. One additional component often associated with educational products is an appeal to credibility — the landing page design focuses as much on the product as the qualifications of the person offering the materials. If you're trying to sell a course on real estate investing, your visitor wants to know that you're a successful real estate agent who's in a position to pass on your expertise.

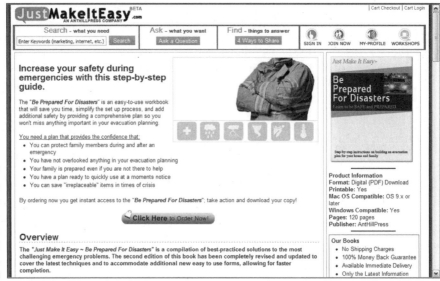

Figure 1-2:
A landing page promoting a virtual product.

✔ **Generating leads:** Some landing pages get contact information from a visitor to encourage a future purchase, rather than a purchase today. These types of pages can be very effective if you can contact the visitor and close the sale. However, getting visitors' contact information can be difficult because people are extremely wary of e-mail sign-ups. They fear these sign-ups lead directly to a tenfold spam increase in their e-mail inboxes.

One strategy is to have visitors sign up for newsletters or other free features — the e-mail address they provide for the newsletter or other free feature then becomes the e-mail you use in following up on the lead. Simple but elegant.

Lead generation can be very effective, especially if the product is too expensive, has too many options, or has high shipping costs. Antique cars are a good example of a product that's ideal for a lead-generating landing page.

Identifying and Knowing Your Audience

To launch an effective online marketing campaign, you have to understand who your potential customers are, which is done by developing a customer profile. A *customer profile* is used to clearly identify your target customer. You need to have a clear vision of your target audience to write effective ads, choose the correct keywords for your search engine optimization strategies, and of course, design your landing page. (You can find more information about developing customer profiles in Chapter 8.)

When marketing online, people tend to consider *everyone* as a potential customer. After all, the Internet provides a potential worldwide market. Admittedly, online marketing makes it possible to get customers that fall outside your customer profile, but these are the exception and not the rule. Customer profiles are used to pinpoint your customer and provide the framework for all online marketing efforts.

Successful landing pages are typically designed with a specific type of visitor or audience in mind. Remember, landing pages (and their associated ad campaigns) are intended for targeted marketing. The visitor type you're aiming for dictates the landing page type and design used. Examples of visitor types may include

- ✔ Job seekers
- ✔ Employers
- ✔ Women over 50
- ✔ Residents of a specific geographical location
- ✔ Athletes
- ✔ Teachers
- ✔ Musicians

These are, of course, just a few of the many customer categories that you may be working with. (Left-handed vegans from Skookumchuck, anyone?) As part of developing your online marketing campaign, define your key customer and demographic. How? You have many methods to choose from, but one of the more commonly used methods of tracking customer demographics is with Web analytics.

When you first start your landing page or troubleshoot an unsuccessful one, identify your specific market. Your online marketing efforts are dictated by who your actual customers are.

Web analytics

Gather as much information about your audience as you can to really get to know them. You can't always get customer information easily, but fortunately, you have some powerful tools at your beck and call. Whenever someone visits your landing page, you can log a significant amount of information about that person, such as

- ✔ The pages the visitor viewed
- ✔ The Web browser they use
- ✔ How long they view each page

✔ Whether they're a repeat visitor

✔ The visitor's Internet Protocol address

Logging the information is an easy task; interpreting the results is a different matter. Here Web analytic software comes into play. All the information you log on your site can be reviewed and interpreted by analytic software. You can then use the information the Web analytic software gleans from all the raw data to help identify the demographics of your visitors, such as their surfing habits and what they like and don't like in your landing page.

Web analytic software ranges in price and functionality, with lower-end software providing simple reports and the more advanced software providing an almost overwhelming number of configurable options. Some of the features provided by analytic software include

✔ **Real-time statistics:** View in real time how visitors respond to your landing page. Are the page layout and the heading working? These statistics allow you to see what's working and what needs to be adjusted for your customers.

✔ **Keyword cost analysis:** Starting a keyword campaign with Google AdWords or another online marketing effort costs money. Keeping track of your keyword costs can be tricky, especially if you are running multiple landing pages. Web analytic software can help identify where your highest keyword returns are helping you put the money in the right places.

✔ **Visitor path tracking:** Do visitors complete the desired transaction? If not, where do they stop? Analytic software identifies how visitors navigate your site. This includes which pages they spend the most time on and what navigational areas may need troubleshooted. Correct path navigation is critical, particularly when tracking the visitor path to the actual purchasing page.

✔ **Trend identification:** Do more of your sales occur at night, or during the weekend or weekday? Web analytic software can be configured to help spot trends in sales. Identifying trends can really help focus your landing page to a specific demographic.

✔ **Affiliate tracking:** You can see which affiliates refer the most traffic and the traffic types they refer. In affiliate marketing, an ad is placed on one site (the affiliate), and directs traffic to someone else's landing page. The affiliate is paid for the leads that are generated by hosting the ads.

✔ **Geographical tracking:** Where are your visitors from? You can track by country or even specific state. Figure 1-3 shows an overview of a geographical analysis done by Google Analytics, a popular Web analytic software program. The darker areas (California and Texas) represent the areas providing the most visitors.

Figure 1-3:
Geographical
Web
analytics.

✔ **Printable graphics and charts:** Need to show your landing page results visually? Web analytic software can prepare charts and graphics displaying a range of demographic information.

✔ **Browser tracking:** Some Web browsers may perform better for you and therefore, should be your focus for ad campaigns. Web analytic software enables you to quickly see which Web browsers are generating the most traffic. (You can see the Web browser statistics for one particular landing page with Google Analytics in Figure 1-4.)

These are just some examples of what Web analytic software can do. However, more advanced software can do much more than this. The information that Web analytic software can produce is critical in understanding your demographic, and it's worth your time to investigate and figure out how to use Web analytic software.

Web analytic software isn't hard to find. Both Google and Yahoo! provide analytic software for their advertising ventures. Many third-party Web analytic software packages are available, however. Simply type **Web analytic software** in your favorite Web browser and you'll find many — even a few free and time-trial versions. That may be a good place to start to review the types of features and benefits you can see from using such software. Or check out Chapter 12, where we talk a bit more about your Web analytic software choices.

Figure 1-4: Google Analytics software displaying Web browser statistics.

Identifying customer expectations

Regardless of the groups you focus your marketing efforts on, they have expectations of your landing page. When these expectations are met, the landing page works toward customer satisfaction. Customer satisfaction can be achieved when your visitors find what they expected to find. Depending on the type of customer you're marketing to, specific expectations vary. Younger clientele, for example, may want to see the latest technologies used, whereas teachers may want to see your credentials for promoting a particular product.

We cover the specifics of managing your customers' expectations in Chapter 9. However, some general customer expectations that need to be established on your landing page include the following:

- A friendly approach
- Knowledge about product/service
- Relevant information that's easy to find
- Effective use of technology
- Professional service
- Follow-through
- An easy-to-navigate interface

When customer expectations such as these aren't met, sales, conversions, and traffic all fall. You can track how effective you are in meeting these specific expectations with the help of the Web analytic software we mention earlier. For example, if visitors can't navigate your site properly, they'll be frustrated and go to a different site. The Web analytic software identifies navigational trouble spots. After you correct these spots, your landing page can better match customer expectations.

We've all heard the expression, "The customer is king." This is definitely true of visitors who come to your landing page. They have clear expectations of what they want and need to find on your site. To get your conversions anywhere near where you want them, you have to be able to meet your visitors' expectations. Take the time to review your site critically through the eyes of a potential customer.

Identifying product benefits

One key in determining who your audience is — and how to appeal to them — is to clearly identify the benefits of what you offer. For example, if you sell a product on your landing page, clearly identify for yourself the most important benefit of that product. With that (clear and concise) information in hand, it's much easier to identify the target market and to create the framework for developing your entire landing page.

For example, if your landing page sells smoke alarms, safety is the benefit. From here, you can focus your landing page on families and the safety your product can provide them. Perhaps your landing page would use images of children sleeping, of emergency vehicles, or a picture that appeals to the security your product provides. To appeal to emotions, you may not use a picture of the actual product, but rather of the benefit of that product.

In addition to outlining the benefits of your product, clearly identify its key features. The feature list you generate is used as the main selling features outlined on your landing page. In this smoke alarm example, the alarm may have features such as a warning beep if batteries are getting low, an automatic LED that flashes with an emergency, and so on.

To get a handle on identifying product benefits and features, as well as on how this helps develop your landing page design, complete Table 1-1 as a warm-up exercise.

Table 1-1	Product Benefit Exercise		
Product	*Benefit*	*Features*	*Potential Audience*
Rechargeable batteries			
Mountain bike			
Baby booster seat			
Recyclable shoes			
Flat bottom boat			
Your potential product			

Whether you're just designing your landing page or fine-tuning an existing one, performing this exercise on your product/service can go a long way to increasing your sales.

Chapter 2

Understanding Online Marketing Basics

*O*nline marketing, also known as Internet marketing, e-marketing, and Web marketing, is a new frontier in sales and advertising. Although online marketing shares some similarities with traditional marketing, it also has unique differences. Online marketing brings with it new terms and new jargon — SEO, PPC, banner advertising, and viral marketing to name a few. To succeed in this new marketing arena, you can't get around the fact that you're going to have to familiarize yourself with all the new terms and jargon — the basics of online marketing, in other words.

This chapter focuses on the common online marketing elements, teases out a lot of the new terms, and then goes on to show you how landing pages fit into an online marketing campaign. (That's why you're looking at *Landing Page Optimization For Dummies* rather than *Online Marketing For Dummies*, right?) The chapter also looks at a cornerstone concept of marketing — customer life cycle management.

Understanding Online Marketing Terms and Definitions

It seems like any industry brings with it a host of terms and definitions specific to that industry. You know these terms as jargon, and online marketing has more than its fair share of unique and often-cryptic terms. In this section, we explain and decrypt much of the jargon used in online marketing. After all, you're going to find it hard to increase conversions if your ROI isn't being maximized because of failing PPC or SEO — and it will be especially hard if you have no clue what we just wrote.

Online marketing, like many other areas tied into information technology, is full of jargon and acronyms. For anyone new to the field, it must be overwhelming. To help prevent confusion, be sure you take the time to understand the terms we list in just a bit. Trust us; you're going to see these terms in most online marketing materials you read.

Be sure to check out the glossary at the end of this book. You'll probably come across a slew of acronyms as you work with landing pages further down the road; keep this glossary handy so you can make your way through the acronym thicket with relative ease.

- ✔ **Landing page optimization (LPO):** A *landing page* is the Web page your visitors arrive at after clicking an online ad or an e-mail link, or following a search engine result or any form of an offline advertising campaign, such as radio ads. The landing page is an extension of these ads, which are designed specifically to generate interest and persuade the visitor to take a desired action, whereas landing page optimization involves all the techniques you'd employ to make the landing page as effective as possible.

- ✔ **Search engine optimization (SEO):** SEO is the process of increasing visitors to a Web site or a landing page by improving positioning with browser search results. Typically, the first couple of results displayed after a browser search get more traffic and clicks from visitors. So, the better your search engine position, the more traffic you're going to get. The act of SEO is the practice of tweaking a Web site or a landing page to help ensure that it appears early in the search results. SEO has become very popular with online marketing; in some cases, it's the only aspect of online marketing chosen by some companies. In truth, SEO is only part of an online marketing campaign.

Many companies don't have what we (Mike and Martin speaking here) consider a robust and well-established online marketing plan. Many try to skate by with plans that rely almost entirely on SEO. Not smart. SEO is actually only one element to an online marketing campaign — and although it can increase traffic, it may not always increase qualified buyers. We tell you what you need to know about SEO marketing in detail in Chapter 14, as a matter of fact — but we'll also clue you in on other (equally crucial) components of an online marketing campaign.

- ✓ **Business to Business (B2B):** Sometimes referred to as e-biz, B2B refers to online marketing designed to exchange products and services among businesses. This may be a manufacturer to a wholesaler or a retailer.

- ✓ **Business to Customer (B2C):** B2C refers to online companies that provide products and services to regular consumers. Amazon.com is an example of B2C, selling products to the consumer.

- ✓ **Banner ad/button ad:** A *banner* ad is a form of online advertising embedded into a Web site. Essentially, a banner ad functions as a graphical ad that also links to an external Web site. Advertisers pay to place banner ads on Web sites in an attempt to attract traffic to their own site. Advertisers can pay just a few dollars to tens of thousands of dollars to have their banner ad placed on a Web site. The cost is determined by the ad placement and the amount of traffic the site gets.

  Button ads are similar to banner ads but are smaller in size. Both button and banner ads can be used to increase brand awareness and increase traffic. (You can find out more about banner and button ads in Chapter 15.)

- ✓ **Click-through rate (CTR):** The CTR is a method of gauging success for online advertising campaigns. The CTR represents the number of clicks your ad receives divided by the number of times your ad is shown. For example, if you had a Google ad displayed 200 times and 2 people clicked it, the CTR would be 2 percent.

- ✓ **Cost per click (CPC):** The CPC represents the amount you (as an advertiser) pay each time a user clicks your ad. For example, Google AdWords has a CPC pricing system that determines how much you pay each time your ad is clicked. Keeping your CPC low is essential when first developing your online marketing campaign.

- ✓ **Conversion rate:** Conversion rate refers to the number of visitors to a Web site who perform a desired action. This may be a sale, an e-mail signup, or some other action. Online marketing is all about the conversion rate. Everything you do is designed to increase your conversion rate.

- ✓ **Pay per click (PPC):** PPC is an online advertising strategy whereby you (again, as an advertiser) pay a Web site for a visitor's ad click that sends him to your landing page. Many of the folks who host PPC ads — Google and Yahoo!, for instance — don't charge you until the visitor actually clicks to your site. PPC ads often work with *content matching,* when your ads are displayed on Web sites that actually have something to do with the ad content. For example, if you've written an ad touting your special recycling bags, your PPC ad may show up on sites related to recycling or "green" topics. The hope here is that visitors to the Web site may see your PPC ad and end up clicking through to your site. (We talk about PPC in greater detail in Chapter 16.)

✔ **Pay per lead (PPL):** PPL is an online advertising payment model in which an affiliate is paid upon qualifying sales leads. A *lead* may be anything from an e-mail address to a completed form. After the conditions for the lead are met, the advertisers pay up.

✔ **Pay per sale (PPS):** In PPS online advertising, an advertiser pays only when a sale is made. As you might imagine, a PPS model is attractive to advertisers because payment occurs only when a sale is actually made. PPS isn't a favored agreement with affiliates and sellers because they have to rely not only on someone following through with a purchase but also that the referral landing site is of a quality sufficient enough to encourage that sale.

✔ **Unique visitors:** When marketing landing pages, be concerned with two types of visitors — unique visitors and repeat visitors. *Repeat* visitors come to your site to view new products or services, check for updates, and so on. *Unique* visitors either haven't been there before or haven't been there for a specified period of time. Creating a landing page requires that you come up with something that appeals to unique visitors and then keep coming up with cool stuff that makes the page fresh for repeat visitors. (If you're curious, Web managers identify unique visitors based on the IP address information found in the log files, and sometimes through cookies.)

Tracking Down Online Marketing Myths

Understanding what online marketing is can be made easier by knowing some common myths about it. The following section reviews some commonly held misconceptions and shines a little light.

Myth #1: Build a great Web site or landing page, and visitors will come

Many individuals and companies spend thousands of dollars creating their Web sites and landing pages. After such an investment is made, there's an expectation that, by creating this wonderful gateway to the worldwide market, you've ensured that thousands of potential customers are just going to *flock* to your site. This may have worked in *Field of Dreams,* but that was Hollywood, folks. In the real world, this *build it and they will come* stuff is simply not true.

The truth is that it's possible to spend thousands of dollars and countless hours beautifying your site and fine-tuning your landing page, all to no avail. Keep in mind that millions of well-designed Web sites and landing pages out there are completely ineffective when it comes to converting visitors into customers.

Nothing is passive about online marketing; it doesn't involve simply putting up a site and waiting for customers. Successful online marketing involves a calculated, intelligent, and creative marketing strategy.

Myth #2: More visitors to your site translate into more sales

Myth #2 gets things about 70 percent right. The 100-percent truth is that drawing more *qualified* visitors to your site translates into more sales. SEO marketing can bring tons of visitors to a Web site's landing page, but such folks aren't always the types of visitors you can then convert into customers. PPC and affiliate marketing, however, can isolate and target a very specific clientele.

When it comes to creating successful landing pages, one of the tricks is to launch advertising campaigns designed to attract *qualified* visitors — visitors who are searching specifically for what your landing page has to offer. We know clients who attract thousands of hits per month to their Web sites and yet are stuck logging virtually no conversions. This is a classic example of ineffective acquisition efforts, in which acquiring all the visitors in the world means nothing if none of those visitors makes the leap to becoming a customer. (Not sure what *acquisition efforts* actually means? We give you the scoop in the section, "Acquisition," later in this chapter.)

Myth #3: The more content on a site, the better

Content is very important on a landing page. However, brevity is often the key. You can easily locate a landing page full of text that no one really takes the time to read. Some landing page developers feel that it's a great idea to share how bright or well-read they are, or they insist that the more informa-tion you can squeeze into a site, the better. Not true. In your capacity as a Web-surfing being, you read headings, gobble up short sentences, and love white space on a page. You're a *scanner,* in other words, and it makes sense to develop landing pages with that in mind. (As for strategies for presenting landing page content more effectively, we empty out our Web content bag of tricks for all to see in Chapter 6.)

Myth #4: Offering a broad range of products/services on a landing page translates to more sales

When developing a landing page, you're always tempted to squeeze just a few more products onto the page in hopes of increasing your chances of actually selling something. A word to the wise: Stuffing pages to the gills typically doesn't work. Too many options can confuse the visitor and cause her to leave. Generally, a landing page works best when a focused ad or search brings visitors to a focused site.

To see why landing pages devoted to specific products work, look no further than the acquisition process itself. When developing your acquisition campaign, you're trying to get the attention of qualified visitors, that is, those that are looking to buy. The more general you make your site; the more visitors tend to browse instead of buy.

Myth #5: The right product/service will make me rich

We've all seen landing pages sell products we never imagined in a million years would ever sell (Snugli, anyone?). Then again, we've seen outstanding products that struggle to sell at all. The fact is, good products or services do not always sell, and substandard ones sometimes do.

If you happen to discover a product that isn't necessarily strong and selling well, take the time to study the associated landing page. What kind of language is on the page? What attracts you on the site? Landing pages that sell products successfully need to be studied; those successfully selling mediocre products and services need be studied twice as hard because clearly they must be doing something right. Imagine what you can do with a good product *and* a great landing page.

You're sure to encounter many other myths and misconceptions that follow along in online marketing's wake. Our list here is in no way an exhaustive list, but we did want to touch on the major ones so you get a better idea of what *true* online marketing is all about.

Understanding the Customer Life Cycle

An integral part of landing page optimization is understanding your customer life cycle. The *customer life cycle* refers to the relationship an online customer develops with you and your business. This relationship may be ongoing over a period of years, or it may be a one-time visit to your Web site. The purpose of the customer life cycle is to identify the key stages in a customer's involvement with your company. These stages are

- ✔ **Acquisition:** Getting visitors to your site.
- ✔ **Conversion:** Having visitors perform a desired action on the site, such as a sale.
- ✔ **Retention:** Having the customer return for future business.

Each stage builds on the next — you can't have conversion without acquisition, and you can't have retention without conversion. No shortcuts. These three elements of the customer life cycle form the framework from which a successful landing page is designed. Figure 2-1 shows the relationship among acquisition, conversion, and retention.

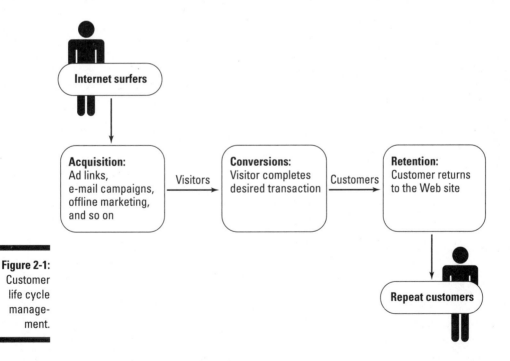

Figure 2-1:
Customer
life cycle
manage-
ment.

If a secret exists to landing page optimization, it lies in understanding the relationship among acquisition, conversion, and retention. Each of these three elements requires a separate skill set and strategies to be effective. Those willing to take the time and energy to master each of these elements can create a successful and income-producing landing page.

Acquisition

The phrase *build it and they will come* in no way applies to online sales and landing page success. Getting visitors to your landing page is a strategic operation, carefully thought out. *Acquisition* refers to the strategies you use as part of that operation — all in the name of getting visitors to your landing page. Acquisition is hard work, requiring a mixture of organization skills, dedication, and creativity. You can choose from many acquisition strategies — some are more effective than others — but put them together and these strategies are the foundation of your landing pages' successes.

As far as landing pages go, nothing is as important as acquisition. If you don't have visitors, you don't have customers. In fact, acquisition is so important that it's inspired a whole new industry. Acquisition consultants and specialists have sprung up offering their services to organizations seeking to increase their online sales effectiveness. These specialists don't come cheap; that cost reflects the importance companies place on acquisitions.

We're sure you'd rather not have to pay thousands of dollars to acquisition specialists, and fortunately, you don't have to. These specialists took the time to understand how acquisition works and spent many hours tuning and fine-tuning their acquisition strategies. You can do the same — with a little help from us, of course.

In your researching, you're sure to find a number of acquisition strategies (both offline and online) that you can use to generate traffic. We discuss a number of such strategies throughout this book, but we thought this is a good place to introduce the ones we consider as the major choices. Here, to start things off, are the online options:

- **Pay per click (PPC):** PPC is an Internet advertising model that uses clickable ads presented anywhere on a Web page that link to your landing page. The PPC ads are associated with the keywords used by a Web browser and are purchased by an advertiser. (Basically, you, the owner of a landing page, would purchase PPC ads based on keywords associated with your landing page. Users surfing the Internet would then see your ad when they search the Web with those keywords.)

PPC is *pay* for click because you, the advertiser, pay for specific keywords to use. Essentially, the more the keyword is used in searching, the more you end up paying for it. Choosing the wrong keywords and paying too much for them will surely sink your acquisition efforts. PPC ad campaigns can be very complex, involving hundreds of keywords and daily tracking procedures. Used effectively, PPC is a powerful way to acquire traffic to your site. Used ineffectively, PPC is a great way to lose a tidy bit of change without achieving any real benefit.

Keep in mind that when working with PPC ads, the ad must be relevant to the search and the landing page must be relevant to the ad. For example, when searching for running shoes, the accompanying ads should refer to running shoes, or at least to footwear. You already know that the person is searching for shoes; your ad for shoes attracts him, and the landing page entices him into a sale.

As you might imagine, PPC is a very important topic for landing page optimization, which is why we devote considerable coverage to PPC in Chapter 15.

✔ **Affiliate marketing:** As we mention earlier in this chapter, affiliate marketing is essentially commission-based selling. In affiliate marketing, an ad is placed on one site (the *affiliate*) and directs traffic to someone else's landing page. The landing page owner tracks visitors referred from the affiliate's Web site. The affiliate is compensated for any referrals that become customers or complete a required transaction. Figure 2-2 shows how affiliate marketing works.

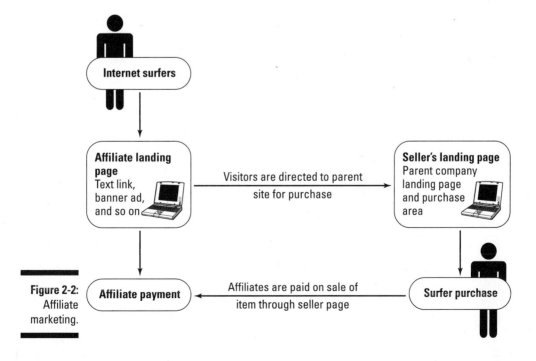

Figure 2-2: Affiliate marketing.

✔ **Banner advertising:** Many Web sites are designed to leave space for banner advertising, which is how many make money from their sites. A banner ad is typically a short, rectangular ad placed into a Web site. Naturally, the advertiser has to pay to have the ad on the Web site. The cost can range greatly — and often hinges upon the Web site's popularity and the ad's location on the site. Banner ads often tend to be flashy, in the never-ending attempt to grab attention, but in fact, if you add too much zip and zing to a banner ad, you can make it quite distracting and ineffective. Well-placed ads are important, but a well-designed banner ad can often be just as crucial when it comes in driving traffic to a landing page.

You can find more information on banner ads and how they can be used effectively in Chapter 15.

✔ **E-mail campaigns:** Acquiring online visitors with bulk e-mail can be tricky because folks tend to label such mailings as spam. To get around this, you can try purchasing very targeted e-mail lists so that your e-mail campaign ends up targeting only those people you think would be interested in your product/service.

Quite honestly, our advertising campaigns have seen little return from this type of advertising. However, e-mail campaigns directed to those who have actually been to the site and then given their e-mail addresses is another matter. After a visitor gives you her e-mail address, you can keep in touch with offers, newsletters, updates, and so on. Maintaining e-mail communication is a very effective strategy for ensuring repeat business. So, when you do have a visitor, even if you don't make the sale right away, getting the e-mail address is a good start. Getting an e-mail address is one of the keys to customer retention.

We could go on and on here because quite a few online acquisition strategies are out there that you can use — blogs, social networking, and search engine positioning, to name just a few. But we have to move on and talk a bit about some viable offline acquisition methods used as well. Here's our short list:

✔ **Radio ads:** Just this morning we heard a radio ad for an online craft shop, specifically for a type of easel they're selling. The easel sounded like good quality, although we don't paint and really couldn't tell a good easel from a bad one. But there was a problem with this ad: The site where you could actually buy the easel was mentioned several times, but to our ears, it could have been Corma.com, Corman.com, Cora.com, or some other variant — we couldn't say for sure. This ad was money wasted. The thousands of us who heard the ad have no idea where to go to see the easel. Now we'll be putting off painting yet again, missing out on an opportunity to unleash our inner Rembrandts.

Although radio ads can work, the auditory nature of the beast makes it a bit of a challenge. Realistically speaking, the silver-tongued radio announcer of this easel ad could spell out every letter of the Web address with incredible articulation, but if you're listening in your car, you're not going to risk a fender bender by scrambling for paper and pencil — and more than likely you'll forget the Web address by the time you return home. Not good.

- ✔ **Magazine/print ads:** Print ads can be very effective. Imagine the ad for easels in an art magazine or a craft store newsletter — just the thing to tear out and put on the fridge for future reference. Just remember that whereas targeted print ads do get results, they can be costly, hard to track, and may not always provide as a good return on investment as hoped.

- ✔ **Indirect marketing:** Putting out flyers is a proven method of getting the word out about a business or product. It's relatively inexpensive to place a flyer in the weekly newspaper for circulation, which could result in your easel ad ending up in thousands of homes. Now, hundreds of those homes may have no interest in easels whatsoever, but some small percentage of those homes you've (indirectly) marketed may be interested in buying an easel, and your ad may be timely.

Again, our listing here is far from exhaustive. You have lots of other offline marketing options that you can use to promote landing pages — everything from attending trade shows, TV advertising, newspaper ads, and more.

Conversion

Acquisition involves getting visitors to your landing page — a simple enough concept, and yet oh-so-hard to carry out effectively. A *conversion* occurs when a visitor performs a desired action. This may be signing a form, buying a product, or registering with the site. A conversion, basically, is a visitor performing what you want them to do.

Throughout this book — and in any other landing page documentation you may end up stumbling across — perhaps the most used term you'll see is conversion rates. *Conversion rates* refer to the rate of conversion that your landing page is accomplishing — how many visitors are performing the desired action, compared to those who leave without performing the desired action. This is expressed as a conversion rate versus a *bounce* rate — the rate at which people hit your site and then leave right away.

The goal of landing page optimization is to increase conversion rates — a goal that isn't always easy to achieve. When it comes to increasing conversion rates, you have much to do — including plenty of research, testing, and retesting. Much of this book is focused on the strategies, hints, tips, and tricks that you can use to increase conversion rates.

"What types of strategies?" you say. As a brief introduction, some of the strategies you need to be using to increase your conversion rate include

- **Keep the landing page simple.** Keep the path to purchase as uncluttered as possible. And, for the record, just because you can zip it up with color, flair, and flash doesn't mean visitors will be impressed. The simpler your page is, the better it will perform.

- **Give out your information.** This is only fair. You're asking them for an e-mail address, other contact information, and even a credit card number. For your part, include your contact details. Doing so goes a long way toward making people feel more comfortable when dealing with you.

- **Be specific about the product.** Remember, people are used to shopping in stores where they can pick up a product and look it over. You can compensate for this somewhat by being clear about the product. Talk about its characteristics — its color, its weight, or anything else you'd want to know if you were buying it.

- **Display your return policy.** Give your visitors a clear getaway plan. If they don't like what they get, they should be able to return it hassle-free.

- **Use testimonials.** Testimonials reinforce your validity, but on one condition — the testimonials have to be real. If a site visitor spots a fake testimonial, your credibility is going to take a beating.

Okay, those are our five quick tips to increase conversion rates. To get more — because these five are just the tip of the iceberg, just enough to give you an idea of the types of strategies used to increase conversion rates — keep reading this book and pay particular attention to the chapters in Part II.

Retention

Retention is the third key element of a successful landing page campaign — right after acquisition and conversion. *Retention* involves maintaining the relationship you've established with your customer. After all, it *is* easier to get a repeat customer than to try and find new customers.

You have several strategies available to you when it comes to retaining customers. (Perhaps it goes without saying that first among them is to provide a quality product/service.) Your retention strategy begins as soon as your visitor becomes a customer. We've found that two key retention methods have been particularly effective for us: e-mail and newsletters. The next few sections explain why that is.

E-mail retention

Although it's never particularly easy to get an e-mail address from a visitor, your odds rise exponentially after that visitor becomes a customer. Without question, part of your retention marketing strategy should include getting the e-mail addresses of your customers. You can then use the address to send product updates, new releases, coupons, thank you cards, and more. New product offers in e-mails to past clients is a great way to get conversions.

Keeping in touch shouldn't cross the line in which you start to become annoying, however. Listed here are some of the types of e-mails you can use to encourage customer loyalty:

- ✔ **The Thank You e-mail:** Typically sent soon after the sale, thanking them for their business. The e-mail is typically short and to the point.

- ✔ **The How Did We Do? e-mail:** We've found these e-mails to be very useful. The feedback can be used to fine-tune the landing page and streamline the purchasing process.

- ✔ **The Company Survey e-mail:** Thinking about introducing new products or services? The Company Survey e-mail is a great way to get product feedback and gently introduce your customers to your new offerings.

- ✔ **The New Offer e-mail:** Do you have a new contest? A blockbuster sale? A dazzling new product? New Offer e-mails have a great track record for sales retention.

You can probably think of several other types of e-mails that can be sent, and some e-mails will be closely linked to the type of product/service being offered and the relationship with the client — so much so that we probably can't even imagine what such e-mails would look like. Whatever type of e-mail you come up with to meet your particular situation, it's important to keep in touch with your customer base if you expect to have any success in increasing your retention possibilities.

Newsletters

Free newsletters to your customers are definitely a good way to keep in touch. Newsletters don't need to be fancy, but you do need to keep them up to date so that customers are clued in on what you're doing right now or can hear about interesting developments that they may be interested in.

Want some quick ideas about how you can encourage customers to return? One way is to regularly offer fresh and interesting information to your customer. This doesn't have to be much; try e-mailing a tip of the day, trivia questions, or interesting facts pertaining to the product/service they purchased. The idea is to keep you (and your products) in their minds.

Managing Your Expectations

Many people, when starting out with online marketing and developing their landing pages, come to the plate with misinformed expectations. This can lead to unrealistic sales projections and ultimately, dissatisfaction with your online campaign. Setting realistic expectations is one of the keys to achieving online success. Some products do naturally better than others. Some landing pages take time to have a voice that works for the reader to take action. It takes time — and doing things in moderation — to make a landing page successful.

Many people claim to know the secret to getting high conversion rates and are quite willing to sell you those secrets. The truth is that there's no such thing as a 100-percent conversion rate; it's a little like Sasquatch — everyone's heard of it but no one's actually seen it. Our advice to you: Forget about unrealistically high conversion rates. Aiming for that 100 percent can be frustrating and cause you to adjust a landing page that's actually performing quite adequately.

So just what is a good conversion rate? This is a difficult question to answer. The truth is it all depends on many factors: the product type, the economy, the product cost, the marketing campaign, and more. So when we talk to clients about conversion rates, we talk in very general terms because you'll always have exceptions. In general, you can expect conversion rates to be somewhere between 0.5 percent on the low end and 10 percent on the very high end. On average, you're likely to find yourself with conversion rates between 2–3 percent.

In very simple terms, this means that for every 100 visitors to your site, 2 to 3 of those should end up buying something — which is precisely why acquisition becomes so important. The more focused visitors you can drive to your site, the greater your odds of securing these conversion rates.

There's no such thing as a failure with landing pages but only lessons to be learned. With proper tracking and record keeping, each setback gets you closer to creating the landing pages that get the best results for your product.

To help in creating realistic expectations, you need to have some understanding of the types of visitors you're going to have. We've identified four types of visitors: the *No,* the *Yes,* the *Probably Not,* and the *Maybe.* With the No visitor, no matter how well designed the landing page is, you won't convert him. A targeted acquisition campaign should weed out most of the No's, but they do slip through. You really don't need to focus much on the No visitor.

On the other end of the spectrum is the Yes visitor. They have credit card in hand and will buy even from a poor landing page. These are the people who are searching for a specific product, see your relevant ad, click to the landing page, and follow through to a sale with little convincing. This is typically not a large group, but a focused acquisition campaign can find these types of visitors so that you get an easy conversion.

In between the automatic No visitors and the easy Yes visitors are two other groups. These are the Probably Not and the Maybe visitors. You can get your conversion rates up and target your campaigns by a skillful approach to these two groups. The Probably Not visitors look for any reason not to buy — poor writing on the landing page, complicated purchasing system, confusing layout, you name it. They have the cursor on the Back button ready to leave your landing page. This skittish group can be converted with a well-designed landing page, but it's going to take some effort. One of the tricks to landing these slippery visitors is to review your landing page through the eyes of the Probably Not visitor. Take the time to pick apart your site, looking for any reason to click off. (Maybe a font or a color bugs you or a slow load time, anything that would give you pause.) If you're honest, you'll find areas that don't work for the Probably Not visitor. In truth, most of us are, deep down, the Probably Not kind of visitors.

The Maybe visitors are a little more forgiving than the Probably Not ones. They spend less time looking for a reason to leave and more time identifying whether the product/service is what they need. Typically, they're less concerned with form and format as they are with the end result. Of course, a poorly designed site will lose them as well, just not as quickly. They're looking to buy, and your landing page just has to take them over the top.

Chapter 3

Preparing for Your Landing Page

. . . .

. . . .

*P*eople spend millions each year on landing pages and Internet marketing campaigns with little or no results to show for it. Some time ago we came across a quotation — who knows where, who knows when, and we don't have a clue who first said it — which expresses this idea quite pithily:

> *Each year I waste half of my marketing budget; the problem is, I am not sure which half.*

—Anonymous

This quotation is a classic because it sums up the sentiment for many online business entrepreneurs. Although this chapter may not prevent you from wasting your marketing dollars, it does lay the framework to at least find out where that money is wasted.

Simply put, one common denominator that successful landing pages have is a plan. The ongoing sales of products from landing pages doesn't happen by accident; rather, landing pages follow a plan, complete with advertising schedules, marketing goals, timelines, and more. Those landing pages that fail are often a result of a failure to properly plan. This chapter is all about planning for your landing page and online business. This is done by clearly identifying the goals of your landing page, defining a clear market analysis, outlining achievable goals, developing a financial summary, and evaluating your progress.

Developing Your Landing Page Plan

Imagine that in your rush to build your dream house, you show up at the hardware store and just start buying lumber, doors, nails, screws, and windows. You have no blueprints, just an idea in your head of what you want the house to look like. This is what it's like to build a landing page without a plan; it's conceivable that, like that dream house, you could actually manage to build it, but without a blueprint, the finished product isn't going to be the best it could be. Again, you *can* create a landing page without developing a plan first; hundreds of landing pages are built every day without any thought to the overall plan. In general, however, those people who don't properly plan become discouraged and end up dropping their online marketing business. (Not a good outcome, by the way.)

Just because you have a great product and a flashy Web page doesn't mean visitors are going to show up to your site with credit card in hand. Having a successful landing page is hard work, and much of your success comes down to preparation and a plan. Don't be fooled by one of the more common e-commerce myths out there, which postulates the following:

> "Successful online sales start with a great Web site."

Don't believe it. Your best chance of success is to develop a plan before you do anything. If your landing page is suffering and struggling to make conversions, go back to the drawing board and make your business plan. The marketing plan really is your blueprint to success. If you don't have a clear idea of who you're marketing to, how to market to them, and the resources you have at your disposal, you can't see the full potential of your landing page.

You have lots of options when it comes to creating your own online marketing plan. Which one you choose is probably less important than actually having one. In this chapter, we lay out a few of your options, detailing some of the more common elements you should consider including in your landing page marketing plan, such as the business summary, the market analysis, your marketing and landing page goals, the pieces of your financial planning puzzle, and the oh-so-important landing page evaluation.

Taking the time to develop a marketing plan isn't the most glamorous part of your landing page efforts, but it's arguably the most important. We find that, on average, those who take the time to carefully write out a business plan and stick to it are far more likely to make the landing page a success. With that in mind, we strongly urge you to take the time to create a landing page marketing plan.

Writing your business summary

One element you want to include in your marketing plan is the *business summary,* or the *executive summary,* which provides an overview of your entire landing page marketing plan. *Overview* is important here — a business summary is in no way intended to provide specific details of the plan, just the highlights. The summary is intended to be read by you (to verify that you stay on track with your goals), by potential investors (who may need a snapshot of your goals and marketing direction), and by anyone with significant involvement in the project (to ensure that everyone's on the same page). If readers need more details of the marketing plan, they can turn to other elements of the plan. For the most part, however, someone should be able to pick up your summary and have a clear idea of what you're trying to do, the resources you have at hand, and your all-important timelines.

Here's a list of the kinds of things you should set out to accomplish in a good business summary:

- ✔ Explain the product/service you intend to provide.
- ✔ Identify your conversion goals.
- ✔ List your marketing methods (search engine optimization, AdWords, and so on).
- ✔ Detail your marketing budgets.
- ✔ Note the names of all people involved in the project.
- ✔ Write down your projected timelines.
- ✔ Document how you plan to achieve your goals.

Writing the summary after you complete the more detailed marketing plan is often easier. Then you can simply cut and paste the highlights into the summary document. The length of the business summary varies, but one to two pages is a nice average.

We find that the summary document is not only for potential investors or business partners but also for partners and spouses. Why? Because developing a landing page from start to finish requires a huge time commitment. Allowing spouses to read the summary gives them a better idea of what you're trying to accomplish by spending those countless hours in front of the computer screen. The summary document is a good way to bring those around you up to speed and get them on board.

Okay, time for you to create your business summary. Knowing exactly what to include in the summary can be difficult, so to get started, consider how (in one or two paragraphs) you'd answer the following questions:

- ✔ **What type of business are you offering?** Are you selling a product online? Promoting an offline store? Are you selling information? The business summary needs to be clear on exactly what type of business you have.
- ✔ **What's your mission statement?** A *mission statement* is a brief description of the purpose of your company. Why are you starting a business? What is your reason for being?

✔ **What are your goals and timelines?** Of course, you want to convert your site visitors into customers and make some money, but the big question is when — perhaps even more important, how much? For a good business summary, your goals need to be clearly defined with timelines attached, such as "My company will have 1,000 unique visitors to the site within 6 months."

✔ **Who's your demographic?** The business summary needs to include a description of your demographic. Be as specific as possible: female athletes, plumbers, Basque shepherds, and so on.

✔ **What's the market demand for your product?** In this section, provide a quick overview of the competition and market demand. Be specific about which other companies provide the same product or service. Answer how you're different from the competition and spell out what the potential demand for your product is.

✔ **What's the format of your business structure?** Are you incorporated or a partnership? The business summary needs to include company information, such as who's involved and what they do.

Don't want to start your business plan from scratch? Many software programs are available that provide templates for your business plan. Many of these have trial versions that you can download to test before you buy. You can find these business plan template applications with a simple online search. One great place to start looking is with the Microsoft Office templates at `http://office.microsoft.com/en-us/templates/default.aspx`. Here you can find many business related templates.

Market analysis

One of the primary reasons to develop a detailed marketing plan is to clearly identify your intended market. You can easily state that your product is good for anyone, but saying so really doesn't help with the targeted marketing strategies you need to use with your landing pages. Do the work involved to clearly identify your key primary market as well as your secondary and/or tertiary markets.

For your marketing plan, it's critical that you take the time to clearly identify your primary market. You need to know exactly who you're marketing because *how* you market is intimately tied up with *whom* you market to. (One of the constants in this book is our conviction that the ways and means of marketing will change depending on the demographic involved.) To take an obvious example, the background, color, image style, and language of a landing page would be different if your key market was snowboarders compared to women over 50. Your presentation is dictated by your audience.

Within the marketing analysis, look for demographic information, such as

- ✔ How old your customers are
- ✔ What gender they are
- ✔ Where they live
- ✔ Whether they have children, pets, or extended family
- ✔ What they do for a living
- ✔ What their level of disposable income is
- ✔ What their hobbies are
- ✔ What motivates them
- ✔ What the size of your target market is

When identifying your market, remember to focus on one or two small niche (or targeted) segments of a market instead of a large general market. Niche markets have less competition and provide a better focus. (For more information on identifying your target market, see Chapter 8.)

Your market analysis needs to identify your target market, but it should also highlight and summarize other market-related areas, including

- ✔ Market trends and patterns
- ✔ The competition — what's already out there and how it's being done
- ✔ Market demand for your product
- ✔ The challenges involved in bringing your product to market
- ✔ How the current economic climate impacts your market

As far as competition goes, identifying what your competitors are doing well and maybe not so well is important. You need to find your unique sales position with all your competitors. Determine why you're special: What is it about you that makes you better than the competition? Is it your shipping rates? Your customer service? Your price point? Whatever it is, find it and focus your marketing efforts on your positive and differentiating points.

All too often, people don't take the time to really develop an understanding of their market. Don't fall into the trap of assuming you know your market. Market research is the only way to really get to know your potential customers and the market you're trying to get into.

Marketing and landing page performance goals

A key part of creating your landing page marketing plan is to clearly identify what success looks like for you. For example, what do you consider to be a successful conversion? Is it

- ✔ Getting visitors to the shopping cart?
- ✔ Having visitors sign up for a newsletter?
- ✔ Having a survey filled out?
- ✔ Generating an actual sale of a product or a service?
- ✔ Downloading of information?
- ✔ Getting e-mail addresses?

You can measure success in plenty ways; you have to find the one that fits for you. After you know how you're going to measure success, identify clear goals, timelines, and service actions. (*Service actions* in this context are the specific methods by which you can obtain your goals within a timeline.)

When it comes to defining your goals, many people use the SMART method of goal setting. SMART goal setting goals must be

- ✔ **Specific:** Goals must be set as specific as possible. Often the timelines to achieve the goal are included as part of the goal.
- ✔ **Measurable:** To be effective, goals must be measurable. For example, you may gauge the successful completion of a goal based on conversions or number of visitors to your site.
- ✔ **Attainable:** Goals have to be attainable, or within your grasp. Your goals need to be within reach, that is to say that you can accomplish them within a two-, three-, or six-month period. Don't set yourself up for failure right out of the gate by setting goals that reach into the far-distant future.
- ✔ **Realistic:** Realistic goals are ones that are *doable*. Perhaps you aren't going to get rich in three weeks, but you may get rich eventually. Keeping goals realistic helps prevent you from becoming discouraged.
- ✔ **Timely:** Goals need to have timelines attached. This keeps you motivated and helps prevent too much procrastination.

After a goal is developed, a service action or plan of attack is attached. As an example, we could list the following:

Goal: I will increase site visitors from 500 to 1,000 by June 15.

Service action: To increase visitors, I will spend $300 per month on Google AdWords to drive additional traffic to the site. Also, by May 15, I will post 50 articles on my site to increase my search engine optimization (SEO) positioning.

Taking the time to develop goals and service actions really does give you an advantage over the competition for online marketing. Doing so provides you with a focus and keeps you on track. By documenting your goals and service actions, you make it possible to evaluate your progress and make appropriate changes (if necessary) to stay on track.

Financial resources

One of the most important parts of an Internet marketing plan is your budget. Now, we know that the mere mention of *budget* often causes people to run away in a panic, but in terms of your business plan, knowing what resources you have at your disposal is critical when developing your plan of attack.

We know as well as the next guy that creating a budget isn't always easy to do, but it's important to be as specific as possible. Your plan needs to include how much money you have, your revenues, your expenditures, and even projections of future revenue and expenses.

Right from the start, you're going to have start-up expenses. You need to identify all start-up expenses, but be forewarned; you may have a lot to include, even if you plan to run a home-based business. Some of the start-up costs typically include

- ✔ **Business-related fees:** Business-related fees include everything from accounting fees, to business licenses, copyrights, non-disclosure agreements, insurance costs, and more.

- ✔ **Sales-related fees:** Will you have shipping costs? Container costs? Will you need tracking software, shipping insurance, or phone support? Ideally, you'll have a product that can be downloaded easily, deftly avoiding many sales-related costs. When you have to ship a physical product — rather than send a virtual product over the Internet — you're going to have major sales-related costs.

- ✔ **Infrastructure-related fees:** Infrastructure costs include elements like a phone, warehouse fees, computer hardware, office upgrades, software, and so on. Infrastructure fees typically include the costs associated with getting a business up and running.

> ✔ **Ongoing technology fees:** You probably already pay for many technology fees — stuff like high-speed Internet connection costs, extra phone lines, fax lines, Web hosting costs, Web development costs, cell phones, PDAs, printer cartridges, hardware upgrades, and more — so it's probably wrong to call them start-up fees, but you're going to have to pay them anyway.
>
> ✔ **Business supply fees:** Will you need business cards? Office supplies? Parking? Office rent? Filing cabinets?

The start-up cost list when you start to put things on paper seems almost endless. Of course, if you start your online business out of a home office, some of these costs are mitigated. Many costs, however, are still there, and perhaps you didn't consider them carefully. For example, our accounting costs per year for an incorporation are almost $2,000, plus bookkeeping at about $400, and insurance costs run about $600. That's $3,000 just for those three costs. How many online products at $19.95 or $29.95 would you need to sell just to pay off these three bills?

People have a tendency to say, "I work from home, so I have low overhead." There's a huge difference between *low* overhead and *no* overhead. We've seen people sell fairly well online with their landing pages, but because they didn't have a firm grasp on their incoming and outgoing costs, they went under.

The funny (or perhaps not-so-funny) thing about your landing page budget is that no matter how careful you are in creating it, something always comes up you weren't expecting. This may include software requirements, hardware failure, or maybe even a Web hosting fee increase. The best way to deal with these financial nuisances is to have a contingency category built in to your budget. You may not need it, but it sure is comforting to know it's there.

Have you ever wondered how much to charge for your product? Of course, you have to consider what the market will bear and what other products like yours are selling for. But you also have to consider your costs. You have to sell a lot of e-books at $25 if your operating budget is $500 per month and you hope to draw a salary. If you want to make $1,500 per month and your monthly bills are $500, you need to sell 80 e-books at $25 each to manage your goals.

Now, what if you wanted money for a vacation, a new car, or to pay down a credit card? How many e-books would that take?

So what can you do? Charge $150 for an e-book? Probably not — but if the outlook for making money online was so bleak, you wouldn't need *Landing Page Optimization For Dummies*.

The good news is that when you get the hang of making a plan and developing a landing page, you don't have to stick to a single product. If you build one successful landing page, you can build countless others.

Landing Page Yoda

Some years ago, we tried to sell something online; it was one of our first efforts, and things were going poorly. We asked a friend, who we refer to as the *Landing Page Yoda,* for a little help as to why our page wasn't working. "Difficult to see, it is," he said. No, not really. Actually, he just asked for our business plan and financials. Of course, we didn't have them. We expected him to look over the page, suggest a keyword here or there, change some fonts, and we'd be off. His consultation involved a thorough review of our business plan. Right from the start, our initial landing page was doomed. Our costs were too high for our price point, our marketing budget was way to low, and we had no money for contingencies, which were sinking us. Even if our landing page was selling, its effectiveness was usurped by a poor plan and no clear financial goals.

We know that developing a plan is often tedious and working out the financials can take a bit of the wind out of your "sales." As consultants, we can say without hyperbole that the plan is an integral part of your success. If we were hired as consultants for your landing page, then (like our Yoda) we'd ask to see your plan and financials; it's your roadmap to tell us where you're going and how you intend to get there. The plan and financials are our way to know whether you're on the wrong path right from the start.

As Yoda might say, *"Grave danger, you are in. Impatient, you are. Rush to your HTML, you must not."*

We've found that the online marketing thing can snowball on you. First, you make a product, people love it and want another one, and then another. By taking advantage of repeat business, you have three landing pages with three products each selling copies per month. With your success, you start to branch out and sell products made by other people and take a cut.

This is how things seem to work: Some landing pages find their success with a single or limited number of products; others seem to morph into a larger business and do really well. Someone much wiser than we are once said, "Work hard and plan for success."

Your detailed financial plan

When it comes to making your financial plan, you have many ways to go about it. You don't really have a right or wrong way; it's just a matter of finding a way that works for you.

In this section, we provide a table of expenses you can expect to have for your online business. Not all will apply; others you may have. We strongly encourage you to fill out Table 3-1 to get a clear idea of what you can expect.

Table 3-1	Financial Cost Analysis	
Expense	**Cost per Month**	**Description**
Office rent	$	
Office equipment — fax, computer, and printers	$	
Phones — long-distance fees and separate line	$	
Web site setup expenses — cost of planning, research, and outsourcing (if needed)	$	
Web site design — hiring a company or doing it yourself	$	
Art and multimedia — logos, purchase of images, freelance artists, or your time	$	
Hosting costs — monthly cost of hosting (depends on your traffic and site size)	$	
Domain costs — your domain cost (on average under $20 a year for each domain you use)	$	
Market research		
Search engine listings and optimization — PPC (pay per click) and SEO	$	
Alternate marketing and promotion — article writing, domain, classifieds, YouTube adverting, and so on	$	
Design and printing of marketing materials	$	
Salaries and wages — employees, contractors, and yourself	$	
Office supplies — paper, pens, printer ink, and business cards (the usual stuff)	$	
Utilities — lights, heat, and cooling	$	

Expense	Cost per Month	Description
Vehicle expenses	$	
Insurance — home and office	$	
Credit card clearing fees — from 1.5 percent to 5 percent per transaction on average	$	
Total:	$	

Okay, we don't go into any more details on the financial end of your business. Remember, however, that you can't optimize something that isn't set up for success from the beginning.

Time to turn attention away from you and onto what your competition is doing.

Researching Your Competition

Somewhere out there, in some corner of the Internet, lies your competition. Someone provides a similar service or sells a similar product. How are they doing? How much are they charging? Where are they located? You need to know. Nothing like a little healthy competition to get you excited and focused. Someone out there is trying to take your sales, and you have to make sure she doesn't.

Typically, finding your competition isn't hard; a few searches and some online snooping serve you well. Don't be hasty, however, because you need to be thorough. You may find it beneficial to create a competition index in a spreadsheet to keep track of the competition. A competitive analysis, as shown in Table 3-2, can give a great snapshot of where you stand currently.

Table 3-2		Product Competitive Analysis		
Criteria	You	Competition #1	Competition #2	Notes
Price point	$	$	$	
Selection				

(continued)

Table 3-2 *continued*

Criteria	You	Competition #1	Competition #2	Notes
Support options				
Landing page navigation				
Company reputation				
Types of advertising used				
Return policies and guarantees				
Site features — services and add-ons				
Checkout and carts				
Payment options				

Keep an eye on your competition throughout your planning stage and for the life of your Web site. Keeping a journal of Web sites is an excellent way to keep track. Be sure to visit the sites on your list from time to time to see whether they've changed their offerings, have started any special deals or promotions, dropped any products, or made any changes to their site. *Remember:* They're trying to optimize their sites as well, just like you.

Part II
Building Landing Pages

The 5th Wave   By Rich Tennant

"Games are an important part of my Web site. They cause eye strain."

In this part . . .

In Chapter 4, you discover the key elements of a landing page — the pieces that need to be in place for the landing page to be effective. These key elements include the fold, headlines, calls to action, and body text.

Chapter 5 explores beautifying your landing page — using colors, fonts, and images on your landing page. Chapter 6 is all about developing a writing style to use on your landing pages, plus we kick in a little grammar lesson free of charge.

Finally, Chapter 7 talks about building trust with your visitors. When it comes to optimizing your landing page, one key area to focus on is the trust elements you include on your site.

Chapter 4

Identifying Key Landing Page Elements

*L*anding pages are comprised of several elements, which combine to make the whole. Each of these individual elements fit together and — if done correctly — form a complete sales page. Knowing what each of these landing page elements are and what they're designed to do is essential when you develop your site.

All too often, key elements of landing pages are missing — or if they're present, they're not used effectively. If this happens, you'll almost certainly experience a drop in your conversion rates or lose all sales. Not good. Our advice: Make a checklist to ensure that all necessary elements are part of your landing page. You may ask, "And how do I know what to put on the checklist?" Simple. Just read this chapter, which does all the work for you by examining these key landing page elements and highlighting where, what, and why they're used.

Working in the Fold

Arguably, the single most important landing page element is the fold. The *fold* is the viewable area on the computer screen that visitors don't have to scroll to see more content. This is known by several names, including *the fold, above the fold,* or *viewable area.* The concept comes from the world of traditional newspaper printing in which the newspaper was folded horizontally and stacked. To stay *above the fold* meant that your content stayed above the point where the newspaper was folded for display. Similarly, staying *above the fold* on a Web site means that your content is going to be visible without a visitor scrolling.

The fold area provides visitors with the first impression of your site and is intended to quickly highlight what you have to offer. A corollary to all this is that if the fold does *not* capture a visitor's attention, you're not going to have enough of those wonderful *conversion* moments — when a Web site visitor is transformed into a customer. Typically, visitors to Web sites don't scroll down the page to find more information (or that crucial Buy Now button) if the fold area doesn't quickly entice them.

Scrolling of any sort used to be frowned upon for a landing page. However, with word processors, the Internet, and other applications, users are used to vertical scrolling. Although the fold rules still apply, visitors are more willing to scroll vertically if the fold is attractive. However, horizontal scrolling is a different matter. We strongly recommend that you avoid horizontal scrolling at regular screen resolutions. Visitors tend to leave the site if lots of horizontal scrolling is required.

The fold is one of the most important areas of your Web site because it contains all the information needed not only to impress your visitors but also to get them to carry on to the sale. In terms of content, the fold must match your visitor's product expectations and quickly convey to the visitor that she's in the right place. If visitors click an ad to get to your site, the ad content must match the fold content. Your visitors don't want anything fancy; they just want the straight-up information they're looking for.

Most visitors are impatient and want their information quickly. If you don't put the info right in front of them, chances are they'll hit the Back button and go find someone who will.

The fold is typically a very small viewing area and must be used wisely to take advantage of what the visitor sees. In Figure 4-1, you see an example of a standard fold area in a 1024 x 768 screen resolution. The scroll bar along the right indicates more is to the page than at first glance.

Designing a well-organized fold area has a major impact on the success of your landing page. Because the fold could be the only part of your page the visitor will ever see, the space needs to be used effectively.

Time to get the obvious stuff out of the way: First impressions are always very important. This is especially true if you want to make an online sale. If you put your best sales pitch at the bottom of the page or important information is buried where the customer has to hunt for it, how can you expect him to take action? You'll lose the sale even if you have a great product or service.

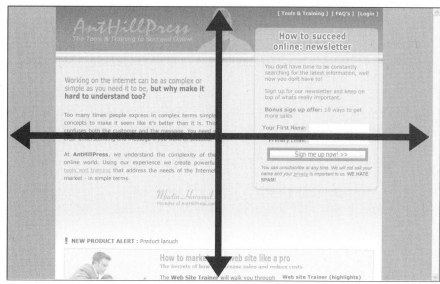

This is why, when it comes to landing page design, start from the top and work down. Arranging your page from top to bottom provides a flow and a consistency to your message.

Three fold secrets

Well, maybe these aren't exactly secrets, but we have three tips for designing elements (text and graphics) that will be placed in the fold. We've found that ignoring any one of these three areas will certainly have a negative impact on conversions.

- **Write for (human) scanners:** We know that the average visitor only scans Web text; therefore, it's critical to position your main textual points within the top fold. In the writing world, this is an *inverted pyramid* — critical points are presented first and then the details come later, should the reader want more information. Everyone is a scanner these days— you scan TV channels, magazine articles, radio stations, and of course, Web sites. Scanning is just a part of how people filter out the good or necessary information from the unnecessary. You have to design the text on the fold with scanners in mind.

- **Watch out for page load times:** The Communications Workers of America released the *Report on Internet Speeds in All 50 States* in May 2008, which states that of the 230,000 connections tested for speed, 15 percent of users are still on dialup! With roughly 15 percent of the North American population still using a slow connection speed, a big challenge is creating a fold area that loads fast. How fast? You should be looking for load times of somewhere between 3 and 4 seconds. That's not a lot of time.

- ✔ **Keep it simple:** Use common technologies that avoid requiring visitors to download patches or plug-ins. If some percentage of your visitors are required to download and install plug-ins to view your landing page features, you can bet that a good percentage of those folks are going to back out of your site as quickly as possible, never to come back.

Must-have fold information

Knowing what the fold's all about is one thing, but knowing what you should fill the fold with is another thing altogether. First and foremost, to make an effective fold area, you have information that's relevant and important to the visitor organized and available. The information presented above the fold is the key to her staying or leaving. To make sure she stays, include as many of the following elements as possible in your fold:

- ✔ **The heading:** The heading is the sentence at the top of your page that your visitor often sees first. Scanners have no choice but to see the heading, which might be all they see. The heading's purpose is to attract your visitor's attention and entice him to keep reading. As you might expect, the heading is an integral element because almost everyone reads your heading and it has to catch their attention.

- ✔ **A value or proposition statement:** The value or proposition statement is a concise, clear sentence stating the expected results your visitor is going to get from using your product or service. Developing a clear value statement is your first step in establishing why a visitor should buy from you. The more specific a statement you can make, the better. (***Note:*** This statement is sometimes combined with the heading.)

- ✔ **Benefit statements:** Don't confuse benefit statements with your value statement or the product features. Benefit statements show how your product or service solves an immediate problem. These statements go right to the heart of the matter by answering "What's in it for me?" Benefit statements often address base motivators, such as saving time, making money, increasing business, improving looks, and so on.

- ✔ **A call to action:** Just as it sounds, the call to action is an action, often in the form of a statement or a page button to click, that you tell your visitors to do. Be bold. Tell your visitors exactly what you want them to do.

- ✔ **Price/sign-up:** You want your visitors to take action and you have a call to action, but if your action area is below the fold, how can they act? Buy Now or Sign Up to Our Newsletter areas need to appear above the fold or be easily accessible to the site visitor. The easiest way to offer such accessibility is usually by means of a button that takes them to a cart checkout page, sign-up page, or more information.

✔ **Images:** People are attracted to images, and (especially when selling a product they can't touch) they want to know what your product looks like. Images can be very effective in demonstrating a product and can help visitors become more connected to it when they see pictures of people using it.

✔ **Navigation:** Navigation is considered part of the information you offer because it provides links to pages important to visitors, such as pages devoted to contact info, privacy policies, and guarantees. These all play an important part in the decision-making process that (hopefully) leads to someone actually buying something from your site. Importantly, landing pages typically have a different menu and header navigation format than the rest of your site; the idea here is to have your visitors linger for a while on your landing page, rather than enabling them to click away to another part of the Web site.

When you design your fold area, not all items need to be presented to the visitor. The most important include these elements: the heading, the value or proposition statement, and the call to action. You don't want to overload the visitor with too much clutter and make it hard to see the important information.

These elements combine to create an effective fold. Visitors are going to buy your product or sign up to your newsletter more often when your landing page presents your product or service clearly and focuses on them. The bottom line is this: Effective use of these elements lowers your visitor *bounce rate* — the rate at which visitors say "Hasta la vista, baby," without any further action on their part.

The text above the fold is often brief and to the point. Additional and more detailed information needs to be included below the fold for those who want to know more about your product.

Defining your resolution needs

We're not talking New Year's resolutions here, but rather computer screen resolutions. When designing the fold, two questions that are often asked are "How much area do I have to work with?" and "Does the fold differ from visitor to visitor?" These questions can be answered only by looking more closely at the issue of screen resolution, especially in terms of how it affects how the fold works from both the designer's and visitor's perspectives.

When it comes to your visitors, keep in mind that you're dealing with their screen size, not yours. Screen size is measured by their *resolution level,* which specifies the number of *pixels,* or points of light, the computer screen displays. Resolution levels range from low (640 x 480) to high (1024 x 768 or more). The higher the resolution, the more viewing area that's achieved.

A *pixel* is the smallest visual element on a screen, whether on a computer monitor or a television screen. Pixel is derived from *pix* for *picture* and *el* for *element.* Your monitor has thousands of pixels, which eventually produce what you see onscreen.

When it comes to identifying the common resolution settings used by Web browsers, you have plenty of places online to look. For example, the folks at www.W3.org found that for the last four years, the majority of users use a 1024 x 768 resolution. Table 4-1 highlights screen resolution users.

Table 4-1		Display Resolution			
Year	Higher than 1024 x 768	1024 x 768	800 x 600	640 x 480	Unknown
2008	38 percent	48 percent	8 percent	0 percent	6 percent
2007	26 percent	54 percent	14 percent	0 percent	6 percent
2006	17 percent	57 percent	20 percent	0 percent	6 percent
2005	12 percent	53 percent	30 percent	0 percent	5 percent
2004	10 percent	47 percent	37 percent	1 percent	5 percent

In Table 4-1, you can see that in 2008, the 1024 x 768 screen resolution was the most commonly used. With this knowledge, you can design your landing page and the fold to ensure that the page functions correctly with this resolution.

You may also see differences in displays, depending on the operating system used. Although the relative screen resolution doesn't change between a Mac and PC system, for example, how they set up that data *does* change. A standard iMac resolution is 1680 x 1050, whereas Windows usually uses 1024 x 768. If you want to be really thorough, consider who your target market is and what system — Mac or PC — they'll likely use to view your landing page.

To make the issue just a little more complex, if you plan to target a specific type of market — say, portable devices like iPhone, iPod Touch, or BlackBerry — you may have to go with a special, smaller landing page because these items have much smaller screen sizes then a typical home online user.

Table 4-2 gives you the average resolution of four common devices: Windows systems, iMac, iPod Touch, and BlackBerry Storm. As you'd expect, the smaller the device, the smaller the resolution.

Table 4-2:	Standard Screen Resolutions
Device	*Resolution*
iMac	1680 x 1050
Windows	1024 x 768
BlackBerry Storm	480 x 360
iPod Touch	480 x 320

We definitely recommend that you review your landing page with the resolution you plan to use. For example, look at your landing page on iMac and see whether it works — that's to say, see whether the information is still in the fold without scrolling. Each screen resolution is going to show a fixed amount of space, as shown in Figure 4-2. By knowing what will appear in all viewing areas, you can ensure that the most important part of your message is being delivered to everyone that visits your site.

The overlay shown in Figure 4-2 is available for download as desktop wallpaper from www.anthillpress.com — with this handy tool, sizing your landing page correctly is a snap.

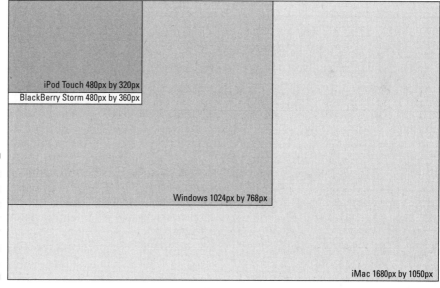

Figure 4-2:
Screen resolution comparison of four common devices.

Testing your fold viewing area

To ensure your fold has all the information needed for every visitor, test it. The simplest way to test what visitors see is to set up your monitor to mimic your visitor's experience.

If you have a dual-monitor arrangement, set up your second monitor with the preferred screen resolution and leave it that way during your testing period.

To change your monitor resolution in Windows Vista, use the following steps:

1. **Click the Start button and then choose Control Panel⇨Appearance and Personalization⇨Personalization⇨Display Settings.**

   The Display Settings window appears.

2. **Under Resolution, move the slider to the resolution you want.**

   Obvious choices here are 1024 x 768 or higher, as that is what most of your visitors will be using.

3. **Click Apply.**

   Your screen auto-resizes to the new resolution.

To change your screen resolution in Mac OS X, follow these steps:

1. **Choose ⇨System Preferences.**

   The System Preferences window appears onscreen.

2. **Select the Displays icon to open the Resolutions Screen.**

3. **In the Resolutions list that appears, select a new resolution.**

   Your screen auto-resizes to the new resolution.

By changing the screen resolution to that of your visitors, you start to experience the landing page as they do. You can't expect to meet your visitors' expectations if you don't know what they're experiencing!

Some monitors or graphics cards don't allow you to change your resolution to the level needed. (This is especially the case when you try to get to the upper levels of the resolution limits.) To get around this, you can resize your browser to the proper size. This gives you a simulation of what people see.

Checking out your competition

Some companies do an amazing job of organizing and designing a fold. To get to this point, company employees have no doubt spent hours developing and testing their fold. A great way to wrap your mind around what others are doing with their fold to reach their success is to check out your competition. As well as seeing some great work, you also see folds that are dismal. These are the ones that load slow, use too many graphics, have non-relevant text, and more. These sites are great to study because they allow you to see how ineffectively some folks use their landing page elements.

When you visit other sites, whether for business or pleasure, keep a notebook handy for observations. If something amazing catches your eye, jot it down. The fold is used not only in landing page design but also all around you. Take a minute and look at this book's cover. The invisible fold here is what would be visible on a bookshelf or a store display. Again, you'll find all the important information falls above that line. Any well-designed book cover gives you enough information to decide whether you actually want to buy it, just as any well-designed Web site gives you the information you need to determine whether a longer stay is really worth your while.

Troubleshooting your fold

Having trouble with your fold? Listed here are a few things to check if you suspect your conversion rates — the longed-for sales to signups — are due to fold problems:

- ✔ **Advertising doesn't match your fold content:** You simply *have* to tie in your advertising with your landing page content — no ifs, ands, or buts. Not matching the customer's expectations creates high bounce rates and low returns. Visitors want to see the information they need right in the fold.

- ✔ **Poor matching of search terms (keywords):** Visitors often use specific words in their search engine to find what they're looking for. (No surprise there.) If your page is a result of one of their searches but has nothing to do with what they searched for, you need to choose a better focus for your page content. That means focus your keywords.

- ✔ **Expecting people to scroll past the fold:** Some designers forget they're dealing with regular people and assume visitors are just going to make their way through the whole page to find the important stuff. Do not make this assumption. Limit vertical fold as much as possible and avoid horizontal folds.

- ✔ **Oversized images:** When trying to impress your visitor, a pretty common tactic is to aim for the fences by placing a jumbo-sized image on a landing page. Common but oh-so-wrong. Jumbo-sized images pose a problem for a couple reasons, but here's two: One, if the customer has to scroll to see the image, it loses much of its effect; two, if it takes too long for the image to load, a visitor may just give up and leave. (Not exactly what you'd hoped for, right?)

✔ **Getting too fancy:** Just because you *can* create Flash animation and other zippy elements doesn't mean you *should.* Fancy elements and graphics can delay load times and draw away visitors from the content they're actually looking for.

✔ **Header is too large:** The header is the top area of a Web site or landing page that identifies your company's brand and makes it instantly recognizable to your visitors. This area is typically a thin bar at the top, but many developers bump up the size of the header area way too much. When you don't factor in header size or navigation formatting, you take space away from the fold information area. This forces the visitor to scroll just to get the basic information.

Figure 4-3 shows what happens when the header containing the top graphic is too large for the viewing area. This design pushes the information down to the point where it cuts off the message and doesn't show the call to action. A design like this makes the header graphic more important than the message.

Figure 4-3:
An oversized header forces important information below the fold.

✔ **Too much text copy:** Overloading the text at the top and trying to get too much in front of the customers all at once is going to overwhelm them, which means you're essentially burying the information the visitor needs to make a quick decision.

✔ **Not testing your final landing page to see whether it fits in the fold:** Folks who design Web sites are often in a rush to get things done — aren't we all? — so they often forget to do the final testing on their landing pages. Take a few minutes to check whether all information is available for the visitor in the fold.

By looking at the common fold problems we list here, you can recognize difficulties with your current landing page efforts or quickly find areas that are slowing down your potential sales.

Working with Headings

A *heading* is the attention-grabbing text on a landing page. The purpose of your heading is to immediately attract your visitor's attention. After you have her attention, you have a better chance that she continues reading. Lose her in the heading, and she's likely to leave.

Most of the time, your heading is the sentence at the top of your page, right where the average visitor looks first. Newspapers provide a good example of good and bad headings. Take a look at today's paper. Which headings capture your attention?

Writing attention-grabbing headings is often not easy and takes some practice, but after you get it down, it's a huge asset to your landing page development. If you can't write good headings, you may need to hire a professional to help. Professional writers — sometimes known as *copywriters* — are experts at writing content, headings, and just about anything you need for your site.

There are many advantages to using a professional writer, but foremost among them is the fact that writing pros write professionally: they avoid misspelled words and awkward sentences; they know the right language to capture the attention of your audience. Deciding to use a professional writer is the first step; actually finding the right one for you is the next. Listed below is a quick checklist of things to consider when hiring a professional writer:

- ✔ **Review the portfolio:** Professional writers should have Web sites that offer published samples of their work. Take the time to review their online portfolios to see whether the writing style matches what you're looking for.

- ✔ **Interview your writer:** You'll be working closely with your writer and you need to be able to work well with that person. Get to know them on the phone or by e-mail to see whether it's a match.

- ✔ **Review their services:** What services does the writer offer? Blogs? Brochures? Web content? Ad content? Press releases? Article writing? Well-rounded writers will have experience in a variety of areas: be sure their resume shows a variety of accomplishments.

- ✔ **Determine turnaround time:** Some writers are great but are unable to meet deadlines. You may not be able to wait for content, as you need to get the product to market quickly.

✔ **Compare costs:** There can be a huge difference in the price between professional writers. When choosing a writer, you'll need to find the one that meets your budget.

You could save a bit of money by coming up with good headings (and other content) on your own, but maybe you're not feeling too sure of your writing skills. Time for a copywriting boot camp! Check out the Copyblogger Web site (www.copyblogger.com) or the helpful folks at justmakeiteasy.com for articles and training materials on how to improve your copywriting skills. And if you want more on writing, check out Chapter 6 in this book, where we focus more on the art of writing for your landing page, including tips on writing headings.

It's simple: If visitors don't stop to read, you have no chance selling *anything* to them. So getting their attention so they read what you have to say is your number one priority.

Placing your heading

The text within the heading is critical, but where you place your heading within the fold is just as crucial, as is how you style the text. Naturally, the heading lives at the top of the fold, but *where* at the top? (This may sound like nitpicking, but trust us — a few inches here can make a huge difference.)

Here are some locations and style tips that have proven to work:

✔ **Above the fold:** A no-brainer — your heading simply has to be located above the *fold* — the viewable area on your site that a visitor first sees before he scrolls. For slow load times, the heading should be one of the first things to load. If it catches a visitor's attention, he'll be more patient and curious for the rest of the page to load.

✔ **Unique font:** Your heading needs to stand out over the other text on the page, not in the sense that it overwhelms everything else on the page but rather as a way to tell visitors *read me first.* You can often add that extra oomph to text with a larger font type and a different color.

Okay, we did say you should go with a different font and color for your heading, but don't take this as a license to go with eggplant tones with cerulean accents — you have limits, in other words. Some headings you'll see on your Web wanderings are the fashion equivalent of a pale blue leisure suit — and equally as attractive. Keep the fonts readable and somewhat traditional. Colors don't need to be overpowering and loud to attract attention — think subtle and classy.

✔ **Font size:** The font size can be almost anything you need for the layout. Often, the font used in the heading is larger than the body text. When larger, the size shouldn't overwhelm the visitor or take up too much of the fold space. A font too big looks ridiculous.

Okay, we just can't get behind some fonts when used on a landing page, especially in a heading. These include Comic Sans, Brush Script, Courier, Algerian, and Broadway to name a few. We know a developer who uses Comic Sans exclusively on all landing pages and in all e-mails he sends us. Now, consistency is often a good trait, especially in restaurant food, consistently using Comic Sans for headings is a visual disaster as far as we're concerned (just don't tell him we said that!). We suggest sticking to proven fonts. (You can find a detailed discussion of fonts in Chapter 5.)

✔ **One of four positions:** Headings are usually found in four different positions on a page:

- Right side of the landing page
- Left side of the landing page
- Centered below the header
- In place of the header

In place of the header? Yep. Sometimes landing pages do not even need a header and the heading appears as the first. Like the other heading placement options, they need to be tested to verify which one is the best. Testing and split testing landing pages is discussed in Chapter 12.

In Figure 4-4, you can see an example of a heading justified to the left. This position gets a high amount of exposure because it's generally the first place the eye lands. The layout you choose depends on the heading length, the image size, and how they sit together on the page.

Seriously, don't forget what we said earlier about Comic Sans.

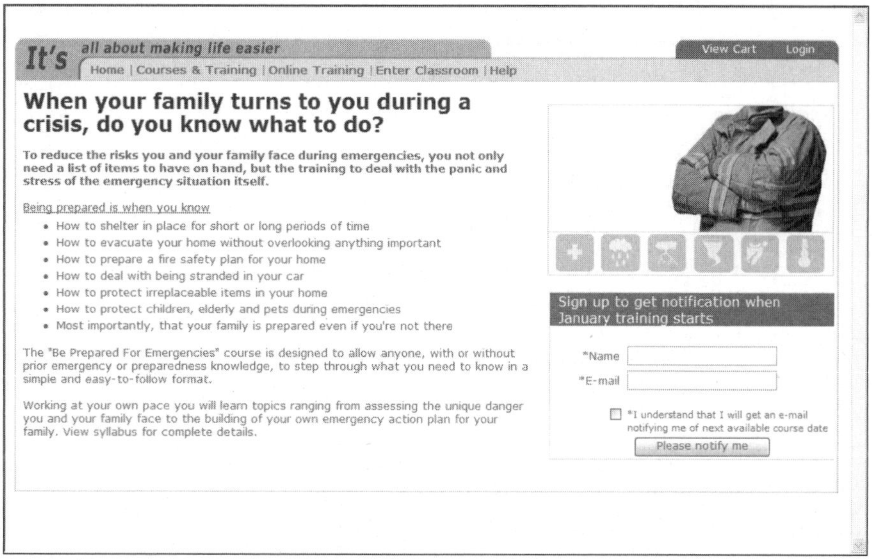

It's all about making life easier

Home | Courses & Training | Online Training | Enter Classroom | Help

View Cart   Login

When your family turns to you during a crisis, do you know what to do?

To reduce the risks you and your family face during emergencies, you not only need a list of items to have on hand, but the training to deal with the panic and stress of the emergency situation itself.

Being prepared is when you know

- How to shelter in place for short or long periods of time
- How to evacuate your home without overlooking anything important
- How to prepare a fire safety plan for your home
- How to deal with being stranded in your car
- How to protect irreplaceable items in your home
- How to protect children, elderly and pets during emergencies
- Most importantly, that your family is prepared even if you're not there

The "Be Prepared For Emergencies" course is designed to allow anyone, with or without prior emergency or preparedness knowledge, to step through what you need to know in a simple and easy-to-follow format.

Working at your own pace you will learn topics ranging from assessing the unique danger you and your family face to the building of your own emergency action plan for your family. View syllabus for complete details.

Sign up to get notification when January training starts

*Name

*E-mail

☐ *I understand that I will get an e-mail notifying me of next available course date

Please notify me

Figure 4-4:
Heading to
the left.

Each visitor demographic is sure to respond differently to any particular page layout you come up with, so do your own market testing for heading placement. This varied response means that some landing page layouts are going to work for some products but not for others, so you need to figure out what layout is going work best in the long run for what you want to achieve.

The secret to creating perfect headings

We've noticed that when we stick *secret* into a heading, more people tend to read it. Everyone wants to be in on the secret — and you're no exception because you're reading this — so here it is: When trying to perfect your heading, do a lot of research and take the time to locate a collection of effective headings. You may need to go as far as to make a scrapbook of both online and offline headings that capture your attention. Use this collection to inspire you on your way to the perfect heading.

Marketers and writers alike often use this trick to get them in the mindset and bring up ideas from deep within your creative soul.

To create your own heading repository, follow these simple instructions:

1. **Create a Microsoft Word document (or a document created in some other word processing program) and place it on your desktop.**

   With a file ready-to-hand, you're more likely to actually use it, which means you can take full advantage of it.

2. **Find examples of successful headings online.**

   Use your favorite search engine to track down your specimens. Use search terms, such as *top headings, successful headings,* and *award winning headings.*

3. **Copy and paste the headings that catch your eye into your Word doc and then keep looking.**

   When online, keep an eye out for headings that attract your attention and copy these to your Word doc.

4. **Save your own headings.**

   When doing your own landing pages, keep successful headings in your repository too and mark them as *successful.*

Over time, you'll create a large heading repository that you can then use to draw inspiration from. Simply look through your heading repository, find one you want to try, and rewrite it to fit your need. Remember, the idea is to adapt a model for your own needs, so don't plagiarize other people's work; just use your sample heading as a springboard for your own entry in the World's Most Effective Heading contest.

Table 4-3 has a list of proven headings that you can use to start your own heading repository. Many more can be found online if you search for *100 best headings ever written*.

Table 4-3	Twelve Successful Headings
Headings	
How to win friends and influence people	
Why some foods "explode" in your stomach	
When doctors "feel rotten," this is what they do	
Guaranteed to go through ice, mud or snow — or we pay the tow	
Have you a "worry" stock?	
Is the life of a child worth $1 to you?	
Six types of investor — which group are you in	
Pierced by 301 nails . . . retains full air pressure	
I lost my bulges . . . and saved money too!	
Here's a quick way to break up a cold	
76 reasons why it would have paid you to answer our ad a few months ago	
Former barber earns $8,000 in 4 months as a real estate specialist	

To avoid copyright infringement, be sure that you're using someone else's heading as a starting point, not an endpoint. In other words, make your own variation, not a direct copy.

Table 4-3 highlights some headings that have proven successful. Table 4-4 shows some headings found online that could've used a tad more work before being making their way online.

Table 4-4	Nine Rather Questionable Headings
Headings	
Grandmother of eight makes hole in one	
Nicaragua sets goal to wipe out literacy	
If strike isn't settled quickly, it may last a while	
Stolen painting found by tree	
Panda mating fails; veterinarian takes over	
New study of obesity looks for larger test group	
Local high school dropouts cut in half	
Carpet tunnel syndrome is often misdiagnosed and misunderstood	
Giant Sale — two for one!	

Determining heading effectiveness

An effective heading keeps visitors on your page longer, as simple as that. Create an effective heading, and your bounce rate decreases and your time-on-page tracking increases. If you don't believe us, take a look at Web site log files — the evidence is laid out for you in black and white. (Not sure how to read tracking statistics and Web site logs? Check out Chapter 12.)

You can also test the effectiveness of your heading with the *split-testing* method in which you alternate two different headings between page visits to see which one is more effective in creating a conversion. Products, such as free Google Analytics, offer a split-testing option specifically for landing page testing. (For more on Google Analytics, see Chapter 12.)

You have to put in some work to get the right heading for your landing page; you'll probably have to write, test, and repeat several times before finding a heading that works well for you. Over time, and with tracking and monitoring changes, you'll see a steady increase in the positive response to your heading.

Troubleshooting your heading

Just can't seem to get your heading to perform as you want? Here's a quick checklist of things to consider — and things to avoid:

- ✔ **Avoid headings that blend too much with the page.** Headings need to stand out. Often, keeping them the same size and color as regular text or blending too much with your look can hamper your page's impact. Be bold in the heading, but not shocking.

✔ **Don't rely on headings that are too long.** Sometimes first time writers try to pack too much into their headings, which become complete paragraphs of information. People want quick, concise information.

✔ **Don't use headings that don't match the advertising content.** Matching headings with what your visitors expect to find is one key to making a heading effective. Headings need to tie directly into your advertising efforts. General headings aren't as effective as headings that speak directly to the target audience.

✔ **Be careful when you place text over images on the landing page.** This effect is used with magazines all the time, but the effect doesn't always work as well online. If you plan to place text over an image, make sure you test the result. Bottom line: Always keep headings simple.

✔ **Don't make headings too hard to read.** You find more and more "hip" types working with opposite colors — a black background with white writing, for example, which is pretty much the opposite of what you'd expect. This can actually make it harder for the reader to read the words. The more difficult the heading is to read, the less likely he is to read it or anything else. Remember to use easily readable fonts.

✔ **Be sure to test your results.** Not testing your landing page is a common mistake. Just be aware that changing your heading can have a major impact on the success of your landing page, so who in his right mind wouldn't test to see what works and what doesn't?

Understanding Body Text Essentials

The *body text* is the largest part of your landing page and includes the listed benefits that your visitors are going to receive from your product or service. We cover the body text format and suggest how to formulate your body text in Chapter 6, but we want to get some body text basics out there for your perusal.

Readers won't necessarily read your body text, or at least not all of it. People are all scanners these days; most don't read everything they come across, and they tend to filter out content quickly. This fact of life is why you need to structure your body copy so the reader can easily find what she wants quickly. More specifically, you need to remember that body writing is done in chunks or small paragraphs, making it easier to scan and read.

When you develop body text, it's always helpful to have someone else — preferably someone else who's not intimately involved in the project — read it over. You can always figure out what you're trying to say, but will the same be true for a more impartial observer? Getting feedback from a more neutral party can be very effective in determining whether your body text really does hit the mark.

General body text guidelines

The text used as body text on landing pages requires a different approach and formatting style than what you'd use for books or magazine articles. For many, reading onscreen is more difficult or less familiar than reading actual print. To overcome any initial resistance on the part of site visitors, keep the following in mind:

- **Paragraph size:** Keep your paragraphs relatively short with a maximum of 3–4 lines, utilizing short, punchy sentences. You want the text to be easy to read and to the point. Save the fluff and details for below the fold.

- **Bullet points:** Whenever possible, use a quick bullet list to highlight important values and benefits. Lazy readers love bullet points. (Notice that this section is in bullets, not that you're lazy or anything.)

- **Font effects:** Use **bold** and *italic* to draw attention to important parts of the text but don't overuse the Formatting toolbar. Font effects help with skimming the page, as long as they're used only to draw attention to points that are truly important. Use the <u>underline</u> sparingly because people associate an underline with hyperlinks.

The body text length doesn't have any hard and fast rules. Certainly, the text placed within the fold has to be succinct and brief. You also can't have text all over the fold, but rather it has to be strategically placed. Additional text is often placed below the fold but this, too, needs to be sales-focused and needs to highlight the content needed to make the sale.

Avoiding text pitfalls

As you'd expect, if you followed our earlier comments about developing your fold and your heading, be on the lookout for a few things when working with the text body:

- **Chatty rambling:** Don't waste your reader's time. Chances are she'll read only bits and pieces of your copy, so get to the point fast. Cover facts and benefits and avoid stories and analogies.

- **An incomplete sales pitch:** Every landing page should be a complete sales pitch. Don't expect your readers to return for a second installment or click to another page.

- **Complicated text:** Over-involved body copy is copy that must be read from top to bottom. Avoid this trap by having your most important points at the beginning and ending of paragraphs. A 20-second skim should be just as effective in selling to your reader as a 2-minute read.

✔ **Overwrought appearance:** This is more of a design issue but is important to mention when you plan your writing. Keep fonts, colors, sizes, and spacing consistent. Don't rely on stylistic tricks and over-the-top effects to make your points; you want the copy to be easy to read, rather than confusing and overwhelming.

✔ **Grammar and spelling:** Although you want to keep the tone and writing style at your reader's level, you also want to ensure you follow basic English rules. To correct any spelling and grammar mistakes you may have introduced into your body text, copy and paste the text into a word processor and take advantage of its spelling and grammar check features.

✔ **Language:** Although you may choose to use slang to appeal to the reader, you need a healthy balance of professionalism and conversational speak. Also avoid the use of highly technical terms and jargon.

Creating a Call to Action

Call to action is another key component of the fold. *Call to action* is the text used to attempt to get the visitor to take immediate action, such as Click Here Now!, Cast Your Vote Now!, or For a Limited Time Only!.

To get a better sense of what a call to action is, think of a late night infomercial. During the infomercial, you're asked repeatedly to have your check or credit card ready. You're infused with a sense of urgency because you'll get that great free gift only if you call the toll-free number within the next few minutes. This infomercial format actually works. Now, we know infomercials aren't everyone's cup of tea, but truth be told, they do work — which is why we stress that a version of this type of call to action needs to be included on your landing page.

Keeping it simple

A call to action is most effective when it's not too complicated and doesn't have too many options. You want your visitor to take a single action, such as Buy or Sign Up, not have multiple options, such as Check Out Our New Web Site or Call to Order Our Catalog. To be most effective, keep the message focused on a single action.

Here are a few things to keep in mind when you look at your call to action:

✔ **Be specific:** Tell your visitors you want them to click, buy, or sign up. Remember to use action words to generate excitement.

✔ **Give a reason:** Tell your visitors why it's in their best interest to do the action you request, such as Click Now to Save Money!.

✔ **Give a sense of urgency:** The goal of many landing pages is to generate an immediate sale, which is why a call to action often includes a sense of urgency.

A good call to action reflects what you're trying to do with your copy. If your copy is leading a visitor to buy, tell them to buy! A call to action can be as simple as Buy Now or as complex as a step-by-step process.

Testing different headings is a good idea and so is creating various calls to action to discover the most effective one. You hear different calls to action daily on the radio, on TV, and of course, on the Internet. Some are more effective than others in encouraging action. Some familiar calls to action are shown in Table 4-5.

Table 4-5	Calls to Action
Call to Action Examples	
Click here to get a full night's sleep in just 4 hours.	
Subscribe now for free tips for doing your own taxes.	
Watch this video on organizing your desk and office space.	
Are you safe online? Click now to find out!	
One week until Valentine's day. Reserve a room now!	
Buy a season's pass and never wait in line again!	
Click here to save now!	

Calls to action are designed to lead people to act. Choose your language accordingly.

Troubleshooting your call to action

Many of the calls to action you see and hear just aren't that effective. To keep your calls to action from becoming calls to inaction, avoid the following call to action no-no's:

✔ **Not testing your call to action:** Every element on your landing page is going to benefit from testing, including your calls to action. Failure to test your call to action results in a mediocre visitor response and takes away from your potential visitor conversion.

- ✔ **Unclear actions:** To be effective, your call to action needs to be clear and to the point. If you want your visitor to buy your product, say Buy Now or Add to Cart, rather than Come Experience the Benefits of Our Product or Try Something New Today.

- ✔ **Misdirected calls to action:** Be sure your call to action takes the visitor to the right page for what the action implies. If the link says Add to Cart, it'd better go to your cart page and not to another information section.

- ✔ **Placing your call to action out of the fold:** Make sure that your call to action fits into your fold area. If people decide not to scroll further down on your page, they should still to have the opportunity to act on your call to action — something they can't do if they can't see it.

- ✔ **Blending your call to action with surrounding text:** If your call to action looks the same as your body copy, then when visitors skim the page, they could miss it. Make the call to action stand out with buttons, fonts, and colors. (Just remember that your call to action doesn't need to be in huge font with screaming pink and orange colors. Stay classy, in other words.)

Using Images in the Fold

Images are a great addition to the fold. The correct image can portray to the visitor a sense of professionalism and trust as well as provide additional information about you and your product. As they say, a picture is worth a thousand words — and like every other element in the fold, images can either attract and retain visitors or repel them.

You know as well as we do that images can have powerful connotations. They can do the practical stuff — show the size and characteristics of an object — but they can also *suggest* a lot, such as when you show a person enjoying your product and its uses. Many visitors expect to see the product they're buying, and it's a good idea to fulfill such expectations.

When you deal with visitor expectations, the best practice is to keep your images simple until you have a firm grasp on how to use them. If you have to choose between a stock product shot and a phenomenal picture that just happens to take away from the message you're trying to impart, go with the stock product shot.

The quality and type of image used within the fold ties in with the trust a visitor feels toward the company. Poorly chosen images (or images of questionable quality) bring down the visitor's impression and shows that the company doesn't care about how its product is represented. For more information on choosing and placing images, refer to Chapter 5.

Using animated images and videos

Many landing page developers choose to include videos or animated images on their pages and in the fold to help get their message across. Although videos and animated images can be effective, they can also slow page load times and create a visual distraction. Even with these caveats, they can be a great asset to a landing page, both in and out of the fold.

When using these items, be very sure that they're actually adding the sales value you expect. You have a lot to mull over before using videos or animations in your design, so consider the following before you proceed:

- ✔ **Increased load time:** Both of these enhancements increase the load time of the visitor's experience.
- ✔ **Increased design time:** Videos and animation require more work in setup and organization time.
- ✔ **Expensive:** When starting out to get the message right on your sales page, building expensive product videos or animated images might not be the best place to start when you test the effectiveness of your landing page.
- ✔ **Creates a distraction:** Before you even think of using any animated images or videos, remember that your main goal is to provide the customer with a rewarding user experience. Will that flashy animation or video help your customer decide whether to buy from you? Do they build trust, or do they simply distract from the message?

Don't get caught up in the flash and the excitement just because the technology is there to do it. Your goal here is to get the conversion, not impress with the flash. If animated images or videos work for your product, go ahead and use them. If they don't work, don't hesitate to remove them.

Placing your image in the fold

When you use an image in the fold, consider not only what image you use but also where you place it. Here are the three primary image locations when you use images in the fold:

- ✔ To the left
- ✔ Centered
- ✔ To the right

Just as with the heading, when an image is positioned on the left, more importance is placed on the image simply because the eye tends to gravitate toward the left upon first seeing a landing page. If you decide to go with an image placement to the left, be sure that you've chosen a powerful image — one that can sell to the visitor all by itself.

A less common tactic is to place the image in the center of the landing page. This puts the image front and center, reducing the area for text but increasing the importance of the image. When you put an image center stage, make sure it gets your message across clearly.

When placing an image in the fold area, test to see what works. The only way to really know is to test and retest your site. One great way to test is to use split testing. With split testing, two or more sites are created, put online, and tested live to see which one performs the best. Split testing is discussed in Chapter 12.

Image mistakes to avoid

Several mistakes are common to image use within the fold. Avoid the following when you design a new page or check against your current landing page design:

- ✔ **Going for too fancy or too casual, rather than the elegantly simple:** Beginners often try to get too fancy with their images, or they go to the opposite extreme and rely on online clip art to fill in white space. Keep it (elegantly) simple; try a simple product shot first before you try to make something overly fancy. As for clip art, don't even go there; too often it makes a site look too simplistic or cheap.

- ✔ **Using images unrelated to product or story:** Using an image just because you have an image is a sure way to throw off visitors. Nothing is wrong with white space. Allow your visitor to see your message and not be distracted by unnecessary bits and pieces.

- ✔ **Using images that are too large for fold area:** Your fold is a very finite area. An image that overflows its bounds isn't effective in selling your product or getting your visitors to do what you want them to.

  Test your landing page to make sure that your image fits. Scrolling to see the image or having to scroll side-to-side to see the full effect of your image doesn't help in your online conversions.

- ✔ **Focusing attention on the wrong areas:** If your image can tell the whole story and get the message across quickly, put it in the more important position. On the other hand, if the image is weak or doesn't reflect the right story, putting the image in a prominent place won't win you any conversions. If the image isn't star quality, put it in a less important area of the fold or out of the fold completely.

- ✔ **Using poor-quality images:** You're better off with no image at all than a poor one. Your landing page is an extension of your business; you want visitors to have the best impression they can.

No matter what image you plan to use on your site, make sure you take the time to properly test not only the placement of the image on the page but the image itself on your target market.

Creating Trust

Dealing with money and online transactions can be a tricky issue. One thing's for sure, though: You can't convince someone to part with his hard-earned money if he doesn't believe in you. This is when trust elements come into play. Trust elements are essential to convert those maybe and hesitant visitors into paying customers.

For some, building trust is probably one of the last things you think about when you try to build a landing page, but trust is another one of those critical elements that no successful landing page can do without. Many sales are lost because visitors don't trust the site. One of the big trust items is knowing that if you don't like a product, you can take it back. If this guarantee isn't found within the fold, lots of visitors are going to turn around slowly and walk away from your site.

Regardless of what product or service you have to offer, every customer that visits your site must be able to overcome their trust issues if you want them to eventually buy from you. Your landing page has a big job in store when showing your Web site visitors that they can trust you. Just how big a job is made clear in the next sections.

Establishing trust

Building trust occurs throughout the landing page. Professionalism, first impressions, and content all work together in the fold to build up the trust in your visitor's eyes.

To build the trust, we use specific *trust features* — those elements that talk to your visitor's inner (skeptical) voice. They reassure your visitor that you're a legitimate business and that you'll deliver what you say you will. Trust features include

- Money-back guarantees
- Testimonials
- Contact Us links
- Links to the Return Policy

Before incorporating a trust feature into the fold area, test for its impact on the decision-making process. If a testimonial gets your visitors closer to buying your product than your Return Policy will, focus on what others have to say about you.

Common trust errors to avoid

Gaining trust is a critical consideration for your conversions. Without trust, your conversions will be nowhere near what they need to be. There are a few common trust related errors to be aware of. These include

✔ **Limited trust efforts:** Beginning designers can be so focused on their sales message or look of the landing page that the trust aspect is forgotten entirely. A simple Guaranteed seal or link to customer testimonials can go a long way to establishing trust.

✔ **Inadequate policies:** Visitors want to know what you do with their information or how you handle a return. Your landing page should have easy-to-find links to your Privacy Policy, Return Policy, Terms of Use Policy, and any other legalese that's applicable to your product or service.

✔ **Incomplete Contact Us information:** Because the visitor can't walk into your store and meet you face to face, it's important they know they deal with real people. A contact page is more than an e-mail form; it includes the head office address, phone number, and business hours as a way of establishing your business presence.

Using Eye Path (Heat Maps) in Your Design

The *eye-pathing* method identifies where the human eye instinctively looks on a page. Over time and with much research, an eye-path chart was developed and comes in the easy-to-use form of a heat map. You can use Web heat maps to find the areas of a landing page most frequently scanned by visitors.

Heat maps remove the guesswork of where people look on your page. Made up of various colored regions of yellows, reds, and oranges, you know where to concentrate your strongest selling points so people will respond to your message more often. The darker the color, the *hotter* the spot.

Heat maps are guides only. In real life, many factors affect visitors' surfing habits. By doing your own testing, you can develop hot zones for your unique landing page design. That being said, when you develop your landing page, you can take advantage of human nature and where people look first on the page to improve the conversion on your landing page.

Identifying a heat map

Because a lot of research on eye pathing has been done already — and the equipment required to do such studies is complicated and costly — we suggest using two established heat maps readily available online. Although both sport very different looks, both show very similar information.

Figures 4-5 and 4-6 show two common heat maps in use. Although in different formats, both show very similar patterns of where people look and where the most important critical elements need to be. The warm and hot zones — as depicted with varying shades of orange, red, and yellow onscreen — are where you want to focus your energy. Also notice that most of the hottest areas are above the fold.

When you look at a heat map, the areas of highest eye-contact concentration are shaped like an F. The industry term for this viewing area is the *Golden Triangle,* although it seems more logical to call it the *Golden F.* The human eye reads the content at the top left-hand corner, and then travels horizontally and then vertically along the left-hand side.

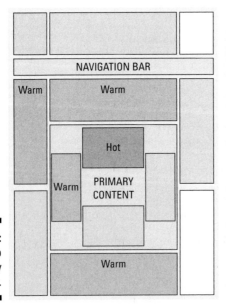
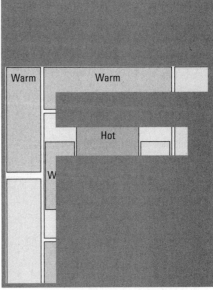

Figure 4-5:
Heat map endorsed by Google.

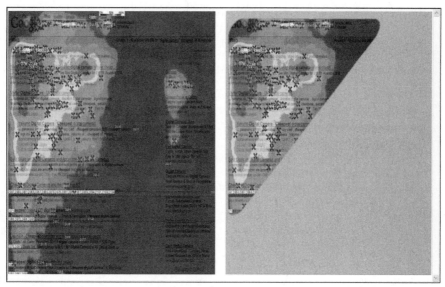

Figure 4-6:
Traditional
heat map.

Heat maps as a marketing analysis tool

One main advantage of using heat maps is that they give insight into what your visitor will do or at least what they are looking at first. You can see what the average visitor is clicking or drawn to. Heat maps also serve the following purposes:

- ✔ **Link clicking:** A heat map can show you specifically what part of a link is clicked more often. For example, if you have a Job Offer — Apply Today link, you might notice *Job* is where the click usually takes place. Watch for behavior such as this to help you fine-tune your navigation and create more effective links.

- ✔ **Performance increase:** A heat map can show you the dead areas of your page. Look out for these two types of dead zones:
  - Links that aren't clicked at all
  - Images that are clicked but aren't active links

  Both of these issues need to be addressed and corrected, whether by creating more compelling links or by linking the image to fulfill what the visitor is looking for.

- ✔ **Maximum ad placement:** Not only does a heat map tell you the best spot to put your most compelling argument, but it also tells you the best place to put ads in order to generate income. Incorporating advertising in your landing page isn't worth the time or effort if the ads don't result in a visitor click. For more information on heat maps and ad placement, refer to a Google tutorial at

```
https://www.google.com/adsense/support/bin/answer.py?hl=en&answer=17954
```

Comparing current heat maps

Eye-path testing and research demonstrates that you have hot zones for your eyes. These hot zones allow landing page designers to get important information in the eyes' path, and therefore, right in front of the visitor.

Figure 4-7 uses an overlay to clearly illustrate the F pattern of hot zones. Notice how the product image, title, price, and call to action buttons fall neatly in the hottest areas.

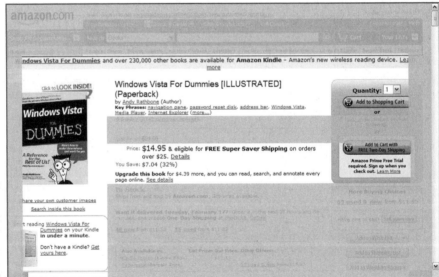

Figure 4-7: An F heat map over Amazon. com.

You can determine whether this is the best use of the space by testing your landing page with and without this element. By placing imaginary hot zones over your page, you can start to visualize what attracts your visitor first.

By knowing how to use heat maps in your landing page design, you can improve your conversions by grabbing the attention of your visitors and putting the important items first.

Doing your own heat map testing

In the quest for the best landing page, you can do your own external testing of what people think of your Web site. If you don't have the budget to professionally test your site, you can use an informal testing method.

Use the following ideas to determine how to conduct your own heat map testing:

- **Select a random group of people.** Try to select people who also fit your ideal visitor demographic.

- **Set up a distraction-free environment.** Set up a computer in an office or an area where participants won't be disturbed. Pre-load your landing page.

- **Show your landing page to participants individually.** Have a person sit down in front of a blank screen, leave the room, and ask him to turn on the screen. Get him to jot down the first things he sees and what stands out. Don't judge the answers. Maybe ask him to fill out a quick survey on what the page meant to him and whether he'd buy it. This way, you get two tests done in one.

This informal way to test is by no means truly scientific, but you'll be surprised at how effective it is when it comes to getting feedback on first impressions and what caught people's eye.

Chapter 5

The "Best Practices" of Landing Page Aesthetics

. . . .

In This Chapter

▶ Using color to entice visitors

▶ Incorporating buttons to grab attention

▶ Choosing reader-friendly fonts

▶ Selecting images that send the right message

▶ Working with photography

. . . .

Your landing page is made up of some basic visual components, with color, action buttons, and text taking up the lion's share. You shouldn't be surprised that having these elements work together is integral to the success of your landing page, but you're probably also aware that actually getting all these elements to work well together can be tricky. At bottom, to determine what buttons fit with what colors and backgrounds, you're going to have to rely on your own creative sense rather than any stock formula you find on the Web somewhere.

In this chapter, we guide your creative sense by going over the basics of incorporating colors, buttons, and images into your landing page. How these elements work together to complement each other sets the tone of your landing page, project's professionalism, and determines the visitor's first impression. (And you know the importance of making a good first impression, don't you?)

Enticing (or Repelling) Visitors with Color

It may not *seem* like it, but color plays an important part in your landing page design. Color can be used effectively to enhance the landing page, making it more appealing or, all too often, it can be used improperly, resulting in a landing page that's a visual disaster. Many developers ruin an otherwise brilliant marketing campaign by choosing a bad (okay, *ridiculous*) color choice. So for those who happen to like Web pages designed with a purple background and flashing bright yellow text, you may need to go to Color Coordination Boot Camp before being let anywhere near a Web site again.

What you're trying to do with your color scheme is to create a pleasant visual experience. Your color scheme should engage your visitor and subtly entice them without distracting with non-complementary colors. There are two extremes at work here — boring color schemes and visually chaotic color schemes. Your visitors are going to reject a site operating at each extreme, so your best bet is to be somewhere in the middle. Color, like other elements on your landing page, requires a logical structure so the brain can make sense of the color on your page. Color choices are not random, they are scientific.

The nutshell overview of color wheels

When most of us set out to create our landing pages, we pick the color scheme we like and if we're lucky and have a good eye for such things, we'll be okay and we end up with complementary colors. If we're not lucky — and it seems more people are unlucky than are — we set up color schemes that are not complementary and clash. A little color theory will help understand how colors blend and work on a landing page.

One of the first places to start with color theory is with the color wheel. The color wheel is a chart of colors of the visible spectrum you can use to show how colors complement each other. The color wheel was apparently created by none other than Sir Isaac Newton. Mr. Newton split white sunlight into green, cyan, blue, yellow, red, and orange beams. He was able to show the natural sequence of color by joining together the two ends of the color spectrum.

The color wheel is made up of three primary colors, (red, blue, yellow), three secondary colors (purple, green, orange), and six tertiary colors (red-violet, blue-violet, blue-green, yellow-green, yellow-orange, and red-orange). Tertiary colors are formed by combining a primary color with an adjacent secondary color.

When it comes to using the color wheel, complementary colors are any two colors that lay directly across from one another on the color wheel. For example, blue and orange, and blue-green and red-orange are complements. Color schemes using complementary colors create contrast and visual balance. Figure 5-1 shows how you'd choose complementary colors using the color wheel.

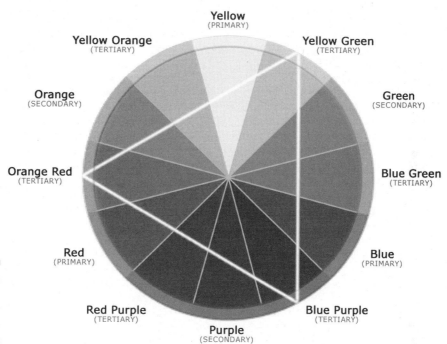

Figure 5-1:
Reviewing the color wheel.

Notice how, in Figure 5-1, red-purple is the complement of yellow-green and orange-green is the complement for blue-green. This forms a color triangle for that color scheme.

The color scheme you choose is very important and becomes part of your branding. Just like your favorite applications that reuse color schemes — think Microsoft Office or Adobe Acrobat — the colors you choose can ultimately identify you. Another telling example is the color scheme used by all the books in the *For Dummies* series. You can identify a *For Dummies* book from across the store without even reading the cover. That's good color marketing . . . and is the type of color identification you should strive for with your landing page. (Still, yellow and black? Who would've thought that'd work?)

A landing page *color scheme* refers to all the colors you choose to use on your landing page. The color scheme includes the colors for the links, buttons, fonts, backgrounds, and more. Choosing a color scheme at first may seem easy, but in fact, it takes a lot of thought and a testing. To make choosing a color scheme that much more difficult, you literally have millions of colors and shades at your fingertips. The good news is most of them are obviously a wrong choice for most applications. On the bad news side, though, it's not just a question of *which* colors you must choose but also how many colors. Using lots of different colors on your site is something to definitely avoid. The *rainbow effect* can look unprofessional, be difficult to read, and turn away visitors.

One of your color scheme's functions is to set the tone of your landing page. Complementing hues attract your visitors, whereas contrasting colors of a light background and dark text make for easy reading for visitors.

In most instances, your landing page is going to be separate from your main Web site. If this is the case, know that you aren't locked into the color scheme of your main Web site. You may want to keep your landing page color scheme consistent with other areas of your site — for branding purposes, for example — but don't feel compelled to do so. You do have the flexibility to try something new for your landing page if a new look makes sense.

According to the "Psychology of Color Marketing," a short marketing course available on Hewlett Packard's Web site at `http://h30187.www3.hp.com/tutorials/viewHowTo.jsp?courseId=19629&printable=true`, colors can attract attention, provoke both positive and negative responses, and stimulate memory. Their research concludes:

- ✔ People are 55 percent more likely to pick up color advertising.
- ✔ Use of color increases retention by an average of 65 percent.
- ✔ Using color in printed material increases readership by up to 80 percent.
- ✔ Color can increase the likelihood of a purchase by 80 percent or more.

These results aren't necessarily surprising. Obviously, color ads are an attractive component for a marketing program; if it wasn't, folks could save a ton of money by producing ads that were all in black and white. When it comes to color selection, the key for you is to choose colors that attract your marketing demographic, colors that represent your company, product, and the feeling you want the customer to have when she visits. Remember, it's all about first impressions.

Choosing the right color scheme definitely requires knowing your audience. If you're marketing weight-control products to seniors, the colors you end up choosing are probably going to be way different from colors used to market snowboards to adolescents. So, be sure you have a clear understanding of who makes up your potential audience before you choose your final color scheme.

The vocabulary of color

Colors can have a different impact on members of different groups, but it doesn't end there. When marketing to different places in the world, research what the colors represent to their cultures. This information isn't always easy to find, but if you have friends from other cultures, you can ask them. (Table 5-1 provides a brief comparison of black, white, and primary colors and what they commonly represent across Western, European, and Chinese culture. Notice how the simple color white can have such opposite connotations.)

Colors don't have the same meanings in every country; be aware that you need to target your color scheme to where you market your landing page.

Table 5-1		Cultural Color Meanings			
Culture	*Black*	*White*	*Red*	*Yellow*	*Blue*
Western	Death, evil, power, elegance	Purity, cleanliness, coldness, elegance	Excitement, love	Warm, cheerful	Calm, soothing, businesslike
European	Funerals, death, mourning	Marriage, angels, peace	Danger, love, excitement	Hope, joy, hazard, cowardice	Soothing
China	Mourning, death	Death, mourning	Good luck, celebration,	Nourishing, royalty	Spring, calm

North American culture also has a general association with colors and their meanings. The meaning of color may vary depending on who you talk to and what you read, but the following list provides a sample of some potential color meanings:

- **Black:** Sometimes associated with death and darkness. However, black can be a powerful, sophisticated color. Black is a serious color that can be easily read over light backgrounds.

- **White:** The color of purity, but it can also imply coldness or sterility. Like black, white can be an elegant color. Using simple white space on a Web site is a great way to keep the page from looking cluttered and can do a great job in attracting visitors to key information. (*White space* is areas of the Web site that have no text, buttons, or other features.)

- **Red:** On the one hand, red can often associated with fire and blood and on the other it is associated with passion and love. All this makes red an emotionally charged color. Red has very high visibility, which is perhaps why it is used for stop signs, fire trucks, warning signs, and sirens. We are programmed to pay attention to red. Seems then like a good choice for call to action buttons.

Different shades of red can mean different things:

- *Reddish (light) brown.* Fall color associated with falling leaves, end of summer.

- *Pink.* Often a feminine color but also suggests love and friendship.

- *Light red.* Valentine's color associated with love.

- *Dark red.* Used on warning signs and stop lights. Calls attention to something important. So you can see, red is a color that will likely find its way onto your landing page in some capacity.

✔ **Yellow:** Generally considered warm and cheerful. Yellow is an attention-getting color, but can be fatiguing for the eye. Black type on a yellow background provides maximum contrast for short, high-impact messages. Dull yellow is not so nice and can often be taken for a color that needs to be refreshed.

✔ **Blue:** Quite the popular color, especially among men. Blue is calm, soothing, and businesslike. However, if used too much, blue can send a cold and uncaring message.

✔ **Green:** The color of nature, providing a feeling of tranquility and calm. Green can also signify wealth and stability. Today, green is associated with recycling and environmentalism. There are many shades of green with different implications as well. Olive green can be taken to suggest peace, dark green with jealously and aqua green for healing and peace.

✔ **Brown:** Another nature color, with a feeling of strength and warmth. Brown can be either down-to-earth or sophisticated. Light browns can work well as a background color.

✔ **Orange:** This color combines red and yellow, so it's energetic, warm, and enthusiastic. Orange is often used to draw attention because it's one of the most flamboyant colors available.

This is just the tip of the color rainbow. What about purple and mauve? Colors pay a significant role on your landing page and as such should require careful thought, planning and testing. Do your buttons work best as yellow or red? Does your demographic prefer back or grey text? If there is one message we would love to get across, it's that color is more scientific than random. Take the time to research and test your color schemes.

Selecting your color scheme

Suppose you develop a landing page for special non-tear recycling bags — bags you'd use to hold the old cans, bottles, and newspapers on the back porch until you can haul everything to the street for pickup. What colors would work for a landing page devoted to such a product? Black background with white text? Blue and silver? Green and white?

You may have a general idea of what would work, but before you can sell those recycling bags, you're going to need to have a bit more information.

Who's your target market?

Are your recycling bags being sold B2B (Business to Business) or B2C (Business to Customer)? Regular consumers may expect something different from a color scheme than if you're selling recycling bags to wholesalers. If you don't think about whom you're building your landing page for, how can you design a page that will appeal specifically to them? Young, old, male, and female all have different preferences that will appeal to them. In addition to preference, colors have to be chosen for practicality. For example, older eyes need a strong contrast between the background and text colors to make reading easy.

Before you finalize your color scheme, make sure you understand who your target audience is.

How long is the design expected to last?

Consider whether the design and color scheme is going to be around for the life of the business, such as the logo and corporate identity, or if the scheme is intended for a short life span. Color schemes are sometimes more bold and experimental if they're for a seasonal promotion, trial, or special promotion. For longer running campaigns and for company branding, stick to traditional, professional, and complementary colors.

What message do you want your design to convey?

Colors can appeal to your visitors' emotions. Do you want your color scheme to convey a calm message? If you're selling books or scrapbooking supplies, a calm message may be just the ticket. If you're selling snowboards, motor bikes, or all-terrain vehicles, a calm color scheme might not be the best way to go. What you really want are bold, exciting colors. (Not that scrapbooking can't be bold and exciting as well, of course.)

Whatever your product, the color is a big part of setting the emotion of a landing page. Stark black and white can bring across elegance if used correctly, whereas blue can project professionalism and a sense of trust. Bright colors lend themselves to a playful environment, whereas earthy tones suggest warmth. Tying the product to an emotion or feeling with color is one of the tricks of the trade when you design a successful landing page.

Eight percent of men and 1 percent of women are estimated as color or tone blind. Colors that are too close in hue may be difficult for them to distinguish.

What's the competition doing?

Not only do you have to consider what your target audience will prefer, but you also need to make sure that your site stands out when compared to your competitors. If you take the time to visit your top competitors' Web sites, you can get an idea of the kinds of colors that the target market is drawn to while putting your own little twist to make your site memorable. This type of research is vital in choosing effective colors.

Getting help online

The Internet provides many resources for colors and marketing . . . but be sure to take some of the free advice with a grain of salt. Some of the info is helpful, but much of it can seem contradictory. To give you a head start in your color research, Table 5-2 provides a list of Web sites that you can reference for creating a complementary color scheme for your landing page.

Table 5-2	Online Color Sites
Web Site URL	**Description**
www.colorschemer.com	Offers a downloadable color wheel to help you choose complementary colors for your landing page.
www.colorblender.com	Free online tool used to test colors and color matching.
www.colourmod.com	Great site for color conversions and assisting you to pick the exact color scheme for your landing page.
www.kolur.com	A color palette gallery you can use to choose the perfect colors for your landing page.
www.ideo.com/visualizer.html	Use this site to test text and background colors. Play with it until you find one that works for your site.

Being practical with color choices

One common error to avoid with your landing pages happens when you use too much color; a second common error occurs when you use colors that are just too bold. Colors can definitely enhance your site, but the primary function of the landing page is to make it easy for visitors to find your information. A color scheme you come up with shouldn't interfere with this goal. The colors you choose are important for setting the tone and impression of your landing page, but you mustn't lose sight that the purpose of your page is to get your visitors to read your message. To accomplish this, keep the following in mind:

- ✔ **High contrast colors, such as dark text on a light background, are easier to read.**

- ✔ **Too many colors are distracting and make it difficult to find the content you want your user to see.**

- ✔ **Color schemes don't necessarily have to be bold.** Subtle colors can be just as effective when it comes to conveying the emotion you're aiming for.

- ✔ **Watch the use of punchy colors.** We'd be the first to say that bright yellow or orange, when used *sparingly,* can be very effective in attracting visitors to elements of your site, but we emphasize *sparingly* here. Although great attention grabbers, using bold colors too much reduces their effectiveness.

- ✔ **Red is a power color.** Red's great for stand-out items, such as phone numbers and buttons. Be choosy when you pick out your reds, though. Your red needs to be a true red, not a red with a pink or purple hue.

If you just can't decide on a color scheme, stick to black text with a white background. This color scheme is simple and can be very effective when color call-out buttons and banners are used.

By no means is this section the be-all, end-all when it comes to online color use. We give you the the basics in terms of what you need to consider when you design your landing page if you really want to hit your visitors with the most impact. You're going to need to do some experimenting to see what works with your particular situation.

Attracting Visitors with Buttons

You may not realize it, but the sales button you use on your landing page can make or break a sale. Just by changing the color, text, or button position, you can up your sales conversions in a major way.

Testing is the only true way to ensure you have the right button, but you can get a head start by scouting out the landscape a bit first. When you begin your testing, take the following two aspects into consideration:

- ✔ **Button color:** Fifteen percent of the top e-commerce sites use the color red for their purchase buttons, which may give you some idea how much faith folks put in red. (Answer: A lot of faith.) Do remember, though, that blue, orange, and green are close runners up.

> ✔ **Rollover cover:** A *rollover effect* occurs when an image changes color when your visitor moves his mouse over it. You may want to try changing your button color from red to green during the rollover to try to increase conversions.

Speaking with your buttons

Short and to the point is the goal for all your buttons. Not only should you be able to complete an entire thought in just a few words, you can also greatly influence your conversions by changing just a single word. Changing your button label from Buy It Now to Get It Now could make a big difference, for example. You can also get the same message across with a single word, such as Buy, Order, or Purchase.

You may want to avoid Buy, which implies a done deal, whereas something like Add to Shopping Cart gives the customer the feeling that she can reconsider her choice. Always test your wording, but consider avoiding any words that are associated with spending money; go instead with words that imply value, immediacy, or importance.

There's a fine line between buttons that say too much and those that don't say enough. For visitors who aren't familiar with online ordering or using the Internet in general, your button message must be very clear. Use Click Here to Order rather than just Order to get the point across to any level of online visitor.

Buttons don't need to stop at a typed message. Experiment with icons, such as arrows, a shopping cart, or a credit card. Anything that draws the eye without distracting from your message can be used to your advantage. Your buttons are a very small, but important, part of your overall landing page success. Test their effectiveness just as you test your headline, call to action, and body copy elements. Buttons can vary widely in shape and size (see Figure 5-2 if you don't believe us) so you have a lot to pick and choose from. The only way to be really sure that you've found the one that works for your Web site is to follow the basic guidelines we present in this chapter and then test and retest the buttons you've chosen for your landing page.

Pushing all the right buttons

Testing takes time, energy, and planning but to get the right action on the page, it's worth every effort. To conduct a focused test, make a short list of specific items you want to compare for effectiveness. Consider the following for your button testing:

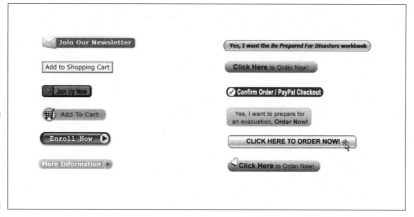

Figure 5-2:
Sample landing page buttons.

- **Color:** Button colors should be bright, contrasting, and eye-catching. Avoid button colors that are adjacent on the color wheel. For example, if your page is orange, don't use yellow or red buttons.

- **Location:** Try and place your action buttons above the fold (the fold area is discussed in Chapter 4). Visitors shouldn't have to scroll to do what you want them to. You can also duplicate the button and have it next to the product specs or other main focus of the page below the fold. This increases the chance of the button actually being noticed and clicked.

- **Word choice:** What your buttons tell your visitors is crucial to conversions:

  - *Make your buttons an action.* Use verbs, such as Sign Up, Download, and Add to Cart, to tell visitors what to do.

  - *Offer confidence.* Reinforce the action with a money back guarantee or privacy disclaimer to help your visitors to trust you.

  - *Create a sense of urgency.* A limited time offer creates the need to act now and nudges your visitors into buying or doing today.

- **Size and shape:** Make your buttons easy to see and to click. Be sure your buttons are on the larger side but don't be afraid to test different shapes. Check out what the big retailers use. Chances are, your visitors are already buying from these established brands and therefore, are familiar with the buttons they use. There is no harm in using what is popular to offer a sense of the familiar.

- **White space:** Give your buttons room to breathe. Keep a healthy margin of empty space around your button so it isn't crowded or overwhelmed.

Choosing the Right Fonts

Just like color, fonts can make a big difference to the look, feel, and tone of a Web site. Deciding which font to use may seem rather routine because you're limited to the number of fonts you can use, but even within the limited number of choices available to you, the one(s) you pick need to get across the best first impression you can give.

You may ask, "Why am I limited to the number of fonts? Lots are out there." This is true; your computer may have hundreds of fonts to choose from . . . but the number of fonts that actually display correctly on everyone's computer is a different matter altogether.

The fonts you choose for your landing page must be *browser-friendly* — browsers can display your fonts the way you intended them to be displayed. Major players in the browser field, such as Internet Explorer and Firefox, are designed to display True Type Fonts, such as Verdana or Times New Roman. These fonts are preinstalled with your operating system when you purchase it.

When a font is used that isn't standard with most operating systems, the Web browser is going to substitute a different font. When this happens, all the time and attention to detail you took in laying out your page so that it looks "just so" is likely ruined.

So which fonts are your best bets? We wish it was that simple. PC and Mac machines display fonts differently, and the progress made by newer machines as the technology has developed has increased the number of browser-safe fonts. Nevertheless, we feel comfortable saying that to get your message to look like you want it to, to the widest audience possible, consider one of the following fonts:

- Arial
- Arial Black
- Courier New
- Georgia
- Lucinda Console (Monaco on the Mac)
- Tahoma
- Times New Roman
- Trebuchet MS (Helvetica on the Mac)
- Verdana

Don't despair! If you had your heart set on using Goudy ExtraBold somewhere on your site, you can still use it (or any other font type you want) in an image, so you can still follow your corporate identity and artistic flair. Just don't have too many images because this could slow down the visitor page load time.

Selecting reader-friendly fonts

The goal of your landing page — aside from sales or leads, of course — is to get your visitors to read your message. Fonts that are full of flair, yet clumsy as all get out tend to turn away visitors because they're hard to read. Keep the font type simple to make reading easy.

Choosing reader-friendly fonts goes beyond sticking with the simple. Even browser-safe fonts — as we define in the section, "Choosing the Right Fonts," earlier in this chapter — have their limitations. Take Table 5-3, for example. Lucinda Console has a style with more space between the letters, whereas Georgia letters are closer together. For long copy, words that are too squished are difficult to read, whereas words that are too spread out cause your page to carry on forever.

Table 5-3	Comparing Browser-Safe Fonts	
Font	*Readability*	*Character Style*
Arial	Easy to read but only at bigger sizes.	Streamlined, modern look.
Arial Black	Easy to read at any size.	Very clean and versatile.
Comic Sans MS	Easy to read at any size.	Comic Sans is informal and friendly but over-used looks ridiculous and amateur.
Courier New	Okay in smaller doses, not widely used.	Based on a typewriter face; used for sample computer code.
Georgia	Very good at any size. Designed for online reading.	Modern, friendly, and professional.
Lucinda Console	Easy at any size.	Very simple and straight-forward.

(continued)

Table 5-3 *(continued)*

Font	Readability	Character Style
Tahoma	Ideal when small text size is needed.	Sturdy and assertive.
Times New Roman	Great at 12 point and higher.	Serious, formal, and businesslike.
Trebuchet MS	Easy at any size.	Streamlined and modern but friendly.
Verdana	Excellent. Easy to read in all sizes.	Modern, friendly, and professional.

Managing font sizes and spacing

No rule exists concerning font sizes when you build a landing page. Visitors can adjust the font size displayed on their screens by changing the text size in their viewing options. Even with this ability, a good rule of thumb is to use larger rather than smaller fonts to ensure that your message is easy to read.

To get the most out of the text display, Web designers are turning to Cascading Style Sheets (CSS) to manage the heading, sub-heading, and body text elements. CSS gives the designer control over the presentation of the font type, size color, and formatting. For more on CSS and Web design, check out *HTML, XHTML 7 CSS For Dummies,* by Ed Tittle and Jeff Noble (Wiley).

Although no standard exists when it comes to font sizes, the following options are often suggested for the main page text elements. (***Note:*** Different font sizes are recommended for different elements.)

- ✔ **Body text:** 10 point or 12 point
- ✔ **Main headings:** 14 point, 16 point, or 18 point
- ✔ **Sub-headings:** 12 point or 14 point
- ✔ **Captions:** 8 point, 9 point, or 10 point

Table 5-4 shows why different font sizes are recommended for different elements. Here you can see that although you can easily read a Georgia font at 12 point (pt), it's very difficult to do so at an 8pt size. Just goes to show that choosing appropriate, reader-friendly sizes is just as important as the font itself.

Table 5-4	Browser-Safe Fonts at 8pt, 10pt, and 12pt	
8pt	*10pt*	*12pt*
Arial	Arial	Arial
Arial Black	**Arial Black**	**Arial Black**
Comic Sans MS	Comic Sans MS	Comic Sans MS
Courier New	Courier New	Courier New
Georgia	Georgia	Georgia
Lucinda Console	Lucinda Console	Lucinda Console
Tahoma	Tahoma	Tahoma
Times New Roman	Times New Roman	Times New Roman
Trebuchet MS	Trebuchet MS	Trebuchet MS
Verdana	Verdana	Verdana

Using Images to Focus Attention

In the early 20th century, the phrase "a picture is worth a thousand words" became well used in American print. Even pushing 100 years, the saying is still true, especially when it comes to a landing page. Until the day when you can harness taste, smell, or touch on the Internet, the words and images used are going to remain your main source of engaging the visitor.

Images tell a story and serve to reinforce what you say with your text. Your text must get across the message on its own merit, but it can be enhanced with a well-chosen visual. For example, a landing page that promotes an open-market job fair benefits more from an image of a mix of people co-mingling around information tables rather than an image of a one-on-one interview in an office setting.

Sending the right message

As a landing page developer, be aware of the emotional focus of your page. Is your landing page about something somber, happy, or adventurous? The images must complement the feeling you're trying to promote. This sounds obvious, but unfortunately it isn't at all hard to find images used that don't complement the page.

Choosing the right picture can take some practice. For example, if you create a landing page to sell security alarms, it's much better to show a picture of a house or even children in the house than it is to show a picture of the alarm. Each picture sends a slightly different message and therefore, has a different emotion attached to it. You might ask, "So why not include all the pictures?" Simple. The fold area, the area a visitor first sees when arriving at your site, is only so big, and you really have only enough space on the fold for a single picture and a single message. Other pictures can be used elsewhere on the landing page, but the picture on the fold is key. (For more on the fold area, see Chapter 4.)

Of course, you can try any image that you feel sends the right message. Be forewarned, however, that the wrong image and emotional appeal is sure to drive down your conversions. Don't take our word for it. In the security alarm example, imagine using an image of a clown breaking into a house and compare it to the results of showing a picture of a house with obviously safe and contented children in it. Seems ridiculous, but this is a true example. Who is really going to be motivated to buy an alarm to prevent the increasing trend of clown breaking and enterings?

When looking at potential images for your landing page, ask the following:

- ✔ What emotions come to mind — happiness, seriousness, fear, sadness, adventure, or hunger?
- ✔ Does the image appeal to your specific demographic?
- ✔ Are you interested in reading more when you see that image?
- ✔ Does the image match what the text discusses?

As always, when you use your images, ensure that the picture can't be considered as libelous, defamatory, or humiliating. If you choose to use stock photography, be sure to research the usage rights. Photos you take must also have the permission of the person photographed to avoid any legal issues.

 Print the picture and give it to a few people so they can give you their impressions of the image. Allow people to see the image standing alone and get their feedback on tone, who it's for, and what it says to them. See how close this feedback matches what you're planning to use the image for on your page.

Directing with images

Not only do images get across a feeling or tone, they can be used to subtly guide your visitor's eyes where you want them to go. One of the tricks you can use on your landing page is to use the direction of the parts of the image to point to a part of the message, button, or product. This is subtle, but your eyes follow a logical path and directing the eye path with a picture is a neat trick.

In Figure 5-3, the side Themes menu points to the headline. You may not have noticed it at first glance, but after you see it, you can't mistake that this was done with complete intent.

Figure 5-3:
A side menu title points to the headline.

Selecting images for your Web site

Using the right image for your landing page can do a lot to make it more effective, but how should you actually choose one? Should your image be artsy? Dramatic? Sophisticated? That all depends on what your landing page is trying to accomplish.

A good picture grabs the attention of your reader. In our experience, the most effective attention-gaining pictures tend to include the following:

- ✔ Brides, babies, animals, and famous people
- ✔ People in odd costumes or situations
- ✔ Pictures that tell a story
- ✔ Romantic
- ✔ Catastrophic pictures
- ✔ Seasonal pictures, such as Christmas scenes at Christmas time

Attention-grabbing graphics are important, but if they're aimed at the wrong people or give off the wrong mood, they don't help engage your visitor. Know your demographic!

Selling a product takes a certain kind of picture as well. Effective pictures are of the product itself, the product in use, or the benefits the product gives the end user. Graphics that enlarge or enhance product details are also an effective landing page addition.

How do you know if you have the right picture? Most of the time, you can't tell unless you try different pictures and test which ones provide the best results. To do this, you can use a technique called split-testing, where multiple landing pages are tested to see which ones perform the best. You can find details on split-testing in Chapter 12.

Working with photographers

Having pictures is one thing, getting high-quality pictures is another. Many landing page developers choose to get professional images from qualified photographers. This is particularly useful if selling a unique product such as camel saddles or leather socks. It would be difficult to find these pictures if you didn't take them yourself. Remember, the pictures you use on your landing page — and specifically the fold area — must be high quality and professional as well as showcase your product well. Why spoil an otherwise outstanding landing page with poor quality pictures?

Not only does the image quality say something about who you are as a businessperson, but also it can be the difference between convincing your visitor of your product superiority and losing the sale. You have the difficult task of impressing a variety of people in all walks of life without even meeting them.

Doing your own photography

With today's digital cameras being so accessible, taking your own photographs is always possible. Photography for the Web usually involves small-scale projects, such as product shots, so you can use that digital camera of yours. While a detailed discussion of digital photography falls outside the scope of this book, here are a few tips to remember when taking your own stock photos.

✔ **Get the lighting right.** Many images appear grainy (due to a lack of light) or washed out (due to too much light). If you do take your own pictures, take the time to test for the right lighting. If using a flash, try bouncing the light off a wall or a ceiling. If the product is small, consider building a *light box,* a device designed to regulate the light for a picture. (Instructions for building your own light box can be found at www. studiolighting.net/homemade-light-box-for-product-photography.)

✔ **Don't trust your LCD screen.** After you take a picture and review it in the mini-LCD screen on your camera, everything looks great. When you get it back to your office, you notice it is blurry or objects are in the picture you didn't want. The trick is to use a tripod to ensure the picture is not blurry and take the time to set up the picture carefully.

✔ **Don't take just one.** Taking pictures with a digital camera is cheap, so take lots of pictures. If you take 20 to 30 pictures, you may get one right.

✔ **Use your angles.** Shoot your product from various angles. After you post your picture online, you may find that one angle looks great and gets a better response from your online visitors.

✔ **Use real people.** If you're taking pictures of employees, make them real employees. These pictures look more authentic and look better on your site. Remember though, you will need to get them to sign a release agreement. (For more on release agreements for people in your pictures, read just a bit further.)

Digital photography is an involved topic and if you are going to be taking lots of pictures for your landing page, it is a good idea to research it as much as possible. There are many online workshops that can assist you in creating your own stock photography including workshops at www.just makeiteasy.com/workshops.

If you want to include people in your photos, be sure they sign a release giving you permission to use them. Regardless of the model or what you've told her about the project, always obtain permission to use her photograph in the form of a model release agreement.

A model release agreement is a legal document that outlines the conditions under which one party can take pictures of another. It does not have to be a complicated, long document but it should stipulate payment information, permitted uses, copyright issues and length of use. Some people do not mind if you take their picture and it ends up on a Web site, but it's better to have your paperwork in order to prevent surprises later. You can find out more information on model releases and how to create one at www.danheller. com/model-release.html#3.

Using stock photography

Stock photography consists of existing photographs that can be licensed for a specific use. Hundreds of sites specialize in stock photography and generally group them into categories such as landscapes, objects, and people. If you need a picture of a 65-year-old woman bungee jumping or of two nuns riding a camel, it is much easier to find these online than arrange to photograph them yourself. Two types of stock photography to be aware of include:

- ✔ **Royalty-based:** Allows the use of photos for a small fee. Each time you use the image, this fee is paid and is generally divided among the company, photographer, and model, if any.

- ✔ **Royalty-free:** Are offered for a flat, one time fee. You pay the fee upfront and have permission to use the image as many times as you need.

Royalty-free images are prevalent online because the tracking of royalty-based image use can be an accounting nightmare.

With thousands of stock photos to choose from, you need to know where to begin. Use the following guidelines to choose the image that puts your product and company in the best light:

- ✔ **Choose a supplier.** It doesn't take long to find an agency online that supplies stock photography. These places are a gold mine for finding the right picture for the right occasion. Browse through thousands of high quality pictures looking for the one that you think will be complementary to your site. You can compare cost between these companies, but often you will go with the company that you think has the best pictures. Also keep in mind that it's perfectly fine to buy pictures from several different sources. Table 5-5 at the end of this chapter identifies some of the Web sites that offer stock photography.

- ✔ **Focus on the message.** Just because you have a specific image in mind, you aren't going to find exactly that image in an online gallery. Remember that your priority here is getting your message across rather than tracking down that elusive image of an auburn-haired girl with gray-green eyes in a burgundy shirt holding a cellphone that you're just sure is the perfect image for your product. If you have a clear idea of what your message is, you can find an image to get that across.

- ✔ **Test out your image.** Most stock image agencies offer free complimentary images that you can test in the design and look of a site. They often have the company logo stamped across the front so that it works fine for a test but doesn't work in a live site. Use comps to your advantage. If you test an image in the *real* world, you may discover that the main colors in the image may not work with your site or they may give off a whole different vibe when placed in the context of your site than it did as part of its original image gallery.

- ✔ **Image size matters.** Image size here refers to the image quality or *dpi (dots per inch)*. A printed image, such as for one used for a brochure, requires 300 dpi or higher to get a crisp high-quality print, whereas online the same image would require only 150 dpi to achieve the same level of professionalism. Higher dpi images often cost more, so don't spend more than you need to. One word of caution: An image with too low of a dpi will probably not look good on your site. With this, you run the risk of your pictures looking cheap and that's not attractive.

✔ **Determine your budget and timeframe.** Depending on the agency, the permission rights to use a photograph in your Web site may be an annual fee. If you think you're going to use the image for the lifetime of the site, the royalty-free option is great. But if you want an image that your competition won't have the ability to use and you have the budget, custom royalty-based photos are the way to go.

After you know what to look for, where do you look? Table 5-5 is a brief list of popular stock image sites. For even more choice, simply use your favorite browser and do a search. Just remember that if an image is listed as being for sale, you don't want to chance the legal consequences of using it without permission. (If you're really looking to save money, some of the sites listed in this table have a selection of free-for-use photos.)

Table 5-5	Stock Photo Web Sites
Web Site URL	*Cost*
www.istockphoto.com	Royalty-free
www.fotosearch.com	Royalty and royalty-free
www.corbis.com	Royalty and royalty-free
www.bigstockphoto.com	Royalty-free
www.acclaimimages.com	Royalty and royalty-free

Chapter 6

Writing for Landing Pages

Easy reading is damn hard writing.

—Nathaniel Hawthorne

The engaging writing you read on the most successful landing pages doesn't happen by accident. Rather, everything from the placement of the text on the page, to the length of sentences, to the spacing used, and even to the exact number of words on the page is carefully considered, researched, and tested. The primary goals for those writing landing page content is to first capture and then keep the reader's attention. Not an easy task, which we make clear; but if you do your job right, you can guide visitors from the first heading to the final sale.

In this chapter, we look at the various techniques used for landing page writing. This chapter takes a look at the fundamentals of writing for the Web and some techniques for writing in general. We also identify three key landing page elements that need to be written: the heading, the call to action, and the value statement.

We realize that's a lot to get through, but there's no time like the present. Perhaps the best place to start is with an introduction to writing for the Web.

Introducing Landing Page Writing

Just to be clear: Writing for your landing page relies on the very same core fundamentals for effective writing of any kind. The content needs to be interesting, relevant, and satisfying. The structure needs to be easy to scan and logical, and the style needs to be engaging, clear, and concise. Every message has a larger context, meaning every message has an occasion for being, has a target audience it needs to reach, and has an intended purpose it needs to achieve. If that purpose is to inform and to persuade the audience so that they'll buy something, be aware of the three major appeals (appeals to reason, to emotion, and to ethics) that must work together in order to communicate clearly, persuade honestly, and influence behavior accordingly.

Whether your information is in a brochure or on a Web site, the fundamentals of effective writing we outline earlier must be followed. We spend quite a bit of time in this chapter going over such fundamentals, but we want to make a major point right off the bat: Despite this emphasis on fundamentals, one key difference between Web-based writing and paper-based writing is the way each audience reads.

Writing for the Web readers

Web *readers* should really be called Web *racers*. Many online visitors don't actually read in the traditional sense but race through a site, scanning for what they need. Studies show that Web readers make lightning-quick judgments about the professionalism of a site just by unconsciously reacting to the site's choice of color scheme, its use of font type and size, and its number and type of graphics. For example, if a site uses a comic font and cartoons to sell life insurance, chances are the potential buyer clicks away from this site quickly. The message and the delivery contradict each other, so confusion results and any initial trust is lost. This audience won't even begin to scan the page if it looks unprofessional or untrustworthy in any way. (See Chapter 7 for more about the trustworthiness of a site.)

This, of course, has significant consequences for the effectiveness — or lack thereof — of your landing page. The initial look of your landing page simply has to match the reader's expectations about the product and/or service you offer. For example, if the reader wants to buy wedding invitations, you'll be well on the way to earning a visitor's trust if your wedding planning site exudes elegance. Most buyers who need wedding invitations associate weddings with elegance, so they'll be reassured if they encounter elegance in visiting your site. Imagine a company trying to sell classy wedding invitations from a site that uses gothic script! Unless you're actively targeting that tiny niche market looking for emo weddings, your potential buyers are going to quickly click to other sites that reflect their values and expectations.

Structuring your online communication

The brain can't make meaning if it can't perceive structure. This applies to the grammar of a sentence, the development of a paragraph (or chunk), and the design of an effective landing page. Time to review a few elements of the building blocks of structure, starting with that topic beloved by all 5th grade English teachers — grammar.

Grammar

Effective business writers tend to favor the power sentence (or active voice) because it gives full information quickly and clearly. The *power sentence* starts with the agent of the action (subject; a noun), moves into the action (verb), and then finishes with the receiver of the action (object; a noun).

> Example: Harry's hair tonic stimulates the hair follicles to re-grow new hair.

Tonic is the subject, *stimulates* is the verb, and *follicles* receive the action.

Here's the same sentence in passive voice:

> The hair follicles were stimulated.

Notice that the emphasis is removed from the product and placed on the result instead; — in fact, the product gets no mention whatsoever!

Nevertheless, passive voice is an acceptable sentence pattern in certain situations, but not as potentially complete as active voice. If you ever need to cloud responsibility for something, use passive voice as politicians are apt to do. Here's an example:

> Taxes were raised last year.

This passive sentence removes the doer of this action from the sentence; in other words, you don't know who did the raising of the taxes. If it's the politician's government who raised taxes, the active voice reveals this all too clearly:

> My government raised taxes last year.

If the politician is not proud of that fact, then the using passive voice works well to conceal the doer of the action, so passive voice has its uses, but the wary reader is probably aware of this sentence trick and will hold your passive voice use against you and trust you less. *Bottom Line:* Use the power sentence to give full information in a landing page.

Paragraph development

Paragraphs on landing pages are called *chunks* and tend to contain between four to seven lines of text, including graphics. Chunks are short paragraphs that benefit from having a strong topic sentence, followed by evidence, and concluded with a benefit statement and a transition into the next chunk. A *transition* is the repetition of a key word or phrase that acts a bridge from one idea to the next. Another transition technique is to ask a question and then start the next chunk with its answer. If the answer's the last chunk, it ends with an exhortation (or a call to action).

Chunking is a writing style that essentially splits your text into small pieces, or *chunks,* of information. The goal is to make the text easy to scan for your visitors and to start reading. Newspapers also adhere to the following rule derived from audience psychology: Readers tend to shy away from longer texts but will at least give it a try if longish text is broken into manageable pieces, which gives the audience a sense of achievement after reading each short chunk.

Highlighting landing page hot spots

Recent studies of how Web readers "read" also reveal that they have a strong tendency to look at only the *hot spots* of the interface — which include the headings, beginnings, and endings of chunks and of the interface. Web readers also tend to avoid anything that looks like it might be an ad or an irrelevant detail. Web page readers tend to know what they're looking for and want to be able to find it fast, so their eyes dart to these hot spots. Knowing this, landing page writers need to create helpful headings, strong topic sentences, and clear endings.

Web readers also expect options that print materials can't provide, such as the ability to follow a hyperlink so they can read more about a subject, watch videos about it, or post comments. This potential of landing pages to incorporate interactivity into the reading experience allows for more reader-involvement and hence more room for persuasion.

The Web audience races through any landing page for information in a predictable way, looking at headings, topic sentences, and paragraph endings and skipping long paragraphs. Web readers also often tend to ignore content on the right-hand side of the interface because they assume that commercial clutter and non-relevant content is all they'll find there. All this racing shows that Web audiences are in a hurry and are very quick to decide whether to trust a site long enough to be receptive to the landing page's content.

Even though Web audiences usually can't skim through a site as easily as through a brochure, they should still be able to click to the page or the section of a site they want to read whenever they want to read it. As a result, make sure you've provided easy navigation tools which include clicking options in each paragraph and on the toolbar. Highlight keywords and use labels for each button that set up clear expectations about where that click will take a site visitor. In addition, include a search box on every page that allows the audience to skip to content they wish to read first, rather than having to do the kind of flipping through pages associated with a traditional print document.

After you get your head around the significant differences in reading styles that separate traditional and Web audiences — the fact that Web readers are racers who must click instead of flip, for example — you're ready to generate the actual content of your landing page.

Writing Controlled Content

Landing page content, as with any type of writing, follows a specific process. To create and control that content so that it does what you want, we recommend that you follow these six iterative stages of writing effective landing page content:

1. Planning
2. Drafting
3. Revising
4. Editing
5. Proofreading
6. User testing

The following sections spell out in a bit more detail what's entailed in each stage.

Stage 1: Planning

Before you put pen to paper (or fingers to keyboard), develop your strategy and make a plan. Like any kind of writing, you must determine your rhetorical context — your target audience, your purpose, and your occasion for writing:

✔ **Audience:** Who's going to read what you write? What do you know about them? Do they prefer graphics to text? What's their sense of humor? How much do they already know about your product and/or service? What's their attention span?

✔ **Purpose:** What do you wish to achieve? Is the idea to get an immediate conversion? Do you want to make a quick sale or do you want to develop a long-term business relationship, or both?

✔ **Occasion:** Are you using the best medium for the message? For example, if your demographic is seniors over 75, an age group that typically doesn't surf the Web for their shopping needs, it may be better to rely on your traditional print advertising and use your landing page to generate interest and trust in the company — at least until that age group becomes part of the Internet consumer culture, and they will.

In the planning phase, ask yourself what you think your audience would ask you if they could. Write down these questions to guide your writing and to ensure that your content stays relevant and focused. You're not writing for you; you're writing to be read, so think about what your audience expects and needs in order for them to purchase your product or service online. Know the demographic of your product and/or service and allow that to guide your decisions about what kind of graphics, diction, and font type to use.

Always keep your ego in check. You're not writing for your own enjoyment or bravado; you're writing for your visitors.

Stage 2: Drafting to capture reader attention

Developing strong content means clearly communicating what your readers need to know about your products or services. Draft this information as you would in preparing for any sales deal. Start with something that's sure to attract the intended audience's attention. This *hook* can be

✔ An anecdote

✔ An interesting statistic or quotation

✔ A question or a series of questions

✔ An analogy

✔ A statement outlining the effect(s) without immediately revealing the cause(s)

✔ A paradox

After you have your audience's attention, you must maintain it by solving their problem. Do this by looking at the subject from their point of view: Know your demographic — who they are, what they look like, what they value, and what they want. For example, if you're selling weight-loss programs to middle-class men and women, use pictures of models with whom your target audience will relate. Use before and after shots that show the problem (overweight) and the solution (fat reduction). Couple this with a celebrity endorsement (which develops trust in your company and its products and/or services), and you have your intended audience's attention. Be sure to use the language and tone of your audience.

Even if you get their attention, remember that their attention span is still very short. They're at least willing to read now, rather than just scan the interface, so you must provide content that maintains and builds on their trust. Do this by presenting your arguments about the product and/or service. An effective argument is any claim supported by credible and current evidence. Credible evidence includes

✔ The results of formal studies, case studies, and focus groups

✔ Expert testimonials

✔ Interviews with satisfied clients

✔ Reliable statistics

✔ Logical reasoning devices, such as cause/effect reasoning, deduction, induction, and so on

Make your claim about the product and/or service. Provide your audience with the evidence necessary for them to reach the conclusion that your claims can be accepted as the truth and then explain how this can benefit them. If you go this route, few readers are going to lose interest in what you have to say.

With the right content, you can transform your visitor's *interest* in the product or service into a *desire* for it; in other words, you can change their perception of the product and/or service from a *want* to a *need*. After this happens, the final step is the exhortation — the call to action. This action is the actual sale — which, by the way, must be structured so that the audience doesn't have to click more than three times to finish the check-out process. (We discuss calls to action in the section, "Writing calls to action," later in this chapter.)

Stage 3: Revising

Who knew that role-playing would ever come into the writing process? Time for you to become your customer: Imagine him or her, and become that person. Sounds weird, true enough, but the great 19th-century novelist Charles

Dickens used this technique when he developed his characters. He scared one of his maids so much that she wrote in her diary of how she entered his room while he was pretending to be little Nell so that he could get her dialogue just right!

Now that you're in character, read your landing page as you would if you were your typical everyday landing page reader. Are the headings substantive and helpful? Does each chunk have an informative first sentence? Is there enough evidence for each and every claim? Do the endings explain the significance of your product and/or service or its benefit to the consumer? Can you find the essential information you need in less than ten seconds? Can you find additional information easily? Are you speaking their language, meaning using the appropriate level of diction and specificity? Revision is just that: "re-seeing" what you've done. Revise so that your content is complete, your style is concise and clear, and your structure is logical and easy to navigate.

Stage 4: Editing

Adjust your draft so that your paragraphs are about four to seven lines long each. These paragraphs are referred to as *content chunks* and include graphic images as well as text. Content chunks need to be *deductive* paragraphs — each chunk starts with a clear topic sentence that the rest of the chunk develops or supports with examples, descriptions, definitions, comparisons, contrasts, and/or testimonials. The idea here is to both *tell* and *show*.

Each chunk needs to be reviewed for the appropriate level of word choice, types of examples, and length of sentences. Try to vary your sentence types and length. For example, to make something stand out, write a short sentence after some really long ones. This structural technique is akin to putting something in bold and is reacted to as such.

Stage 5: Proofreading

A misspelled word makes your readers trust you less, so use your spell checker. Also, make sure grammar and punctuation rules are followed properly. Errors in grammar and punctuation detract from clear communication, decrease trust, and ultimately risk the loss of potential customers.

Stage 6: User testing

Put up the landing page and have someone else use the site. Then have that person fill out a simple survey about its readability, ease of use, graphic design, and textual content. Watch your tester, too, to monitor and note any reactions and then adjust your content accordingly — which may mean going back to any of the previous stages This is why we say this whole writing process is iterative: At any stage, you may find that you have to return to an earlier stage to perfect your landing page.

Developing Persuasive Content

Drafting and revising isn't just about the clarity and brevity of your message. If you really want to generate high conversion rates, you must realize the importance of the three major appeals used in persuasion throughout the ages: the ethical appeal, the rational appeal, and the emotional appeal.

The ethical appeal

A writer or speaker must first gain the audience's trust, and anything that contributes to this is an appeal to *ethos* (ethics). Ways to achieve this trust revolve around letting your audience know that you have personal experience with the subject matter. (For instance, I loved the products so much, I bought the company.) Also, citing the experts and using methodologically sound and recent statistics gain your audience's respect. This sends the message that you did your homework and you did it well. If your persona (the writer's mask) is perceived as honest, friendly, and professional, your audience becomes more receptive to what you have to say. People have the tendency to disregard what someone says if that person is disliked for any reason, and this often leads to the logical fallacy of *ad hominem* (arguing against the person instead of the issue,) so try to write politely and respectfully. Other ways to lose trust are to have errors in spelling, punctuation, and grammar, so edit and proofread your page carefully.

The rational appeal

While gaining the audience's trust, you need to engage them emotionally and rationally. An appeal to *logos* (reason) is anything that requires the brain to engage. Any statement with cause-and-effect reasoning or any other logical reasoning device, such as a syllogism, is processed logically. Facts, statistics, and logical reasoning, for example, function as rational appeals.

The emotional appeal

An appeal to *pathos* (emotion) is anything that plays upon the audience's emotions. Usually, landing pages will use an emotional appeal in the beginning and in the ending of the message, but they can also be peppered throughout the body. The bulk of a landing page's message, however, should use rational appeals, not only in order to make the sale in the short-term, but also to maintain the customer's loyalty over the long-term.

Writing the Three Key Landing Page Components

Writing the body of your landing page is often not difficult. The body highlights your product, your company, your service, or whatever information your want to reveal. (You should know all that stuff like the back of your hand.) In addition to the body of your text, though, you have three key elements within your landing page that you're really going to have to nail in terms of writing quality: headings, calls to action, and value statements. You may be tempted to dash off these three elements and then move on, but we strongly suggest you take the time to write them carefully and thoughtfully because they can have a significant impact on your conversions. The following sections point out a few things to consider when approaching the process.

Writing enticing headings

One of the keys to a successful landing page is your heading. In a few seconds, your heading either attracts or repels your visitors. If you don't take the time to figure out how to write great headings, you're making your conversion job a lot harder.

The heading is the first text visitors see when they arrive at your site, which makes the heading key for grabbing your visitor's attention and enticing her to read on. In fact, the heading is probably all that many of your visitors will ever read. This makes the heading one of the more important components of your entire landing page.

When it comes time to sit down and write your perfect heading, the first thing you need to do is identify your audience — and yes, we know we're repeating ourselves, but the point is such an important one that we'll risk sounding repetitive. Your heading text has to speak to your demographic. You aren't likely to use words like swangaz, whip, or whoadie if you're trying to sell shoes to business women. Why? Because those are hip-hop terms. This is of course an extreme example, but knowing your audience is what enables you to determine the appropriate language and strategies to use when trying to relate to your audience.

Just so we don't leave you hanging, *swangaz* refers to a spoked tire or rim; a *whip* is a vehicle; and *whoadie* is an informal way to address a friend. Now if you find yourself reading a heading on a hip-hop landing page, you have a better chance of knowing what's going on.

Assuming you know who your audience is, here are specific examples of various heading strategies commonly used. This is just to give you a starting point to create your own headings. If none of these ideas work for you, the next step is to browse the Internet, newsstands, and magazine racks. Find headings that attract you and modify your favorite headings to suit your needs.

In the meantime, here's a list of eight heading tips and tricks. You can mix and match these heading types throughout your document. For instance, the main heading in the fold area may be one type, whereas the subheadings may be another. The important thing is to ensure that all your headings grab your reader. The following list lays out some strategies for doing just that:

- **Use words in your heading that immediately target your demographic.** This makes an instant appeal directly to your audience.

   Great News for Back Pain Sufferers

   Attention Hunters

   Free to Dog Lovers

   Notice in these examples that your audience is immediately identified. Chances are if I'm a back pain sufferer and I see a heading, Great News for Back Pain Sufferers, I'm going to be interested. Compare this to a heading that reads Getting Older Isn't Easy. If I'm a back pain sufferer, I wouldn't read further.

- **State the benefit to your audience.** The landing page isn't for your benefit, it's for your visitor's benefit. Stating it right upfront is very enticing.

   We'll Save You $500 a Year in Taxes — Guaranteed

   End Indigestion Now

   Get Relief from Ingrown Toenails

- **Make your heading sound like the next best thing, a breakthrough product.** Do you have a better mousetrap? Better fitting shoes? People love to discover something new, so give it to them in the heading. Use words like *new, latest, breakthrough, revolutionary,* or *updated.*

   Breakthrough Hair Loss Remedy

   Get the Latest Music Now

   New Development in Hair Care

✔ **Use questions in the heading.** Questions can identify the audience and can be used to entice.

> Do You Suffer from Amnesia?
>
> Do You Want to Know the Secret to Success?
>
> Do You Want to Know the Secret to a Great Marriage?

✔ **Use how-to headings.** How-to headings are typically very effective. If you're selling a how-to type of product, such as how to build a flat-bottom boat, the how-to heading is a great choice.

> How to Travel to Europe for Less Than $400
>
> How to Cook a Great Steak
>
> How to Discover Your Inner Child

✔ **Use number list headings.** Number lists are great because they enable you to use bullets to make your points — and besides people just love top ten lists.

> Five Ways to Ease Back Pain
>
> Fifty Ideas for Valentine's Day
>
> Seven Secrets to Success

✔ **Issue a command with the heading.** The command basically gives an order and is very direct in what you're asking your visitor to do.

> Buy Now and Save
>
> Don't Miss This Opportunity
>
> Enroll in Our Program Today

✔ **Feature an offer in your heading.** Face it, visitors come to your site to find something. Give them an offer upfront and save them from needing to read more.

> 75% Off Ladies Shoes
>
> Buy One Knife, Get a Second Free
>
> Get Free Trial Software with the Purchase of Our Book

Getting the right heading can be a big task. You can test headings with multiple campaigns or get friends to read them. Two final things we recommend about headings are to never assume you have the right heading until you're absolutely sure it's working and to write your heading first; it often gives you focus for the rest of the document.

Many people try and capture attention by using all caps in the heading. IT MAKES THE HEADING HARD TO READ. Instead, as is done in the *For Dummies* books, your main heading looks better mixing caps and lowercase letters: It Makes the Heading Easier to Read.

Many people try putting humor into their landing pages. This can be very tricky, and for the most part, the risk isn't worth the reward. The reason is simple, humor isn't universal; what's funny to you may not be funny to someone else. In fact, it may be offensive. Humor of course can go with advertising. (Just watch TV if you need any further proof because nearly every commercial on the tube has some attempt at being funny. We once read somewhere that no one wants to buy from a clown, unless that clown is selling Big Macs.)

Writing calls to action

In advertising, the *call to action* is the text that asks your visitor to take a specific action. You may be using the call to action to ask the visitor for an e-mail address, to fill out a survey, to buy a product, or to complete any other desired task. In many instances, the call to action is the text used to get your customer to actually buy your product.

The call to action is important because it gives your visitors clear direction as to what you want them to do. Giving your visitors clear direction is necessary because you don't want them to become lost and click off your site. A well-written call to action implies urgency, encouraging your visitors to click now and not put off the desired action. A few examples of a call to action include

> Sign Up Now
>
> Click Here for a Free_____
>
> Download Your Copy Here
>
> Click Now for Your Free 30 Day Trial
>
> Take a Tour
>
> Add to Cart
>
> Register Now

As shown in the list, the call to action is very clear about what you want your visitor to do. Calls to action aren't about ambiguity; they are clear, focused, and short.

The call to action can be standalone text that's linked, but more commonly, the call to action is a linked button. The button can be various colors and sizes, as shown in Figure 6-1.

You can easily find call to action text and buttons online. When choosing the text to use on your landing page, surf the 'Net and find some that you like. Find the button color and shape that would complement your landing page and then incorporate it into your design.

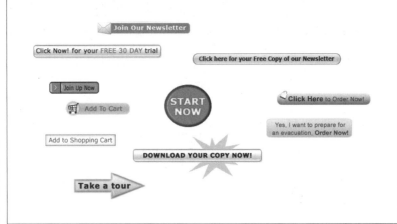

Writing a value statement

The *value statement* is an important part of your landing page; it's a clear statement of how your product/service benefits your visitor. That is, it clearly outlines why your visitor needs your product (or service). Again, to write a great value statement, you definitely need to know your audience. You simply can't outline benefits to someone if you don't know to whom you're speaking.

If you search online, most companies have poor, ambiguous value statements. They're far to general, they don't speak directly to their audience, and they're often more about the seller than the customer. You hear poorly written value statements every day:

> We offer the best waffle maker on the market.

> We are the acupuncture specialists.

> We have the largest selection of socks available.

> We have the best accountants working for you.

> We won't be undersold.

All these examples aren't about the people your visitors are most concerned with, that's to say, they're not about themselves. These value statements need to shift to focus on how they benefit the reader. So, you may be "the acupuncture specialist," but how does that fact benefit your visitor?

In this way, the value statement needs to clearly identify the result to your visitor. Table 6-1 shows what we mean by tweaking headings to highlight the potential benefit to visitors of the advertised product.

Table 6-1	Creating a Value Statement	
Original Statement	*Customer-Focused Value Statement*	*Customer Benefits*
We offer the best waffle maker on the market.	You can make fast, great tasting waffles with the best waffle maker on the market.	Great taste, cooks fast.
We are the acupuncture specialists.	Relieve your back and neck pain with our acupuncture specialists.	Relief from back and neck pain.
We have the largest selection of socks available.	Enjoy comfort, low cost, and one-stop shopping with the largest sock store in the city.	Low cost, comfortable socks located in one location.
We have the best accountants working for you.	Organize your taxes and maximize your returns with our trained accountants.	Get taxes organized and get larger returns.
We won't be undersold.	You pay 50 percent less for carpeting.	Pay half price for carpeting.

As you can see from Table 6-1, it doesn't take much to shift the focus away from the seller or provider and onto the customer. This seems like a simple concept but is often overlooked.

When developing your value statement, take the time to clearly identify the benefits of your product to the customer. Get the focus away from you and on to them. Shift your pronoun usage away from *we* or *I* to *you.*

Five Awesome Landing Page Writing Tips

A great way to end this chapter is to identify five tips for capturing your reader's attention. These tips are commonly used on successful landing pages to grab readers:

✔ **Use text boxes:** Boxes are a great way to call attention to specific text. Understanding that Internet readers are scanners and skimmers, the boxes draw their attention and give you a chance to get across a message.

✔ **Use bulleted lists:** Bulleted lists are great for grabbing attention because

- They're short.

- They're easy to read.

- The eyes are drawn to them when skimming a page.

- You can get your point across quickly.

✔ **Use numbered lists:** Like the bulleted list, the numbered list is a great way to capture skimmers and scanners with short, easy-to-read content. Also, numbered lists are great for establishing sequence of events such as an order of what you want your visitors to do.

✔ **Use questions:** Do you want to save money on laundry detergent? Are you happy with your weight? Questions are a great way to capture an audience. If the question is something they'd ask, they're going to read to get the answer. The use of questioning in marketing is a whole area to study. The right questions can get your visitors from the heading to the sale.

✔ **Keep it simple:** Many of the landing pages you see are cluttered and busy. For many, it's a big turn off. Some are just pages of links, flash, bling, and color. These busy pages are like yelling and white noise. Sites that use lots of white space, simple text, fonts, and colors are just the opposite. These sites aren't the ones yelling, "We won't be undersold!" They're the ones saying, "Hey, we have a great product; come take a look."

Chapter 7

Building Customer Trust

"Trust is a peculiar resource; it is built rather than depleted by use."

—Unknown

*Y*ou know you're honest and that your products and services are legit. You are honest, aren't you? If not, feel free to skip this chapter.

For the rest, proving your credibility and developing visitor trust doesn't happen by accident. You have very specific strategies to follow — and elements to place on your landing page — that help separate you from the shysters, charlatans, and other Internet bad guys out there. If you don't make use of these elements and strategies, visitors have no way of developing any sort of trust in you.

For us to state flat out that your visitors won't become your customers if you don't make the effort to gain their trust may be too black and white. The truth is, not everyone is that cautious — a pool of folks out there will believe *anything.* (Why do you think crooks try Internet scams in the first place? Because they work some small percentage of the time.) However, if you wish to reach a conversion level worth mentioning, you need to reassure your visitors that you aren't another online scam. In this chapter, you explore your options when it comes to reassuring your visitors, which involve getting acquainted with the principles and practices of developing trust with your visitors and customers.

Developing Trust with Visitors

Face it: Most reading this don't have the luxury of an established brand name when it comes to marketing your landing page. Without a brand name, established sales record, or solid reputation, visitors are naturally going to be skeptical and will likely wonder whether you're legit. This hesitation is normal because, believe it or not, not everyone on the Internet is honest. It's true!

Because you already know you're going to have to deal with some buyer hesitation before you even build your landing page, you can take the steps necessary to help alleviate their concerns. This is what we mean when we talk about building trust. We have a couple very specific strategies that you can use on your landing page to help in this regard — nothing too cutting edge, but rather the standard trust elements that have traditionally served to comfort visitors and make them feel secure enough to buy from you. Before we get into specifics, though, take a quick look at what you're up against.

Dealing with (cynical) realities

You already know that visitors to your site are going to be cautious about you. Their fears are likely like the ones you'd feel if you were to buy from a (new to you) landing page. You may ask, "What fears?" Plenty, if you're honest. Each of the following fears has to be addressed to make your visitors comfortable in buying from you:

✔ **Spam, spam, spam:** Most of your landing pages are going to ask your visitors to provide an e-mail address, perhaps because you need addresses for leads or you want an easy way to keep your visitors in the loop about new products and services. The problem is most people are wary of giving out their e-mail addresses because they're concerned about spam. And with good reason.

We assume that many of you have given out your e-mail address to a Web site in the past and soon found your e-mail inbox full of e-mails ranging from notifications of lottery winnings to male enhancement products. Blocking all this unwanted correspondence can be difficult and, even worse, you often end up overlooking important e-mails buried in in the midst of the spam thicket.

Nobody wants unsolicited e-mails, which is one of the lowest forms of marketing on the Internet. To combat your visitors' fears of you abusing their e-mail addresses, reassure them by stating clearly the reason why you're asking for the e-mail address and put in writing that it won't be sold or given out for any reason.

✔ **Concerns over privacy or personal data:** On landing sites, you may ask visitors or customers to fill out survey forms or other paperwork. This may even include credit card numbers and home addresses. You typically ask for this information to get a clear understanding of your customers' demographics.

The problem is most visitors want a certain sense of anonymity on the Internet. They don't feel comfortable being tracked and traced. However, marketers do just that to help you zoom in on your customer base. Being asked to divulge personal data remains a large concern for any online buyer. Knowing that one's personal data is in the hands of some unknown someone or is stored on a database doesn't provide much comfort to the buyer.

To help alleviate these fears, develop and display the rules of how their personal data and information is to be stored and used.

When people buy online, they really can't tell whether they're buying from a company next door or three continents away. This also means that information supplied by them could end up anywhere. Be very clear regarding your location and how you'll store and keep their privacy and information secure.

✔ **Concerns over dealing with a fly-by-night company:** Companies come and go on the Internet. New ones show up, and old ones disappear. This does little to reassure your visitors that your company will be around to back up your products.

Battling this fly-by-night reputation can be difficult. However, you can use several strategies, including ensuring all contact information is included on the site, giving the site a face by providing images of the business location and staff, and adding language describing the nature of the company and how long it's been in business. Combined, these strategies help convey the message that your business will be around long enough to fulfill its obligations.

✔ **Fear of dreaded hidden fees (and unwanted surprises):** Only $19.95. Sounds like a good deal, but many sites make these bold price claims only to hit customers with hidden fees. High shipping costs and other fees appear as if by magic, leaving the customer feeling cheated. Surprising customers with hidden fees or other unwanted surprises destroys trust quickly. Shoppers will actually stop buying if they suspect things will cost them more or if they start the buying process and suddenly see a price increase.

Now, such fees may not be hidden fees per se, according to the professionals in your particular field, but they may appear that way to purchasers dealing with your Web site. What you might expect to appear perfectly reasonable to a consumer might seem suspect to a large proportion of the folks who visit your Web site. The little extras, such as tax, too many shipping choices, package insurance, or restocking fees, may come across as misleading to a customer if not clearly explained at the beginning of the purchase process.

Keep the surprises to a minimum. You're running a business, not trying to trick visitors into buying. Keep them informed of all costs and other pertinent information.

✔ **Fear of product return hassles:** Not everyone is going to love your product, so factor in a certain number for returns. Return policies need to be easy to follow and as hassle-free as possible. Horror stories about not being able to return the products, extra return fees, or ridiculous return policies, such as having the product in the original packaging, have plagued shoppers for years.

All these nightmares make people who purchase online even more wary of who they do business with. Some online companies have resorted to full customer support and a specialized area dedicated to returns to alleviate buyers' concerns.

Customers must know that if the product doesn't live up to the advertising and expectations, they can return it hassle-free. If you can't offer a Return Policy for a product you're selling — or you come up with a Return Policy that is just not workable in the real world — you have to work extra hard to convince the buyer to purchase from you.

✔ **Concerns about viruses and spyware:** Many people fear that purchases of digital content, such as e-books, software, or any downloadable product, may contain viruses or spyware. Most products probably don't and are therefore clean, but that concern on the part of consumers still needs to be addressed.

To battle this (mis)perception, many digital product providers use Virus and Spyware Free icons.

✔ **Identity theft fears:** A few years ago, you never really heard about identify theft. Today, identity theft is one of the fastest growing crimes around, so people are naturally worried about becoming targets. Today, fears about identify theft are one of the main reasons why people don't want to provide their credit card numbers or give out personal information in surveys.

As you can see, visitor fear is well-founded. Not only do you have to build trust for your product, but you're also fighting against credit card fraud, malware (see the following section), the Internet's reputation as being unsafe, and other issues that were there long before you thought of your online business.

The scourge of malware

Malware (malicious software) is one of the great fears of computer users. Malware, of course, refers to viruses, but it also encompasses much more:

✔ **Viruses:** Of course, you've all heard about viruses and likely have a virus scanner on your computer right now. Viruses are software programs designed to damage or influence your computer in some way. There are many types of viruses — *macro* viruses, for instance, corrupt documents. (Just imagine opening all your documents to see that they're unreadable. Talk about a malicious act of malfeasance!)

✔ **Worms:** Worms are often confused with viruses but actually function differently. Like viruses, worms are also software programs that disrupt the user's computer. However, worms are programs that propagate automatically and silently without modifying software or alerting the user. Worms are insidious because they do not require human interaction such as executing a file; instead, they can copy itself from one computer to another over a network. When inside a system, they can carry out their intended harm whether it's to damage data or relay sensitive information.

✔ **Trojan horses:** A Trojan horse is an application that appears to be one thing but after installed, does something else. Perhaps this program looks like an innocent game, but after you install it, it works in the background to allow hackers into your computer.

✔ **Spyware:** Spyware is a software application that runs silently in the background, covertly gathering system information through the user's Internet connection without his knowledge, usually for advertising purposes. Spyware can do a great many things but is certainly not what you want on your computer.

With all this badness out there, it's no wonder that consumers are leery in terms of trusting anyone on the Internet. The following section discusses the specific elements to include on your landing page that help make you appear more credible.

The Elements of Trust

Here's the real meat and potatoes of this chapter. *Trust* elements are those landing page components used to make your visitors feel more comfortable buying stuff from you. You have several trust elements at your disposal, including data use policies, testimonials, third-party logos, and more. In this section, we outline the key trust elements that you can incorporate into your landing page. We start by looking at building trust with the language you use on your site.

Using the correct language

When you write content for your landing pages, ads, or headlines, it's very important to make sure you know the audience with whom you're speaking. You have to use the right language for the demographic and audience you're trying to appeal to. The following are two approaches you can take with the language you use on your landing page:

- ✔ **Speak as an expert:** Many visitors feel more comfortable when they see you as an expert in an area. In order to be seen as an expert, the language of your landing page must exude *expertness* — language that's authoritative and intelligent in ways that build the visitor's confidence in your knowledge. A word to the wise: If you plan on taking this approach, you better actually *be* an expert and not just play one on TV. People will see right through you if you try to fake your content.

- ✔ **Speak as a peer:** You don't always have to be an expert to sell a product or a service. For example, if you're selling a product geared toward adolescents, men, women, figure skaters, shepherds, or police, you might want to use the language they're using. Sometimes being the Voice from On High, delivering words of wisdom to the masses below, isn't going to appeal to an audience. In certain situations (okay, maybe not when soliciting medical advice), people prefer to listen to someone who seems just like one of them. To use this approach, you need to have a very clear idea of your audience. Take the time to find out who your real customers are, how they talk, and how best to relate to them.

Be clear on the language you want to use on your landing page and then use that language consistently. To get your message across and to build trust, be clear on whom you're talking to, how to talk to that group, and the tone to take. (You can get more information on how to identify your customers in Chapter 8.)

Incorporating trust words and phrases

You don't need to be a rocket scientist to figure out that the words you use on your landing page can impact the extent to which your site visitors trust you. Knowing this, you can use different words and phrases that help build trust. You probably also aren't surprised that certain words or phrases are established as particularly effective in earning that trust. For example, in just a few minutes of Web browsing, you stumble across many of the following phrases:

- ✔ 100% guaranteed.
- ✔ Your privacy is our concern.

- ✔ We're here 24/7 to help you.
- ✔ Your privacy is important to us. View our Privacy Policy.
- ✔ We're registered with the BBB (Better Business Bureau).
- ✔ Read a few testimonials from our customers.
- ✔ Visit our store located at *Anytown, USA* if you have any questions.
- ✔ Money back guarantee.

Look at your own pages and what you offer. Do you have words or phrases that up your visitor's comfort level with your site? If not, put them there. Don't give your visitors any reason to doubt your credibility.

Protecting customer information

You must obtain, store, and retain customer information in a professional and safe manner; this is absolutely critical. Before visitors will give you their information, they have to believe that you're trustworthy enough to manage their personal information well — essentially, they have to be assured that the trust they've given you is well-placed and that their information is safe. Few things are more important to online visitors than the use and storage of their personal information. Having a plan and policies in place is important to deal with their concerns.

To help alleviate visitors' concerns over the use of personal information, clearly display how you intend to gather, use, and store information. This type of clear communication goes a long way in making your visitors more comfortable. The following includes a sample of a written Client Policy Agreement.

Sample Client Privacy Agreement

Feel free to take the following and run with it:

> *Company name* will use your personal information obtained with this site, including without limitation, your name, e-mail address, or other information unique to you in the following ways:
>
>> (a) *Company name* may use your personal information to contact you regarding new offers, products, and services. This will be done through e-mail, and you can cancel this service at any time.
>>
>> (b) *Company name* may use your information to enhance and modify the site. Your personal information may be combined with others to more clearly identify our customers' needs and to accommodate those needs.

(c) *Company name* uses cookies and other types of user tracking technologies. Cookies are used to log caches on the site. Cookies can be disabled, but doing so may adversely impact some of the features available on the site. The purpose of these tracking mechanisms is to identify customer surfing habits and make the site better suited for customer needs.

(d) *Company name* will not sell or disclose any part of your personal information to any third party, except if required by subpoena.

This privacy statement example is, of course, just that — only an example. The one you come up with has to be customized to fit your business and landing page. Take the time to write a clear privacy agreement and don't leave out anything. A clear privacy agreement goes a long way in increasing trust.

Securing personal information

You may have seen stories on the evening news telling the sad tale of data — credit card numbers, for example — that have been compromised and may have fallen in the wrong hands. This can happen if the data isn't stored securely or disposed of in a safe manner. Depending on where you live, you have clear regulations of how to hold customer information. Securing information is more than just creating a database and storing it on your computer.

Don't underestimate the importance of properly securing personal information. Gartner recently conducted and found that 39 percent of consumers have already changed their behavior due to worries about their personal data being stolen and 59 percent of those have cut back on online shopping.

You can choose from a number of options to secure customer data, such as:

- ✔ **Encrypt customer information whether it's on a hard disk or being transmitted over the Internet.** *Encryption* means to scramble the information so that if it's somehow intercepted, it can't be read. We recommend that customer data be encrypted when it's being stored in a backup as well.

- ✔ **Limit access to customer information to only those who need to see it.** The fewer people who have access to the data, the less risk there is of it being misused.

- ✔ **Store customer data on a computer different from the one you use on the Internet.** To do this, customer data can be encrypted and stored on a removable hard drive or flash drive.

- ✔ **Ensure your computer is up to date with virus checkers and run scans regularly**. You don't want to fall victim to a Trojan horse or other malware that may compromise your system.

✔ **Develop policies regarding how long customer data can be kept and how it will be disposed.** Many companies have detailed policies which dictate how long customer data can be held and what can be done with it during that time. In addition, the policy typically identifies how data can be disposed of and who is responsible for managing the data.

Maintaining customer data is an involved subject. More information on how you can secure customer data can be found on the Web site of the Federal Trade Commission at `www.ftc.gov/bcp/edu/pubs/business/idtheft/bus54.shtm`.

Using trust icons and logos

Trust can also be expressed with images, logos, and other graphical elements. Trust logos and images let the visitor know you're associated with credible organizations and are accountable to them. These trust icons and logos reinforce your trustworthiness.

Often you'll find these trust icons and logos in the bottom portion of the landing page or checkout page. Trust logos include product providers, protected Secure Socket Layer (SSL) certificates, or other authority sites with the goal of expressing how trustworthy your site is. See Figure 7-1 for sample trust logos.

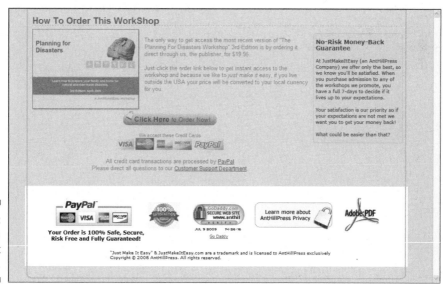

Figure 7-1: A sampling of trust logos.

Data disposal

Mike has the following story:

"Some years ago, I was doing a radio program that took a look at data disposal. In the show, I went to a local IT recycling plant and a few secondhand stores as well, on the lookout for older hard disks. The idea was to see how much data could be retrieved if someone reasonably intelligent put his mind to it. I ran an undelete program on the disks and scanned them for data. In a very short amount of time, I got many personal documents, saved e-mails, pictures — just about any type of data you can imagine. Several documents were lists of passwords, saved Web caches, and more."

Remember: All electronic devices — from flash drives, hard drives, CD-ROMS, cell phones, and more — contain data and potentially personal information. When you dispose of these devices, ensure that the data is truly gone. You can do this in several ways. You could download applications that are designed to cleanly erase all content on a hard drive or flash drive before disposal, but other special applications can be used to re-create the data. If the data that was held on a device was very sensitive, you may need to completely destroy the hard drive or storage device — we're talking pulverize here — to ensure that the data can't be retrieved in any way.

How important is proper disposal? According to professional services firm KPMG, 2008 was the worst year ever recorded for reported data loss incidents. The company's data loss barometer predicts that the number of people affected by data loss around the world could rise to 190 million in 2009, compared to 92 million last year. No wonder your visitors need a little reassurance.

You must have the rights to display the icons. Placing icons or logos on your site without the company's permission isn't an ethical practice and can lead to legal or false representation issues.

Finding icons and logos to use is a relatively simple process. Figure out how you're conducting business, make a list of potential logos and icons to get across the security aspect, and research the business for their icon usage policies.

To determine how you're conducting business, ask

- ✔ Who are you using for your credit card clearing?
- ✔ What company are you using for securing your data through SSL?

    SSL is the lock provided for orders or getting information via a secure form.

- ✔ What companies or affiliate programs are you selling for?
- ✔ Do you have a guarantee logo?
- ✔ Are you registered with any organizations, such as BBB?

Using third-party logos to build your trust is a sound practice, but beware of the potential negative flip side. Not only will customers increase their confidence in you for working with trusted sources, they'll also bring their bias for companies that they've had a bad experience with.

A prime example of this is credit card clearing. If you utilize *PayPal* — a company with a sound reputation, by the way — to do your credit card clearing but the customer has had a bad experience from a past PayPal purchase, that might give her pause. She may like your product but want another way to pay for it. If PayPal is the only option you have for purchasing, you must either accept that some people won't buy because of this brand or you need to offer more purchasing options.

Using testimonials and customer comments

Another strong trust element involves customer testimonials. Testimonials enhance your credibility and provide a third-party endorsement. This spontaneous customer input impresses the visitor with your trustworthiness. Posting comments and testimonials is an online version of word of mouth. Testimonials reassure others that people just like them used the product and liked it enough to take the time to tell you about it. Strong evidence supports the notion that testimonials are one of the most important aspects of a sales page.

You can use testimonials throughout the landing page. They can commonly be found in highly visibly places, such as above the fold (the fold is discussed in Chapter 4), the body area, or in a sidebar menu. To increase the trust factor, Figure 7-2 shows how a testimonial is usually associated with an image of the person who provided it to make the words come from a real person and keep it personal.

Having only a few testimonials per landing page is recommended; often a secondary page is used to offer even more testimonials to review. Over time, you can build a long list of testimonials that will help build trust even for a smaller company.

Testimonials need to be authentic. Resist the temptation to use your mother or Aunt Flo and write a fake testimonial. Kind of cheap, don't you think?

Using customer comments

Customer comments are different than testimonials in that they're often raw, unedited comments from people who have purchased the product or have something to say about the company.

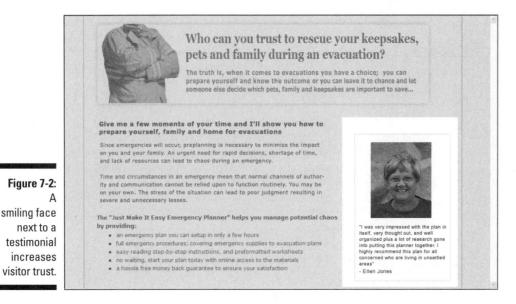

Unlike always-positive testimonials, customer comments can either be favorable or unflattering. This honesty is seen by the visitor as a genuine review of your product or service and builds trust with the visitor. If you have nothing to hide, you must be trustworthy. A good example of this approach is the book reviews on Amazon.com. These are five-star ratings with comments, and customers can put any comment, good or bad of the product.

You generally find that the customer comments used on landing pages are at the bottom of the page. They're placed at the bottom, not to hide them but because as comments are added, the page has a tendency to grow extremely long.

You can collect comments and post them in various ways:

- ✔ As **open posts** that are part of an online public forum
- ✔ As **part of a controlled environment** — with registration and sign in — where visitors can leave a comment
- ✔ As **comments that are updated automatically** and posted to the site
- ✔ As **part of a selection system** in which the site administrator selects when or if a comment goes live on the page

Regardless of your approach, you'll find both pros and cons in the system you choose. Open posting and auto updating is easy to set up and takes relatively no maintenance or person power. However, the comment quality could potentially vary widely, with extremes ranging from crushingly negative to excellent. Creating a registration system, especially with selective posting, enables you to collect visitor information and screen the quality of the posts, but it does take more programming knowledge and maintenance time.

One of the best options when it comes to controlling comments is to make sure you have a clause in your Terms of Use Policy that states that you, as the landing page owner, can use comments at your own discretion and that those posting comments must abide by your terms. After all, you don't need any angry posters making your job more difficult than it already is.

How many comments or testimonials should you aim for on your landing page? We don't have a set number that will consistently influence the customer to buy, but the more you have, the better your chances are at influencing the customer with regard to your trustworthiness. Not only do testimonials concrete proof that your site has lots of customers, but it also gives more than one view of your product or service.

Part of using testimonials and comments effectively involves testing their effectiveness. It may be that some of your testimonials are actually hurting your conversion rates. One of the best ways to determine their effectiveness is using split-testing. Split-testing involves simultaneously testing multiple landing page configuration to see which one performs the best. You can find more on split-testing in Chapter 12.

Using negative comments to your advantage

Dealing with negative comments from others can be hard to take, especially if you feel the comments are unjustified. Just remember, in most cases, the comments aren't aimed at you personally, but at the product or the business. Instead of taking negative comments too personally, review them to see whether they can be used to better your product. A little criticism can be a good thing but a lot of public criticism on your site can sink you. Then what?

One question that always arises when talking about customer feedback is, "Should you censor your comments?" This comes down to ethics. If you choose to censor visitor feedback, remember that independent visitors put the information there; editing their comments may change their meaning and take away from the authenticity.

On the other hand, censoring is required if the comments are defamatory, go against your stated polices, or use indecent or foul language. A strong Terms of Use Policy for your site allows you the discretion to pull (or simply not use) comments that aren't in the best interest of your readers.

Comments need to be (and look) genuine. Some visitors are skeptics by nature, and if they suspect you're adding your own comments — known as *seeding* — or the comments seem too perfect to be authentic, visitors might just ignore them.

Editing comments

So what if the comment has spelling or grammatical errors? The questions become: Who is your target market? What is their education level? Poorly written comments don't reflect a highly educated target market, so you might consider omitting ones with glaring errors.

On the flip side, even highly educated people are just that — people. Some sites choose to leave comments with spelling and grammar errors intact to support the fact that real people are leaving information behind and therefore, the site can be trusted more.

Having a customer comment area can be a tricky addition to the landing page. When it works, it is a powerful trust-building element. If left unattended, negative or malicious comments can hinder your conversion efforts. If you have the time to monitor and edit customer comments, then maybe it would work for you. Otherwise, it may be best to stick to the more controlled testimonials.

Adding content pages to build trust

When you look at trust items, look beyond just the landing page to include the pages connected to it. Strong auxiliary pages give validity to your site while building confidence in your company and the product you're selling.

Your visitor needs to feel your company is secure and real. Visitors want to know they're dealing with a real company run by real people. You can bridge the gaps by including the following pages:

- **Contact Us:** Customers need to know that if they have a question or concern, you can offer assistance. This assistance can be in the form of e-mail, phone, snail mail, or live chat.

  No matter what you offer as your communication channel, make sure that you also indicate your response window and hours of operation. Customers need to know what to expect. For example, if you offer 24/7 e-mail support, you might want to add, "You'll receive an answer within 72 hours."

  Don't offer more than you can do. Customers expect to receive what they're told, and this includes when they'll be contacted. A physical mailing address or a business location brings a sense of authenticity to the business and should be included on your Contact Us page.

  If you don't have a head office or a physical business address, rent a P.O. Box. Many post services now offer full addresses rather than a simple box number. If you choose this option, make sure it's clear on your Contact Us page that this is only a mailing address.

- **About Us:** When building the trust factor, visitors need to know you and what your company stands for. An About Us page can be a simple, single page that covers the basics; or it can consist of several pages that cover mission statements, key employee bios, and a company history.

About Us pages reflect the most professional aspects of your business and are formal in nature. The focus of this area is to get across your professionalism, and what you say proves to visitors that you're a real business worth doing real business with.

✔ **Additional testimonials:** If you have many testimonials, a page that displays them all is a nice addition to your site. This demonstrates that even more people loved your product or service than what shows on the landing page.

Make this page accessible directly from your landing page through links embedded in your body copy or a Click Here to View All Testimonials link right below the testimonial. You don't want to hide testimonials!

✔ **Help and support areas:** Help and support areas are another way to show that you have the customer's best interest in mind. Although this may sound similar to the Contact Us page, help and customer support areas are more than just an e-mail link.

Help areas usually have frequently asked questions (FAQs) concerning return policies, product issues, or other site issues. Use your own experiences as a guide. Think of questions you, as a customer, might ask and then provide answers to those questions. If you receive multiple e-mails with a similar question, include the question (and its answer, of course) in your FAQs.

Using Terms of Sale and Terms of Use as trust tools

Clearly displaying your policies on your site can make a big difference in building trust. Policy pages come in many forms and are typically found with a link at the bottom of your site pages. Some Web sites use one long policy section that covers everything, whereas others use separate policies to cover privacy, terms, and sales practices. Both ways are effective as long as they're accessible and easy to read.

Terms of Sale Agreement

A Terms of Sale Policy identifies such elements as the method of payment, delivery specifics, and shipping and returning procedures. The Terms of Sale Policy is essentially the sales contract between you (the seller) and your customer. Although few people actually take the time to read your entire Terms of Sale Policy, it's still necessary to have one. Visitors will notice the link to the Terms of Sale Policy and be reassured that you have one. Also, if a problem arises, you're covered as long as you've upheld your end of the bargain as stated in the Terms of Sale. See the following for a sample Terms of Sale.

Sample Terms of Sale Agreement

Feel free to use as you see fit:

This Terms of Sale Agreement represents a legal contract between you (the customer) and *(your company).* By purchasing any product or service from our site, you state an acceptance of this agreement.

- **Product Description; No Refunds or Exchanges:** We've made every attempt to display our product online as clearly as possible. However, we do not guarantee that descriptions are error-free. All sales made through our site are final. No refunds or exchanges for items purchased through our site will be made.

- **Display:** All images on this site have been tested and approved to work with a 1024 x 768 screen resolution. The display of the site will change depending on the resolution used. We recommend using the 1024 x 768 screen resolution to see the best representation of our products.

- **Payments and Disputed Payments:** Currently, our site accepts the following payment methods: VISA, MasterCard, PayPal, and beaver pelts. No other payment options are available at this time. We reserve the right to cancel shipment and return payment in the event a payment is disputed.

- **Pricing; Shipping; Pricing Errors;** Other Errors: Prices offered on this site are quoted in U.S. dollars. The listed U.S. price does not include shipping or handling, expedited shipping service, or tax. These fees will be extra.

- **Order Status:** After you place an order, we will send you a personalized e-mail within one business day and provide you with an order confirmation number. When your order is shipped, we will send you a shipment confirmation e-mail with the shipping carrier tracking number, if available.

This is a very simple example of a Terms of Sale agreement, but it gives you an idea of what to look for. Notice in this sample agreement, this fictitious company doesn't offer returns or exchanges. This is common for established companies, but it's a tad riskier for a smaller entrepreneur. How much trust do you think this type of policy would inspire if the source was a relative unknown?

When it comes to the Terms of Sale, choosing what to include is really up to you. We strongly recommend that you write the policy with trust building in mind. If you're confident about your product and service, why not include a 30-day money back guarantee or an Exchange Policy? This can go a long way in making your visitors more confident in you.

Offering return policies & guarantees

Most people have a real sense of security when they see a product guarantee and an easy-to-use Return Policy. These make your visitors confident that you back your product and that in turn, builds trust. Visitors want to know that if they're not happy with the product, they can return it and either get their money back or get another product in return. Returning products is a major concern for visitors when purchasing online. Unlike a physical store, customers are faced with a higher hassle factor. Not only must they do extra work to return the product — the trip to the post office to mail it back to you, for one — they're also faced with a shipping delay when they're getting a new product in exchange.

Strong return polices and guarantees will help with this problem. Your Return Policy is part of your Terms of Sale and outlines how you want the return to be done, how many days the customer has to return the product, and any fees or requirements included to return the product.

The more complicated you make your Return Policy, the less likely that the visitor responds to it positively and as a result, might not make a purchase at all. A complicated Return Policy might say, "Returns accepted only in the original packaging with a $25.00 exchange fee and a four to six week delay while problem verification occurs. Also, we accept returns shipped only on a full moon or when the moons of Jupiter are in alignment."

A Return Policy with too many hoops to jump through does nothing for the visitor's resolve to buy from you.

Guarantees need to be laid out clearly and need to be easy to understand, with a link to your policy on them for more details. If you offer a 100-percent money back guarantee, state exactly what you mean by this and whether any complicated rules are involved, such as those listed in the example earlier.

Guarantees are a great way to add that finishing touch to your trust building efforts. Nothing says more to your customers than knowing that if they're not happy with their purchase, they have a hassle-free way to get a product they like or to get their money back.

 A good idea is not only to have a Return Policy but to also clearly promote it on your Web site. Even promote it upfront in the fold area. You'll find more information on what the fold area is (and what to include in it) in Chapter 4.

Terms of Use Policy

The Terms of Use represents a contract between you (the seller) and the visitor to your Web site. This policy sets the guidelines of what can and can't be done while visiting your site; it's the visitor rules and regulations. Typically, visitors have to obey these rules and regulations, or they're banned from the site.

Depending on the company, the Terms of Use can be a general document, or it can be a very detailed and specific contract. The following is a simple Terms of Use Policy.

Sample Terms of Use Policy

Our little gift to you:

> Thank you for choosing to visit YourSite.com. We've established a series of terms and conditions that ensure that you and others can continue to use the site safely and hassle-free. Your use of the YourSite.com Web site is at our sole discretion. We reserve the right to deny you further use of the site at any time, for any reason, with or without cause.

> To continue to use YourSite.com, the following conditions apply:

> 1. You, the visitor, agree that uploading, posting, e-mailing, or otherwise transmitting data to our site that is harmful, malicious, hateful, threatening, or offensive in any way is strictly prohibited.

> 2. You agree that misrepresenting yourself as another or violating the privacy of another is prohibited.

> 3. You agree to not knowingly upload, post, or e-mail material that contains any form of malware, such as Trojan horses, spyware, or viruses.

> 4. You agree not to use YourSite.com to promote your own business or products.

> 5. You agree to not conduct yourself in a manner that would reflect negatively on YourSite.com and our customers.

This really is the tip of the iceberg for the Terms of Use Policy. If you take the time to read the Terms of Use from a number of different large Web-based companies, you'll soon discover that they can be pages long and cover more aspects that you can imagine. These documents are often drawn up by lawyers and take another lawyer to decode them. They can be the online version of hieroglyphics.

If you have an online business with a few landing pages to support it, you need a Terms of Use Policy. This protects you and the customer and speaks to your professionalism. We recommend you keep your Terms of Use as reader friendly as possible and — like the Terms of Sale — put a link at the bottom of your landing pages for visitors to see and easily access the policy.

Placing Trust Elements in Your Landing Page

Okay, you have all these trust elements lying around ready to use, but where do they actually go? You don't want to hit your visitors over the head with them all at once, but they need to be where they're the most visible. To begin, break your landing page into three areas, the *fold* (the first page visitors see), the *body* (the text areas that appear after the visitor scrolls down), and the *footer* (the bottom of the page). Each of these areas can hold important trust elements. The elements can be moved around a bit, but some general guidelines get things started. To organize your trust items, try the following schema:

✔ **The fold area:** The fold area the area that the visitor first sees without scrolling when getting to your site, as discussed in Chapter 4 — is arguably the most important part of your page. The fold contains not only the key parts to tell visitors they're at the right place, but it also provides your visitors with their first impression of your site. The fold is also the first area to incorporate trust items, such as

- *Your brand:* Distinguish yourself with your logo, if it is recognized. Familiarity goes a long way when it comes to building trust.

- *Trust-building images:* We're talking pictures of your office, staff, or product — whatever it takes to portray yourself as professional and established.

- *Examples of product quality (testimonials, supporting text):* "We're good, here's the proof." The fold is not a huge area but if you can squeeze in a few testimonials, that can work to build trust.

- *Guarantee:* You can boldly state that your product/service comes with a satisfaction guarantee.

✔ **Throughout the body:** If you've captured your visitor in the fold, they're going to scroll down to your body. When visitors are looking for more information on your product or service, they need to be able to find content throughout the body text of the page that reinforces the idea that you're the kind of person worth buying from. The body of the page is the perfect opportunity to offer

- *Messages or testimonials* from satisfied customers.

- *Stats* that back up your claims and level of quality.

- *Details* of your return policies.

- *Captions* under extra images or stats that can reinforce your quality and satisfaction claims.

✔ **The footer:** Never overlook the bottom of the page as a place for trust. If your visitor has read your entire page or skimmed to the bottom, strong footers and trust items can be just enough to push her to trust you and buy from you. Consider including

- Testimonials
- Trust icons
- A Privacy Policy
- Terms and conditions
- Contact information
- Support/help centers

Figure 7-3 offers one take on the footer look.

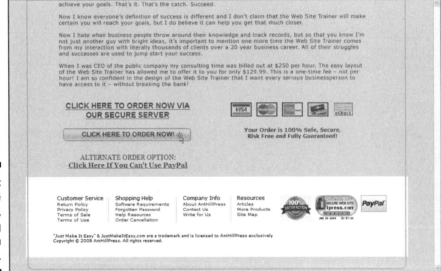

Figure 7-3:
A sample footer, including common trust items.

By incorporating trust items throughout your page, you increase the chance your visitor will see your trust elements, plus you're building trust through the sales process of your page. Each page will need different trust items, and it's important to remember that very rarely can you put every trust item on any one page.

Who your target market is and what stage of the buying process they're in will determine where you need to focus your trust items. Be sure to focus your efforts there and test your page to ensure you're getting your message across.

Five Trust Building Tips

Just like building a brand, building company trust through your landing page takes time. Businesses use many long-term strategies for building trust and go so far as to build trust even before a product hits the market. Here are five things to consider when you try to build trust:

- ✔ **Use experts:** Is there an expert in the field with knowledge of your product/service who's willing to write a testimonial for you? If you sell car alarms, perhaps you know a police officer who gives you the thumbs up. If you're selling a computer workshop, maybe you know an IT expert from Intel who can give you a positive review. Tracking down an expert isn't always easy, but finding one who will give you a promotion goes a long way toward building trust with your site visitors.

- ✔ **Use statistics:** Advertising uses statistics all the time. Often these statistics don't reveal any real truth or conclusions, but they do build trust. Include positive site statistics (wherever you can find them) as well as sale percentages; but don't forget that you can also build trust through statistics, such as the number of satisfied customers you have or the number of people that have signed up to your monthly newsletter. You see this every day in the form of billboards or advertisements proclaiming, "Over 20 million served," or "Bestseller! Over one million copies sold." All these tell the story that other folks out there trust the business or product.

- ✔ **Express your business values and motivation:** If you've taken the time to find out as much as you can about your audience, you can inform them through your mission or value statement of your goals and what you stand for. If visitors share and understand what makes you tick, they can relate more to you and trust you.

- ✔ **Conduct surveys and focus groups:** You can also bolster and build trust by conducting surveys and holding focus groups. During the customer research phase, not only can you share the important data that's collected on your product or service, but you can also offer verifiable information to back up the claims you make on your site.

  Product research surveys are done all the time via phone, mail, in person, or in a controlled focus group. Big business pays for targeted surveys to be completed to back up claims and give credibility to its product, all in the name of building trust with the consumer.

- ✔ **Be confident:** Show the results of using your product/service. Your confidence comes through in the images you choose, the writing you use, and in your total site. This confidence is catchy and will certainly gain the trust of your visitors, both in you and in your product.

Trust Element Checklist

We cover a lot of ground in this chapter. Time to see whether your landing page is gaining visitor trust. Check your landing page against Table 7-1.

Table 7-1	Reviewing Your Trust Elements		
Trust Element Question		*Yes*	*No*
Are you using language that appeals to your audience?			
Can you identify trust words and phrases on your site?			
Do you have a clearly displayed privacy agreement?			
Do you have a policy for handling customer information?			
Do you have trust logos and images on your site?			
Do you have visible testimonials on your site?			
Do you have a clearly listed About Us and Contact Us section?			
Do you have an easy-to-use Return Policy displayed prominently?			
Can you clearly identify how your product/service benefits your audience?			
Are your trust elements placed in the correct areas of your landing page?			
If a friend or colleague reviews your landing page, can he identify the trust elements you use?			

Part III
Getting to Know Your Customers

The 5th Wave — By Rich Tennant

J&R HYPNOSIS CLINIC

Overcome Technophobia
Contact our Web site
WWW.JRHYPNO.COM

"You know, it dawned on me last night why we
aren't getting any hits on our Web site."

In this part . . .

This part is all about getting to know your visitors and figuring out how to design a landing page just for them. Chapter 8 examines the procedures for developing a customer profile, including the steps to create a virtual customer.

Chapter 9 picks up at designing your site with your visitors in mind so that you meet their expectations. After you design your site, Chapter 10 looks at tracking customer responses and includes an overview of the tools you need to do the tracking, such as feedback forms, online forums, and customer reviews.

Chapter 8

Getting to Know Your Audience

In This Chapter

▶ Finding out what a customer profile is

▶ Using marketing segment and personas to your advantage

▶ Surfing where your customers surf

▶ Understanding customer buying habits

▶ Translating the buying process into your landing page

*B*efore you can really develop your landing page into a successful online business, you have to see your page through the eyes of your customers and put yourself in their shoes. (Okay, not literally because the technology for inhabiting the body of another person hasn't been developed; we just mean you really *really* need to understand the perspective of your potential customers to be able to design a landing page for their needs.)

To be able to get this perspective, you have to be completely clear about who your target customers are and what your demographics are. Many landing page developers simply aim at large groups of potential customers, which often leads to unfocussed, generic landing pages. This chapter is all about finding your customers and getting into their heads. (Again, not literally. No Vulcan mind melds here.)

The chapter begins by discussing customer profiling and how you use it to customize landing pages. We examine how customer demographics affect your landing pages, where to find untapped customers, and how developing a mental picture of your virtual customer gives you valuable insights to improving your landing page conversions.

When you're thinking of an ideal customer for your product, think individually; think of one product and then think of the one person you just know wants to buy it. The more you focus on that one person, the better your overall results will be.

Creating a Customer Profile

A *customer profile* is a description of your customer based on various demographic criteria. These criteria may be related to geographical location, gender, age, education level, income range, hobbies, and so on. Now hear this: You need customer profiles to help focus your online marketing efforts. These profiles help you provide your customers with what they're expecting to find on your site and are essential to have if you want to keep your customers to come back.

Before you begin creating your customer profile, decide whether the focus of your landing page is a B2B (Business to Business) or B2C (Business to Customer). If your focus is B2B, you're going to have to know such things as company size, budgets, previous suppliers, and so on. If your landing page is designed for individual customers, the profile's specific to them, including age, income level, education, and so on.

Developing your customer profile isn't a one time task; rather, it's an ongoing process. When your landing page is first under development, identify a potential customer profile. That means focus in on who you expect your customers to be. After you have your landing page up and running, shift your focus to finding out whether the *potential* customer profile you created turns out to be the *actual* demographic visiting your site.

Getting the information

Many of the landing pages you develop are going to be in a pretty constant state of flux — you're very likely to introduce or discontinue products as well as change the design, the URL, or more. Throughout all this change, keep track of who's visiting your site and keep on top of your current customer demographics.

Just like your site, your customer demographic is dynamic. Depending on your product or service, the demographic can shift with the economy, time of year, weather, and more. Keeping track and analyzing your demographic information reveals customer patterns that you can use to your best marketing advantage.

Consider the following methods for gathering your customer demographics:

✔ **Web analytics:** Your landing page can log a significant amount of customer information, including a visitor's IP address, the Web browser used, how long visitors were on your site, and more. This type of information can be used by Web analytic software to develop a profile of your customer demographic. With such software, you can determine where the bulk of your customers live, what they like about your landing page, and what they don't. The details that Web analytic software can provide are essential in developing a landing page targeted at your specific demographic. We discuss Web analytic software in more detail in Chapters 1 and 12.

✔ **Online surveys:** We realize surveys can sometimes annoy visitors, but the potential information they can provide is marketing gold. We recommend making surveys a tad more palatable by offering those visitors who answer a few questions some exclusive tips or a special offer. Not only will you get valuable information, surveys give your site an interactive component. Surveys should never be long and should really require only a few minutes to fill out. The questions on the survey must be carefully chosen to reflect the type of information you seek.

So how many questions to include in a survey? No standard rule here, but as a guideline, customers usually take the time to answer more questions than casual surfers.

The types of questions asked on a survey vary depending on the audience. Table 8-1 shows the types of demographic questions that may be asked in a business survey as opposed to those asked in a consumer survey.

Writing the right questions for a survey isn't always easy. If in doubt, you can buy survey templates online with both business and consumer foci. Simply find a survey that reflects the types of questions you'd ask and place the survey right into your landing page. To get you started, Microsoft offers free survey samples that can be easily downloaded right into a Word document. Try going to `http://office.microsoft.com/en-us/templates/default.aspx` and search for a few of their survey options.

Many people don't take the time to fill out surveys, so making yours as friendly as possible is important. Listed here are five tips to help get a response from your survey:

> *Keep the survey questions simple.* Many people are turned away by lengthy questions and detailed instructions. Short questions with a single focus work well.

> *Offer free incentives.* Everyone loves free stuff, and offering something is a great way to get your survey filled out. Try giving away a free newsletter or a gift certificate. Incentives encourage many hesitant respondents to take the time to fill out one.

> *Post privacy protections.* Some surveys can ask information some people don't want known publicly. Explain how their responses will be used. Be above board and honest about the reasons for the survey. Don't give any reason for people to suspect you're doing something shifty.

> *Keep the format easy to use.* Drop-down lists and clickable buttons are easy and quick for people to respond to. The less users need to use their keyboard to type in responses, the better.

Publish survey results. Depending on the type of survey, it may be appropriate to publish the results of the survey to those who've taken it. If this is the case, tell the respondents this is what you're doing. This is a great way to get the e-mail addresses of those taking the survey because those respondents interested in seeing the results have to give you their e-mail addresses as contact info.

Table 8-1	Customer versus Business Demographic Questions	
Question Number	**Customer Demographic Question**	**Business Demographic Question**
Question 1	What's your age range?	What industry are you in?
Question 2	What's your education level?	How long have you been with your current employer?
Question 3	What's your gender?	What's your current job title?
Question 4	Approximately how much do you spend on groceries per week?	How often do you participate in company training programs?

When you design surveys, it can be a balance between annoying visitors and getting the information you need. One thing some people do is hide the close button on pop-up surveys. We certainly don't recommend this. If you decide to use a survey, make sure that it's easy for people to opt out of and continue browsing your site if they decide they don't want to answer any questions.

Pre-profiling your ideal customer

Stuff like surveys and the mining of Web analytics data tend to occur after the landing page is built and visitors are already to your site. From there, you try to build an accurate customer profile of who the actual visitors are. Naturally, gathering this information when your landing page is in the development stage isn't possible — you can't analyze visitors who haven't visited yet, right?

Or can you? We think that it's not only possible but rather crucial that you develop a pre-landing page profile of your visitors. Every Web site owner should be strongly focused on both current and prospective customers. The ability to find a customer, encourage her to buy from or sign up to your service, and to come back again for a repeat buy are the main purposes of a landing page. The more you know about your customer when still developing your landing page, the more targeted your design, message, and efforts will be.

Here are some tips to help you find your landing page's ideal customer:

- **Define your product or service from the customer's viewpoint.** What problems does your product or service solve for your ideal customer? What needs does the product meet for your customers? How does it improve a person's life or work situation? What does it *do*? (For more on defining your product and service benefits to customers, see Chapter 1.)

- **Define your ideal customer.** In an ideal world, who are your customers? What are they like? After your product and its benefits are clearly identified, you can surmise who will benefit most from it.

- **Figure out where your ideal customer lives.** Your product can help identify where your ideal customer lives. Is it a product or service for rural communities or for urban centers? The focus and look of your site may change depending on the location of your potential customers. Cultural factors come in to play as well if you're marketing across continents.

- **Determine what happens before a customer buys your product.** Determine what the deciding factor for a sale is. What has to happen in work or life to nudge them over the edge of looking to buying? Is it seasonal? Is it a specific time of year or day of the month?

- **Find out how your customer decides to buy.** Knowing your customers' buying strategy tells you a lot about their tendencies. Have they bought this type of product before? Are they impulse buyers or is in-depth research required? What steps do they take to make a decision to act?

Identifying your customers before you have a landing page can be tricky, but if possible, visualize your perfect customer. Pretend you're placing an ad in the newspaper: "Customers needed. Must be . . . ." Must be what? Knowing the answer to that question helps direct the development of your landing page.

Much of your landing page success comes down to how well you know your customer. This knowledge helps you tap in to where you can find more customers and retain the ones you have already.

Defining your customer demographic

Demographics refer to the statistical characteristics of a segment of the population. Customer demographics identify the specific characteristics of your customers, allowing you to focus on a very specific clientele. Customer demographics encompass geographic location and personal information, such as age, as well as life and work specifics.

The two important reasons to have a clearly identified customer demographic are

✔ To identify common characteristics that make up your ideal customer

✔ To identify the geographical area that holds the highest number of ideal customers

When determining your customer demographic, get a hold of a number of pieces of information, including

✔ What's their age range?

✔ Are they male or female?

✔ Are they married? In a relationship? Single?

✔ Where do they live?

✔ Where do they work?

✔ Do they have children? How many?

✔ Do they have pets? What kind? How many?

✔ What is there annual income range?

✔ What are their hobbies?

✔ Where do they shop?

These are just a few of the questions that you may want to know about your potential customers. You can take your demographic research one step further and explore the following personal characteristics and behaviors of your customers:

✔ **Find out about their attributes:** How would they describe themselves? Humorous? Committed? Loyal? What are they passionate about? What are their favorite hobbies or pastimes? Do they collect anything? Cars? Stamps? Coins?

✔ **Find out about their shopping habits:** What determines where they shop? Convenience? Location? Price? How do they prefer to pay? Credit card? Cash only? Are they impulse buyers? Are they loyalty program members?

✔ **Find out about their reading habits:** What magazines do they read? Do they subscribe? Do they read newspapers? Online or print? When do they read the most? Time of day? Seasonal?

✔ **Where do they usually read?** School? Home? Work? Do they read for pleasure or learning? Fact or fiction?

✔ **Find out about their hobbies and interests:** What types of things do they do in their spare time? Are they part of any clubs? Book club? Cooking club? Are they part of any sports leagues? Where do they enjoy spending their time?

Demographics can go beyond behavior and focus on where the customer is in the great game of Life. Questions that center around work, education, and finance give you product price points and message complexity you can use to reach your ideal customer. Categories include

✔ **Work-related questions:** What industry do they work in? Where do they work? How long have they worked there? Is there room for advancement? Are there benefits included? Do they enjoy their work?

✔ **Financial questions:** What's their income level? Do they own their own home or do they rent? What's their occupation? What type of car(s) do they drive? Do they invest? What's their net worth? Do they own rental properties?

✔ **Education-related questions:** Are they high school graduates? How many years of college have they attended? Are they university-educated? Do they have any vocational or trades education? Do they home-school their children? Would they take an online course?

Customer answers tell you whether you need to focus on middle-aged, divorced men who have child support payments to meet or young, college-age women who are just beginning their families.

Market Segmentation

By definition, *market segmentation* is a marketing strategy designed to help you both identify subset groups of potential customers as well as determine the needs of that particular group. It's all about identifying groups and dividing a market into a distinct selection of buyers. The goal is to give you a clear focus of the group you're advertising to and to better understand your customer base. The assumption is that you, as a promoter of a product or service, will be more effective if you target a specific market rather than an *average* customer. For example, a landing page targeting women with school-aged children looks somewhat different from one targeting women in general. After you segment your customers, you can begin to target your online marketing efforts directly to that group. This includes the language you use, your figures, purchasing options, and more.

The underlying goal of market segmentation is to identify your audience. Understanding exactly to whom you're speaking is very important. Are you talking to unemployed fathers? Outdoor enthusiasts? Women older than 50? Only after you've identified your audience can you actually relate to them. Communication fails when you don't know your audience.

You can begin to segment your audience according to four distinct criteria. (Okay, you can really segment your audience anyway that you desire, but these four criteria give a starting point.) They are

- ✔ **Customer location:** Many of your customers may share a common location. Location can be any similar geographic location, such as the same state, province, neighborhood, country, and city.

- ✔ **Customer demographic:** The customer demographic typically refers to such characteristics as age, gender, income level, education level, and more.

- ✔ **Customer behaviors:** Customer behaviors include such elements as brand loyalty, surfing habits, buying patterns, and such. So, for instance, you could create a market segment based on users who frequent woodworking Web sites. If you know you have a bunch of woodworking enthusiasts on your hands, speak more directly to that audience.

- ✔ **Customer lifestyle:** It's common to group customers according to their beliefs, values, and attitudes. They'll explore your landing page if they believe you're like-minded. Again, this can be done only if you know how to speak to your audience.

Personas: Putting a name to the group

Market segments give you a snapshot of a particular group of customers. For example, you might identify your market segment as women, age 50+ from California who like waterskiing and surfing. What if you could narrow down that segment to a specific person?

Personas attempt to do just that. A *persona* is a stand-in or a representation of a larger group. Personas are of course, fictitious, but that's no reason not to treat them like real people. In fact, we highly recommend doing so, even to the point of giving them a real name and coming up with photos for them. Personas are used to help you visualize exactly who your customer is. The information included in a persona may include the following:

- ✔ Picture
- ✔ Name

> ✔ Age
>
> ✔ Location
>
> ✔ Occupation
>
> ✔ Hobbies
>
> ✔ Beliefs
>
> ✔ Values

A completed persona profile can be seen in the following section.

Applying market segmentation and personas

Okay, if you've followed along so far, we've talked about market segmentation, demographics, profiles, and personas. Time to put them all together in one example. Imagine that a client has approached you, asking you to come up with a customer profile for all those potential customers willing to pay good money for his highly detailed set of blueprints for building his very unique product, flat bottom boats. This section walks you through the thought processes involved in coming up with such a profile.

One mistake often made by landing page developers (and others) is to envision the Internet as selling to customers around the world. This is true to some extent, but face it: Large sections of the world aren't interested in your product, simply because they don't fit into your customer demographic. In this flat bottom boat example, everyone in the world can access your landing page and download the blueprints, but your realistic potential market is limited. Many adolescents, college students, Indonesians, aboriginal tribesman, New Yorkers, Yuppies, and so on may not be interested in building a flat bottom boat. Focusing your marketing efforts on any of these groups would be money and time wasted.

So who's interested in plans to make their own flat bottom boat? You know that even though anyone in the world can access your page, you can't focus on everyone at the same time; you need to reduce and pinpoint a particular audience. So, to identify the market, start at the beginning and answer some questions:

> ✔ **What are the benefits of building a flat bottom boat?** Very few flat bottom boats are available on the market. The flat bottom boat is sturdy and can carry significant gear. This makes it great for outdoorsy people. With the flat bottom boat plans, a boat can be made for less than $200.

✔ **What are the potential drawbacks of the product?** Due to the construction material, the flat bottom boat is heavy. Also, to build your own, customers need a large workshop or outdoor workspace and a number of power tools.

✔ **How accessible is the product?** The product is a downloadable set of blueprints. This allows for easy product shipping and isn't limited geographically.

✔ **Who may want this product?** This product is well-suited for handy people who like the outdoors and may want a sturdy watercraft. Customers living around or near water may really like this product. Given the cost of canoes and other watercraft, this durable boat can be made for $200, making it suitable for those with time to build it and a limited budget.

✔ **Who wouldn't like this product?** People not near the water, and those who don't have a workshop or the time to build a boat wouldn't be interested. Also, those who can't lift and transport a heavy boat to the water wouldn't be interested.

As you can see, such questions really start to focus and segment your audience. Can you start to see the market segment for flat bottom boats more clearly? Here's what you know:

✔ To build the boat, the customer needs several power tools.

✔ The customer needs a large workshop; therefore, those living in apartments may not be able to build the product. Homeowners with a garage may be best.

✔ Due to the weight of the product, the customer should live fairly close to water.

✔ The customer may not have a lot of money and is looking for an economical method to get onto the water.

Of course this is a simple example. But even from this, you've ruled out several market segments while identifying others. To conclude the flat bottom boat example, the summary in Table 8-2 identifies the market segment for blueprints for a flat bottom boat.

Table 8-2	Flat Bottom Boat Customer Demographic	
Profile	*Choices*	*Outcome*
Type	Consumer Business	Consumer
Location	Locally within a few miles Within a city In a rural area Within your state or province Anywhere in North America Anywhere in the world	In a rural area Anywhere in the world ***Note:*** Customer should live near water
Gender	Male Female	Male
Age	Under 20 20–35 36–50 50+	20–35 36–50
Disposable Income	Limited Moderate Affluent	Moderate ***Note:*** Needs access to large workshop and tools

The flat bottom boat example gives you an idea of what it takes to identify a market segment. In this example, you can design your landing page around your particular market audience: Outdoorsy people — probably males — who have access to both a workshop and tools. They'd likely live near water and understand the benefit of a sturdy homemade watercraft. From this information, you can begin visualizing a landing page that would speak to this audience. If necessary — and we think it's often necessary — you can develop a specific persona, as shown in Figure 8-1.

In Figure 8-1, you can see that Dwight now represents the market segment you're advertising to. Now you can design your landing page with Dwight in mind. You use images, language, and content that appeal directly to Dwight.

Name: Dwight	Gender: Male
	Age: 45
	Location: Dwight lives in an urban area near a river.
	Occupation: Dwight works as a part-time construction worker and handyman.
	Disposable Income: Moderate
	Overview: • Dwight has a young family. • Dwight loves camping, fishing, and the outdoors. • Dwight never attended college. • Dwight rebuilt his deck last year. • Dwight owns his own home. • Dwight's motto, "I'd rather be outside."

Figure 8-1:
Potential persona for a flat bottom boat.

Establishing Your Customer's Surfing Habits

Tracking your customers' surfing habits can go a long way in determining who they are and what they're into. By establishing these habits, you can find marketing opportunities that you'd otherwise miss — giving you a competitive advantage in the process. This opens opportunities to market directly to the customer you want, greatly increasing the chance your customer will buy.

Surfing habits are based on what types of Web sites your customers visit. This could be magazines, trade journals, and publications your customer reads or social networks they interact with. You can check online to see what e-zines your customers subscribe to and sign up. Browse forums, blogs, groups, boards, and other social network-type sites. The world is at your fingertips. You may think this seems a little like stalking, but really you're taking an active interest in your customers and immersing yourself in their world. This helps you better understand them and better communicate with them.

Follow this plan to find out where your customers surf:

✔ **Look at the customer demographic profile you created.** You can take the information from the customer demographic to determine what type of Web sites would interest your ideal customer. In the earlier flat bottom boat example, you'd look to outdoor sites relating to camping, fishing, and such. Online magazines help you identify what's happening in and around your customers' interests.

✔ **Search customer-related search terms.** Use search engines to narrow the search for Web sites that your ideal customer would be interested in. Are there other flat bottom boat sites? Be sure to use both broad and specific searches to get the best results.

✔ **Check out Web sites that show up from your searches.** Make a list of the top sites that come back from your searches. You're interested only in Web sites that actually have content related to your visitors. What types of images do these sites use? What's their tone? How do they speak? All this can be emulated on your landing paged to attract the right customers.

✔ **Check out blogs and chats.** What are your customers saying? Blogs and chat areas are great resources to find out exactly what's on your customers' minds. What do they enjoy? What challenges do they face? Blogs and chats allow you to hear what your customers are saying, giving you a chance to respond on your landing page.

Understanding the Customer Decision-Making Process

To give your customers what they want with your landing page, you need to have some idea of customer buying behavior. By understanding this behavior, you start to build the bridge among your customer profile, the sales cycle, and the final step of getting customers to commit and buy your product.

When it comes to identifying buying behavior, it isn't black and white; it has a lot of variables. However, five stages have been identified for the customer decision-making process, which is a rather linear process, as shown in Figure 8-2. Unless your customer has an impulse buy or your product is something they purchase routinely, they don't buy something first and *then* decide why they need it.

Figure 8-2 is important for choosing the marketing direction you take. By looking at the whole process and not just the end purchase, you can adapt your landing page and its message to speak to customers in all stages of the buying process. By the time a customer hits the purchase stage, it may be too late for you to influence her to choose you.

Taking a closer look at each stage gives you ideas on landing page strategy. You may want to create a landing page that goes through all stages, or you might want to create a landing page that's already partway through the decision process and use targeted ads to attract those at that stage.

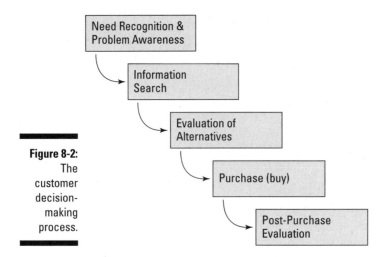

Figure 8-2:
The
customer
decision-
making
process.

Figure 8-2:
The customer decision-making process.

Stage 1: Need recognition and problem awareness

The first stage in the buying process is deciding that you need or want a product or service. Often you purchase products that you've determined will either solve a particular problem or meet a particular need. (How obvious is this paragraph?)

How involved the need or problem is determines the depth of stages 2 and 3. A low involvement purchase — like that chili dog when you're hungry — requires relatively little searching and evaluating. You might go to the fridge or stop at the first eatery you see. Smoke alarms on the other hand, may require research for the best-suited alarm for your needs; will it be battery powered or plugged in to the electrical system, for example. Other high involvement purchases include buying a new couch, car, toupee, or any product or service that requires thought and research. According to this theory, it takes you longer to choose a car than a hamburger.

When people use search engines, they often have an idea of the problem they want and need to solve. If an ad you run appears to meet that need, there's a good chance they'll click to see your landing page. Best Prices on Couches works if someone is looking for a couch. How about Click Now for Smoke Alarms? "Most Realistic Looking Toupee on the Market"?

Stage 2: Product/service information search

The information search usually leads customers to use one or more of the following sources:

- ✔ **Personal:** Friends, family, neighbors, co-workers, teammates, and so on. This is generally a word-of-mouth experience. This is where the great impression you make on past and current customers can pay back in spades.

- ✔ **Commercial:** Commercial information comes from such sources as advertising, salespeople, packaging, displays, and so on. The non-human commercial sources, such as displays and packaging, tend to be visual and colorful. As for the human element — retailers and salespeople — your hope is that they're friendly and knowledgeable and could maybe say a good word or two about your product.

- ✔ **Public sources:** Public sources include television, radio, consumer magazines, newspapers, and so on. These sources usually have a high trust factor. *Consumer's Digest* and other product reviews hold a lot of weight for a customer's final decision.

- ✔ **Hands-on experience:** We've all seen samples, trials, limited-time offers, touching, and so on. Downloadable sample applications are a prime example of this type of information source. Whether food, a gadget, or software, tasting or trying a product can make or break a sale in no time at all.

Stage 3: Evaluation of alternatives

Customers weigh the information gathered and give each a different value of reliability and importance. Table 8-3 runs down a possible evaluation process in choosing a new blender. Notice that quite a few factors influence the consumers' decisions. Are they strictly price driven? Will they buy only brand name items? Or will they take the personal recommendation because it's a good price and has lasted three years?

Table 8-3	Buying a Blender		Price
Product	Source		Price
Blender 1	Same as Mom's Generic, not a name brand Owned for three years without complaint		$19.99
Blender 2	Brand name Positive review in consumer magazine		$59.99
Blender 3	Brand name Sale in flyer Friend has it and says it's okay		$39.99

Stage 4: Purchase

After the evaluation process is complete, a buy is made. This stage is short and to the point. Decide and buy.

One factor that may hinder conversions even if there is a decision to buy is the checkout procedures. You can lose a lot of customers if your online buy process is hard to understand or doesn't flow for the customer. Basically, you lose customers right at the checkout. To find out if this is happening on your landing page, you can use tracking software such as Google Analytics to isolate any trouble with your check out. (Google Analytics and tracking software is discussed in Chapter 12.) It is important to know how many buyers you've lost because they didn't like or couldn't use your purchase system. Your landing page needs to flow, from the fold (discussed in Chapter 4) to the checkout.

Stage 5: Post-purchase evaluation

After the item is purchased, your customers always evaluate. Did they make the right choice? Would they go back and buy that product again? Does the blender meet their needs? Do these pants make them look fat? Does the couch match their living room like they thought it would?

In the case of something consumable, they'll decide whether they'll eat there again or buy that same flavored coffee. When it's an item that's purchased, disappointment can go two ways: It can lead to a returned product and purchasing the runner-up from the evaluation stage, or it can remain as a note-to-self to not buy that brand again. Either way, a happy purchase results in positive word of mouth whereas disappointment brings the opposite. This is why your landing page should include an easy-to-use Return Policy.

Having a good and easy to use Return Policy also helps build trust between you and your customer.

Taking advantage of the sales cycle

Knowing the decision process isn't helpful if you can't translate that into your landing page design. Each of the stages can be directly reflected in your design or online marketing campaign. Here are some ideas to use the buying decision to your advantage:

- ✔ **Stage 1 — Need recognition and problem awareness:** An effective headline creates a need or points out a problem every time. One of the top 100 headlines is a perfect example: Five Familiar Skin Troubles — Which Do You Want to Overcome? Until you read that, you may not have thought you had a skin problem. Chances are visitors will keep reading just to find out if they have one of the mentioned troubles. Do Your Smoke Alarms Actually Work? Hmmm, I think I better find click and find out.

  Images can also be used to get across a need or a problem. This can be twofold, such as having an image that shows only the problem and an image of your product fixing that problem. Images can bring out the emotion, hunger, frustration, or anxiety in your visitors, which hopefully leads them to where they want to overcome such feelings by buying your product.

- ✔ **Stage 2 — Information search:** Placing testimonials on your page gives people that personal touch. Testimonials give feedback from real people and make a nameless company come alive while showing that others liked (and would recommend) the product.

  The top area (fold) of your landing page is like the packaging of a product — both the front and the back of the box, as it were. Just like a product package, you need to have descriptive copy and clear images of the product to entice the person reading it.

  Create articles on your product and place them in online trade journals and Web sites that interest your ideal demographic. Then use this article as a promotional tool. Lead-ins, such as As Seen on This Web Site . . ." make your company more trustworthy and real to customers.

  Depending on your product or service, you can offer a free sample chapter or video of the product in use. This isn't quite the same as a taste test or a hands-on demo, but it's as close as you'll get online.

- ✔ **Stage 3 — Evaluation of alternatives:** Are you the best at what you do? Let visitors know on your landing page. Why, considering all the options available online, should they choose you?

Knowing your customers well helps you relate to them — you'll be better able to convince them that you're the company to go with. Help your visitors evaluate the competition by offering comparison charts or extra incentives, such as limited-time offers. Any little tidbit you can offer to sway your visitor to choosing you is worth the effort.

Offer easy ways to contact you and be sure to get back to customers quickly on any question or concerns they might have. Customer service and personal interaction helps you stand above the crowd.

✔ **Stage 4 — Purchase:** For some reason, many landing pages don't make it clear where and how to actually purchase the product or service. Make it easy for visitors to become customers. Use large Buy Now buttons and an e-commerce system with as few clicks as possible to make the actual buying process that much easier.

Make it easy for visitors to follow through to the checkout and actually buy the product. The fewer clicks it takes to get to the checkout, the better. Take the time to remove any obstacles that visitors may trip over on the way to the checkout.

✔ **Stage 5 — Post-purchase evaluation:** You may think that you've made the sale, so you're done. Not quite yet. Keeping a customer happy before, during, and after the sale increases the chance of a repeat customer, and those are the best kind you can have. Repeat customers tell their friends, and word of mouth is advertising you don't have to pay for.

A great idea is to contact your customer after the sale, but you can do that only if he provided his e-mail address during the purchase process. Provide a special form for feedback, customer reviews, and testimonials so that you can get that critical e-mail address.

Make your Return Policy easy to find and the process easy to do. You're not planning for them to return the items they bought, but if they know you stand by their satisfaction, even if this product didn't suit their needs, they're more likely to return to you for something else in the future and still tell their friends about their great experience.

Knowing Your Audience Checklist

In this chapter, we stress how important it is to take the time to know your audience. Your message is simply lost if you appeal to the wrong group of customers. You can easily go online and find landing pages that are either appealing to the wrong audience or to an audience that's way too broad.

Here's a table to help ensure that you know your audience. You may think we're harping on this point a bit too much, but if you don't clearly know your audience, your landing page won't reach its potential. So, Table 8-4 is a little test to see whether you know your audience well enough to speak directly to them with your landing page.

Table 8-4	Your Audience Checklist		
Audience Question		*Yes*	*No*
If your landing page is under development, have you taken the time to develop a pre-profile of your potential customers?			
Can you identify five specific characteristics of your potential customers?			
Have you identified at least one market segment?			
Can you identify five specific characteristics of your market segment (demographics)?			
Do you understand how your market segment behaves?			
Do you know where your market segment lives?			
Can you locate where your market segment surfs online?			
Can you identify the values and beliefs of your market segment?			
Can you clearly identify how your product/service benefits your audience?			
Can you talk to your audience in their language?			
Can you develop a persona to represent your market segment?			

If you're honest in your answers and can answer yes to the questions in Table 8-4, you're well on your way to developing a strong landing page. If not, go back to the drawing board and, for the final time, get to know your audience.

Chapter 9

Meeting Your Visitors' Expectations

*E*ach and every visitor to your landing page brings with them a certain set of expectations. They expect your page to load quickly, they expect to quickly find the information they're looking for, they expect the content to be relevant, and more. Your job, as the landing page developer, is to isolate exactly what your visitors expect from you and then meet those expectations. If done correctly, you'll reduce the number of visitors who leave your site without a conversion— in landing page terms, which means you're reducing your *bounce rate*.

Providing what your visitors want may sound simple, but it really isn't. You have only a few seconds in which to engage your visitor and have her hang around. How? That's what this chapter is all about: customizing your landing page (or landing pages) for your specific demographic and getting your visitors to hang around long enough to make the conversion. Figuring out what customizations to try can be a bit daunting, but we have several key strategies that you can employ to get a handle on what needs tweaking, from tracking all visitor behaviors to creating multiple landing pages for split-testing and problem isolation.

Trust us: If you can meet your visitors' expectations, your bounce rate will go down. How much that rate goes down depends on how well you meet those expectations.

Dealing With the Impatient Visitor

Landing page success is measured in terms of conversions, which occur when visitors perform your desired action — when they buy your product or service, for example. Conversions happen when you get the right visitor to the right landing page at the right time. At the other side of the scale is your *bounce rate,* which refers to the visitors that click your site who aren't grabbed by what they see and then navigate away.

Bounce rates are measured in percentages — the bounce rate represents the number of visitors who leave your page within a specified period of time, say 20 seconds. You always want to have the lowest possible bounce rate, but how low is good? Bounce rates don't have black and white rules for this, and it depends on your landing page. For instance, if you have only a single page (or only a few pages) on your sales site, your bounce rate is going to be higher simply because visitors are going to explore your site in a shorter period of time.

In general, however, consider the following general guidelines when it comes to evaluating bounce rate percentages:

- **Less than 20 percent:** Wow, that's a great place to be, so pat yourself on the back, secure in the knowledge that you must be doing something right. Keep it up.

- **21–35 percent:** This is the range most live in. Sometimes, it may fluctuate up and down, but the 21–35-percent range is definitely acceptable. In this range, you can consider your landing page conversion a success.

- **36–50 percent:** Okay, this isn't a good place to be in. This is a high bounce rate, and obviously something on your landing page isn't working. Does the advertising match the Web site content? Does your page have significant navigation issues? Trust elements missing? Heading ineffective? Time to start mixing up things a bit. A good place to start is split-testing, which involves running multiple landing pages to see which ones are more effective. We discuss split-testing in Chapter 12.

- **Greater than 50 percent:** Definitely back-to-the-drawing-board time. Bounce rates of 50 percent or more are a real problem. Our guess is that you're just not getting the right traffic to your site, that you're targeting the wrong demographic, and that plenty of elements on the actual site need to be changed. A bounce rate in this range is a major wake-up call for you, telling you that your site needs a major overhaul. Try to re-create your business plan (Chapter 3) and focus in on your demographic (Chapter 8).

Understanding bounce rates and working to reduce them encompasses many factors. If managing and reducing bounce rates were easy, everyone would have a small bounce rate and everyone's site would have awesome selling rates. The cause of high bounce rates on a site can be many things — some of which may not even be under your control.

To speculate though, we think that high bounce rates are a result of two major problems:

- ✔ **Not getting qualified traffic:** Qualified traffic refers to you getting the right type of visitor to your site. This means that you get visitors within your demographic. Having 1,000 visitors per day show up at your landing page is fine, but if your advertising efforts attract visitors who are unlikely to buy from you, you're going to have a very high bounce rate. (For more on reaching your demographic, see Chapter 8.)

  Many people get excited about search engine optimization (SEO) and how it can help you get lots of hits from a search engine. However, "tons of hits" isn't always a good measure for success. SEO traffic is often quite general, and although it may bring visitors to your site, they aren't qualified visitors. They may be there by accident, looking for something else, just surfing, and more. By contrast, visitors brought to your site through targeted advertising are coming in response to your ad and coming to see your specific product, which is far more targeted than SEO traffic. You can expect conversions to be higher from ad-generated traffic than from SEO traffic.

- ✔ **Not meeting visitor expectations:** Visitors coming to your landing page bring with them a plethora of expectations. They want a site that's easy to navigate, easy to read, makes them feel good about dealing with you, and so on. Failing to meet your visitors' expectations will drive them away pretty quickly.

A little more on bounce rates

Controlling and managing your bounce rate can be a never-ending battle for you. One month, your bounce rate may be high and the next, lower. You can be left shaking your head in confusion, wondering whether bounce rates really mean much in the grand scheme of things. Really, how much do things like bounce rates impact your bottom line? To answer that question, consider the following:

Suppose you chose to run a Google AdWords campaign — a popular choice for those who use targeted advertising to drive traffic to a landing page. The AdWords campaign is based on keywords or keyword phrases. With the AdWords keyword advertising system, ads appear as a sponsored link on the Google results pages. You, as the advertiser, select keywords and a short one- or two-line text ad, which is displayed on the results pages when the ad keywords match up with the search keywords.

Each keyword and keyword phrase has an associated cost and, as you may imagine, some are more expensive than others. The keywords you ultimately choose and purchase should appear in your ad.

Suppose, for example, the keyword you've picked will cost you $.10 per click, which means every ten visitors from this ad costs you $1.00. If you have a 90-percent bounce rate, you're spending $.90 for every one potential sale. Remember, just because someone stays to read your page, doesn't mean they'll buy.

Now take a bounce rate of only 20 percent. With this rate, you have eight people who may buy your product instead of just one. That significantly increases your chances of making a sale. Table 9-1 puts this in perspective.

Regardless of the bounce rate, you're paying the same amount of money to get the same number of people to visit your site.

Table 9-1	Bounce Rates versus Possible Revenue			
Cost per Click	Number of Visitors	Average Sale	Bounce Rate	Possible Revenue
$0.10	1,000	$20	10 percent	$17,900
$0.10	1,000	$20	25 percent	$14,900
$0.10	1,000	$20	50 percent	$9,900
$0.10	1,000	$20	75 percent	$4,900
$0.10	1,000	$20	90 percent	$1,900

Tracking your bounce rate

Tracking your bounce rate is very important — if you don't track your bounce rate, you can't possibly calculate how well you're doing. If your landing page already has tracking ability through log files, finding your bounce rate should be fairly straightforward. (We discuss tracking bounce rates in Chapter 12.)

If you're not tracking your conversions through log files, make use of a free tracking program, such as Google Analytics, which generates statistics with respect to your Web site. You can get a lot of useful information — including info on bounce rates — from the data.

You can find the Google Analytics tool by going to www.google.com/analytics.

In general, your landing page has two kinds of visitors:

✓ **General traffic:** Refers to people who stumble upon your site. Often, they've used a search engine to look for a topic, and your page was one of the many results they got back or a general link from similar Web sites.

✓ **Targeted traffic:** Is the kind you want to attract. These visitors want something specific and have come to your site for a reason. Your site may have been chosen at the suggestion of a friend, because an ad you ran matches what they're looking for, or your site was featured somewhere they trust.

When you first open an analytics program, you may be wondering exactly what you are looking at. These programs can appear quite complex but hang in there. Learning to use your analytics program and interpret its results will pay off in the end as they give you important information you need in order to isolate the areas that need to be optimized on your landing page. Figure 9-1 shows an example of bounce rate tracking with Google Analytics.

Figure 9-1:
Visitor tracking with Google Analytics.

Bounce rate reduction: The top 10 list

You likely purchased this book because your bounce rate right now is too high and you're looking for ways to remedy that situation. Many of the chapters you come across in this book provide the strategies needed to help reduce your bounce rates, from Chapter 6 (about writing), to Chapter 7 (about building customer trust), and to Chapter 8 (on developing a customer profile). If you put these strategies to work effectively, you can keep your visitors happy and your bounce rates low.

Right now, though, your landing page may have a bounce rate of 45, 50, or even 90 percent. Those aren't good numbers. Reducing bounce rates can be a difficult task but don't despair, it's possible.

In our experience, the only way to really deal with high bounce rates is to go back to the basics. The following is a top 10 list of things to focus on when your bounce rates get out of control:

1. **Tracking and more tracking:** To reduce bounce rates, you're going to need to get an accurate assessment of where you are *now* in terms of bounce rates and then track the results of your changes as you go along. This type of information is critical to spotting bounce rate trends and success from your efforts. (Google Analytics is just such a tool for keeping track of your bounce rates.)

2. **Focus on qualified traffic:** If your bounce rates are high, you may be attracting the wrong clientele to your landing page. Maybe your ads aren't aimed at the right demographic, or many of your visitors are from SEO efforts that don't necessarily attract potential customers. For example, if you're selling recycling products, focus your ads on sites that promote green initiatives or recycling trends and such, rather than on sites devoted to hunting or cooking. Ads placed on sites that have a clear connection to your product or service have a much greater chance of recruiting qualified traffic to your landing page than if your ads were just randomly placed on unrelated sites.

3. **Know your audience and use their language:** In Chapter 8, we talk a lot about the importance of knowing your audience because different demographics of people are going to have different expectations from your landing page. A site designed with seniors in mind is sure to use a different tone, approach, and language than one designed for college students. Reducing bounce rates can be done by clearly identifying your audience and speaking to them in their language. Are you writing for computer professionals, corporate employees, circus performers, school-aged children? If you do have high bounce rates, it's likely that you haven't clearly identified your audience.

4. **Match keywords and headings:** If visitors arrive to your page from an online search, from another Web site, or from online ad campaigns such as Google AdWords, the first thing they'll look for is the keyword they typed. To be effective, your ad and heading should specifically reference that keyword. For example, if you're interested in finding out about a new cellphone on the market, you'd probably type the cellphone name and brand into a search engine. Up comes 1 of 10,000 pages on cellphones. You click one of the top results or an ad that shows up in the search engine sidebar. The result: a site with a heading promoting cellphone chargers. At first, you're disappointed because this appears to have nothing to do with your search. Imagine, though, that you're a peculiarly persistent kind of Web surfer, and you scroll further down their page to discover the information about the product you wanted.

   Chances are, though, that if you didn't see the information you were looking for right away, you're going to click the back button and go the next search result, making you one of many potential customers that's been lost forever. However, if you saw a heading that included the latest information on the cell phone and brand, you'd be more likely to read on.

   Using keywords in your heading is one way to match visitors' expectations with what they see on the page. If you make use of very specific keywords, a visitor is going to see right from the start that the page is going to be a pretty good match to her search. (Figure 9-2, for example, shows how the intelligent use of keywords in a heading can create a direct link to a visitor's search request: No question that if he's looking for evacuation planning, he's in the right place.)

5. **Match the copy and images to your ads:** In addition to ensuring keywords and headings match, it's also important to match your copy and images to the ads. For instance, if your ads promote a specific product or service, ensure that a complimentary image is used in the fold area. If you have an ad for watch straps, show a watch strap that you're selling. Also, the text in the ad and your copy should match. This goes a long way in keeping visitors happy and reducing those bounce rates.

6. **Communicate clearly with a call to action:** To reduce your bounce rates, be clear in what you want your visitors to do. Use phrases like Scroll Down for More Information, Click Here for a Sample, and Click Here for More Information. Being direct in your language helps visitors find what they're looking for quickly and can reduce frustration.

7. **Reduce page load times:** One of the quickest ways to lose a visitor is to have her wait for your page to load. Sure, you can create impressive Flash pages and you can take a great picture, but if these elements create load time problems, they're simply not worth it.

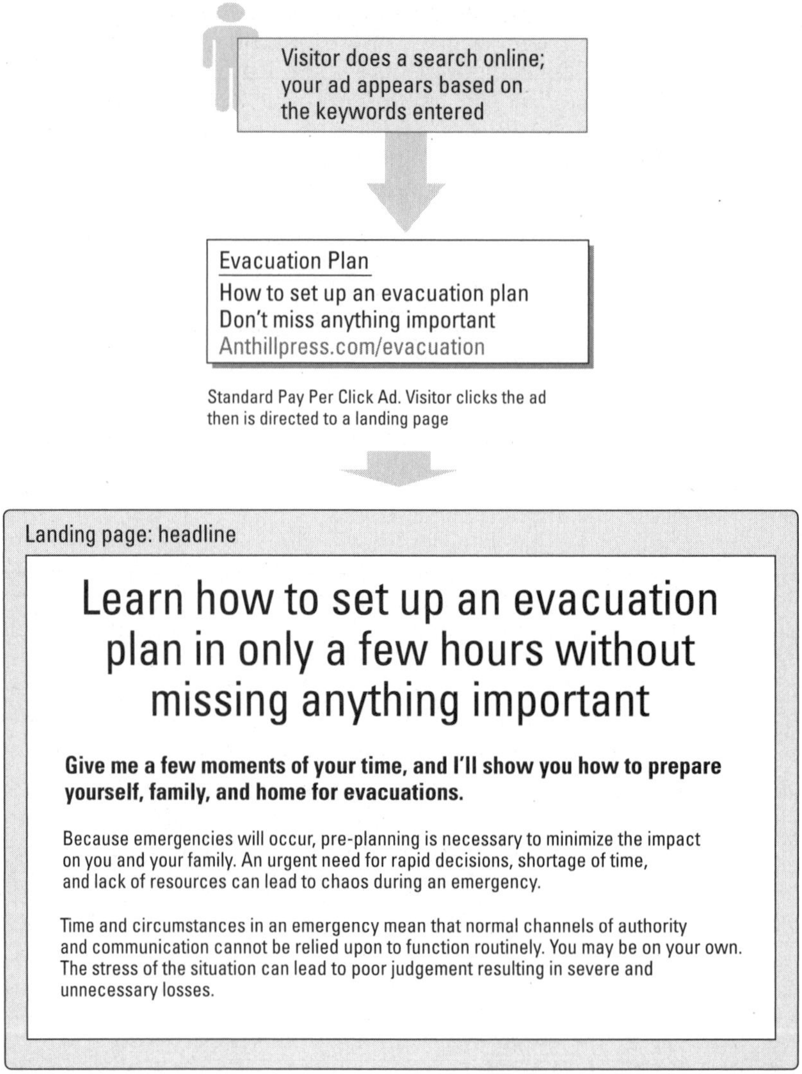

Visitor does a search online; your ad appears based on the keywords entered

Evacuation Plan
How to set up an evacuation plan
Don't miss anything important
Anthillpress.com/evacuation

Standard Pay Per Click Ad. Visitor clicks the ad
then is directed to a landing page

Landing page: headline

Learn how to set up an evacuation plan in only a few hours without missing anything important

Give me a few moments of your time, and I'll show you how to prepare yourself, family, and home for evacuations.

Because emergencies will occur, pre-planning is necessary to minimize the impact on you and your family. An urgent need for rapid decisions, shortage of time, and lack of resources can lead to chaos during an emergency.

Time and circumstances in an emergency mean that normal channels of authority and communication cannot be relied upon to function routinely. You may be on your own. The stress of the situation can lead to poor judgement resulting in severe and unnecessary losses.

Figure 9-2:
An ad with
effective
keywords
in the head-
line.

8. **Use clear navigation:** Your visitors, like us all, get frustrated quickly with poor navigation and a lack of direction. Ensure that your landing page flows logically and that you can follow the routes you want your visitors to go. They should feel that the navigation works for them. To test your navigation, have members of your demographic use your site and give feedback on the navigation. What worked for them? What didn't work? In addition, it's also helpful if you take the time to review the navigation strategies on other sites. Take note of what worked for you and what didn't.

9. **Provide sufficient content:** This may sound like common sense, but many landing pages don't do an adequate job of actually describing the product or service in sufficient detail. We realize your copy above the landing page fold may not hold much descriptive content, but plenty of content needs to be in the body below. Be sure to clearly state the benefits of your product or service and how these benefits are advantageous for the visitor.

10. **Avoid any and all bait and switch tactics:** If you lure visitors to your landing page with false promises (dubbed the *bait and switch*), your site is doomed to fail. Bait and switch involves stating or implying one thing in your ad campaign and providing something completely different on the landing page. This is often done by providing a keyword in your title that makes visitors think your page is about one topic and then switching to something else. After the switch takes place, they realize after reading for a bit that it has nothing to do with the words they identified with in the title. Visitors are frustrated and then leave.

    The bait and switch isn't always intentional. Poor landing page design can give visitors the impression that they're dealing with the ol' bait and switch, even when you really didn't intend to deceive. For example, if the information the visitor's looking for appears too low in the page, he's forced to read more text than he'd expect and feels cheated. This goes back to having a strong above-the-fold area.

When it comes to reducing the bounce rate, you have much more to consider. But the top 10 list we provide earlier is sure to steer you in the right direction and, if followed, will drop your bounce rate significantly.

When you create your landing page, make sure you consider browser compatibility. Not everyone uses IE (Internet Explorer). Download all the major browsers to your computer (Firefox, Safari, what have you) and then check to make sure your page is loading properly in each one. You might be getting a high bounce rate because people just can't see your page. The easiest way to avoid the problem is by checking your pages in various browsers before you put them live.

Also, while we're at it, avoid *redirects* — that Web trick where you arrive at a page only to instantly be taken to another site. Many visitors don't trust being redirected somewhere else. This can happen if you go to a page where you saw Your Bookmark Is Outdated, You Will be Automatically Redirected in 5 Seconds. You want to avoid redirects because people are suspicious of them and they waste time.

Dealing with load times

Slow load times are a problem for visitors — you know that, and we know that. But what actually causes slow load times? Many different things can cause slow load times; some are outside your control, such as bandwidth problems or if your visitor uses slower Internet access technology, but some of the slow load offenders are under your control. Here's a list of things you can try if you want to improve load time performance:

✔ **Reduce the number and size of your images:** When you *optimize* your images, you reduce the physical size of the image in kilobytes (KB). You can accomplish this either by making a smaller image or by reducing the quality of the image. Keep in mind that you don't want to reduce the quality to the point where the images look grainy. Also, be choosy about your images; don't flood your site with too many unnecessary images.

✔ **Don't autoplay videos:** Make sure any videos you may have on your site aren't set to autoplay. If customers have to wait until a video loads before they see the page, this can cause big delays. This is true also of audio content such as site introductions.

✔ **Limit animations and Flash:** The more animations and Flash you have on your site, the longer it takes to load your page. Minimize your load time by reducing said animations and Flash to what is really needed to get your point across.

✔ **Avoid fancy HTML scripts:** Rotating images, text strollers, and the like are HTML scripts that folks add to their Web sites in hopes of adding value. If all that hopping and moving about works for your site, that's great, but we suspect that they're not really adding that much value and they're surely slowing down the load time for the visitor. If a script isn't adding value for the customer, don't use it on your landing page. If you feel you need these items, use simple testing to see whether they actually improve sales.

Test your loading times and your Web site HTML. You can find handy online testers to give you an approximation of problems and perceived load times by visitors. To get you started, check out your load times by going to `http://tools.pingdom.com` or `www.webwait.com`. Keep in mind that many image-editing programs, such as Adobe Photoshop, have a Save for Web feature that shows you optimized images for your online use.

 How fast does your site need to load? Research from a company called Zona identified the eight-second rule a few years back. That's how long it took to lose half of the visitors to your site if your page did not load within that time. With today's high speed network connections, you no longer have those eight seconds. You are more likely looking somewhere three and four seconds. This is why your site needs to be as streamlined as possible.

Keeping Customers Happy: Final Thought

Visitors who find what they expect to find are generally happy visitors. Your mission is to keep visitors happy from the time they view your ad, to the time they finish the buying process, and even to the after sales follow-up. That's a long time to keep visitors happy.

Understanding the typical path a visitor takes will help you recognize potential areas on your landing page that need improving to keep them happy. Every visitor that comes to your site could (potentially) carry out eight separate actions, as shown in Figure 9-3. Follow along as we accompany a typical visitor as she makes her way through the initial ad encounter on to the buying cycle and then to the final after sales follow-up.

Understanding the average visitor path starts with looking at each step individually:

1. Finding and clicking your ad

   Visitors need to find your page. This may occur through search engines, pay per click (PPC) or banner advertising.

2. Reading the heading

   If your visitor hasn't left right away, chances are that the first thing she does on your page is read your heading. This tells her whether your information is what she's looking for. Writing a good heading is critical. We cover the art of writing headings in Chapter 6.

3. Reading or skimming the body copy

   When the heading succeeds in capturing their attention, visitors proceed to read or at least skim the body copy to see whether the information fills in what they wanted to know. (Writing Web content is covered in detail in Chapter 6.)

4. Clicking the Buy button

   If — and it's a big if — your body copy has done its job, your visitor is happy and may follow through by clicking the Buy button.

5. Purchasing your product

   Completing the purchase carries the customer through a specific sequence of steps. This process can be spread over a few pages (require signing up and who knows what else), or it can be as simple as a single click to finish the purchase. We recommend you keep this process as simple and unencumbered as possible. Doing so makes it more likely that visitors will follow the process through to the end.

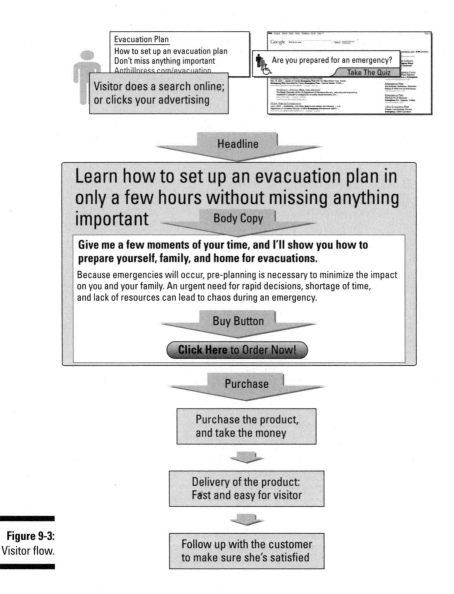

Figure 9-3:
Visitor flow.

6. Taking the money

   Every purchase involves the exchange of money for a product or service. Taking the money might include online credit card clearing, the receipt of a check in the mail, or the use of a third-party clearing house.

7. After sales product delivery

   After her payment clears, ship your product to the customer — hopefully in a timely manner. Delivery methods include mail or digital delivery.

8. Customer satisfaction

Keeping the customer happy involves ensuring his experience was pleasant and he's happy with the product he received. After sales follow-up can occur by monitoring recent return requests or sending a satisfaction survey to recent customers.

The list earlier identifies the steps a typical visitor may go through on your site. Remember, each of these steps has a *failure* point, a point where your visitor may bounce. If you're having high bounce rates, go through these steps yourself or have others do it to help isolate where your visitors are leaving.

Creating Multiple Landing Pages

We talk about the importance of matching keywords and headings earlier in this chapter, but how is this possible to do if you use an ad campaign with multiple keywords? And then there's that point we make about having to match your landing page to your demographic. Well, what happens if you have two or more demographics that you wish to target?

Good, important questions. Luckily, we have a pretty easy answer to both: multiple landing pages. Although multiple landing pages make sense for several reasons, the three reasons that stand out from the crowd are as follows:

✔ **Being able to match keywords to headings:** If you run multiple keywords, you can use multiple landing pages for those keywords. That way, you can accommodate more keywords and target your landing pages for a visitor's keyword search.

✔ **Being able to match landing pages to your demographic:** Many of the products and services you develop and promote are going to have some overlap with various demographics. We always stress the importance of speaking to your audience and knowing your demographic; having multiple pages enables you to accommodate different demographics by tailoring each landing page just for them. Multiple landing pages allow you to customize your page(s) and keep it (them) as specific to your audience as possible.

✔ **Being able to test your landing page design:** Will a different heading work better? What about a different image or logo? Creating multiple landing pages allows you to test different elements to see what works and what doesn't. This is much better than continually testing and modifying your main landing page.

One of the best ways to meet the visitors' expectations is to create multiple landing pages to match each and every ad or keyword you're using in your marketing.

By using multiple landing pages, you can create a message so targeted to your visitors that it's like you're inside their heads and can read their minds. When this happens, customers are more likely to read your materials, thereby reducing your bounce rate and thus increasing your overall conversion rate.

The need for multiple landing pages

The number of landing pages you need is sure to vary, depending on what you market and who you market to. Multiple keywords, visitor demographics, and geographic location all benefit from a multiple landing page strategy. Because many reasons exist to use multiple landing pages, the following sections just touch on the major ones.

Keywords and phrases

When your ad or Web site displays for a visitor because it appears as the result of a search he's initiated with a specific word or phrase, multiple landing pages allow you to center each of your pages around one keyword or phrase. Matching to a keyword is critical because after you know what a visitor's looking for, you can prequalify her intentions. Not sure what prequalify means here? Perhaps an example may help clear up this.

Suppose a user searches for *Adidas shoes.* If that's clearly the case, any landing page he ends up with should — in the best of all possible online worlds — sell only Adidas shoes. His search type *prequalified* him for a specific shoe. Why would you give him a landing page with different types of shoes?

If, however, he searches for a more general term, such as *running shoes,* you have more options. You can send your traffic to a Web site that promotes several types and brands of running shoes or maybe to a landing page discussing how to choose the right fitting shoes and so on. With a general term, you may have to split the traffic to guess what the user may really be searching for.

Think of yourself as Columbo, or if you don't know who that is, maybe Nancy Drew. The point is the keyword is your clue, and with that clue, you have to design a landing page that the visitor is looking for. Some clues are easier than others to decipher, but the keyword search is what you can build your landing page around. At the end of the day, putting the phrase or keyword right in front of your visitor will improve your bounce rate and will also lead to more people actually reading your information. Now, imagine doing this not with one keyword, but with 10 or 20. Similar pages, targeted focus. This is how the real magic happens. You get a keyword search and you just happen to have a landing page as specific as possible to that search.

Visitor demographics

So what happens if you have a product or a service that appeals to two very different demographics? Knowing that you need to talk directly to your audience, how can you do that with a single landing page? It's like going to a concert where both the Wiggles and Eminem are performing. It really would be best to split up that audience. Wiggles fans can be unruly.

Splitting landing pages according to demographic certainly reduces your bounce rates and keeps your visitors happy. Doing so keeps your audiences separate and allows you to appeal and speak to them directly.

Education and occupation

A visitor's educational background and occupation often determine the kind of language she's comfortable with, whether it be unique terminology and/or jargon. Multiple landing pages allow you to make the most of industry-specific lingo or to write to the education level of the reader. Although you don't want to talk down to your visitor, you also don't want to write above her head.

This approach is ideal not only for advertising across different occupational fields, but also for marketing the same product for different age groups. Say you're selling a book that's good for children and for parents. For the children, you want to get them excited about the story, but the parents may really want to hear all about the book's educational merits.

National and international

If you plan to run ads at an international level, different landing pages are essential, not only for tracking purposes but also for cultural differences. The last thing you want to do is offend someone with the incorrect use of color or language.

Even on a national level, multiple landing pages give you an advantage. Even though you're advertising to the same country, people have different predispositions from north to south, east to west. Narrowing your landing page to the part of the country you advertise to can only help your conversions.

Language

Often you probably don't take into consideration that everyone doesn't speak your language. You may be overlooking a huge, untapped market by not offering your landing pages in multiple languages. If you target international markets in any way, offer pages written in the core language of that nation.

Testing new markets and products

Running multiple landing pages is a natural choice when testing new products or markets. Using more than one landing page allows you to test the price point, look, text, and demographics — all with a one-page design that you just re-create multiple times.

For example, if you're not sure whether your product will sell at a new price point, create a duplicate of the current landing page and change the price. Then run an ad advertising the new price point, which leads visitors to this specialized page, showing you whether the new price is effective.

Multiple landing pages can also be used to determine the interest in an existing product or even whether the product is *not* ready for market. To do this, create a page that focuses on a different key point of the product — speed, convenience, size, what have you — and let the visitor response to the various pages show you what part of the product your ready-for-market advertising should focus on or whether a demand even exists.

Deals and promotions

Separate landing pages for every deal or online promotion allow for determining which promotion or deal is actually effective. You can even run them all run simultaneously to see quickly which promotions are the most effective. This works great for determining price points or add-ons that might help sell your product. Examples might be setting up a landing page that offers a Buy One, Get a Second One at ½ Price deal and another that offers a Buy One, Get $10 Off the Next Purchase deal.

Ad types

When you use different advertising methods, such as e-mail campaigns, pay per click (PPC), banner ads, and even traditional methods, such as newspaper spots, you attract different types of people. Using multiple landing pages allows you to concentrate the page focus on the ad medium.

For example, your PPC ads would use a few choice words to attract the visitor, whereas a newspaper ad would have a heading or a tag line to attract him. One landing page for each is the only way to effectively talk directly to your visitor.

Does this mean you might have hundreds of landing pages for you product? Well, it could. Some marketers do have hundreds of pages, but that's a lot of management and resources. Unless you have a lot of time on your hands, it's hard to track so many pages spread over many different products.

Our advice is

✔ Focus on your largest target market, using a single landing page to get them buying.

✔ Introduce new versions of that successful page based on your keywords and ad types.

✔ When you introduce new products or deals, take the time to test them with different landing pages.

You don't have to keep a landing page after it's served its testing purposes. After you know what works, you can roll the improvements into your main landing page and direct people from the old page to your new one.

Creating effective multiple landing pages

Multiple landing pages work by directing your visitor to specific information that matches his expectations when he arrives at your landing page. Several techniques exist to accomplish this, which the following list makes clear:

✔ **Scripting:** This technique involves using a special script to determine which page is displayed for your visitor. When a visitor clicks your ad or link, as shown in Figure 9-4, she's directed to different versions of the landing page and page contents based on the information set up in the link address. Scripting is clever, automatic, and very effective.

✔ **Direct pages:** One of the most direct ways to incorporate multiple landing pages is to literally make many individual pages. This technique is generally used for sales, promotions, or testing page-component combinations. URLs for direct addresses often have no extra variables attached and take visitors straight to the page, such as `www.just makeiteasy/evacuation-plan` or `www.justmakeiteasy/ evacuation-plan-sale`. Each URL represents a different sales page or piece of information.

See Figure 9-5 for a direct pages example. Here, individual ads target different pages, which display different information based on the ad or the deal to be presented. The direct pages approach is targeted and to the point. Again, the point is to direct traffic directly to what they want to see.

Every landing page, no matter how well it's doing, can be tweaked. The more attention you give your landing pages, the lower your bounce rates will be.

Online visitors find your ad

Computer program decides which content should be shown based on ad or traffic type

Landing page: A

Learn how to set up an evacuation plan in only a few hours without missing anything important

Give me a few moments of your time, and I'll show you how to prepare yourself, family, and home for evacuations.

Because emergencies will occur, pre-planning is necessary to minimize the impact on you and your family. An urgent need for rapid decisions, shortage of time, and lack of resources can lead to chaos during an emergency.

Time and circumstances in an emergency mean that normal channels of authority and communication cannot be relied upon to function routinely. You may be on your own. The stress of the situation can lead to poor judgement resulting in severe and unnecessary losses.

Landing page: B

Learn how to set up an evacuation plan in only a few hours without missing anything important

Give me a few moments of your time, and I'll show you how to prepare yourself, family, and home for evacuations.

Because emergencies will occur, pre-planning is necessary to minimize the impact on you and your family. An urgent need for rapid decisions, shortage of time, and lack of resources can lead to chaos during an emergency.

Time and circumstances in an emergency mean that normal channels of authority and communication cannot be relied upon to function routinely. You may be on your own. The stress of the situation can lead to poor judgement resulting in severe and unnecessary losses.

Figure 9-4:
Using a script to generate a page.

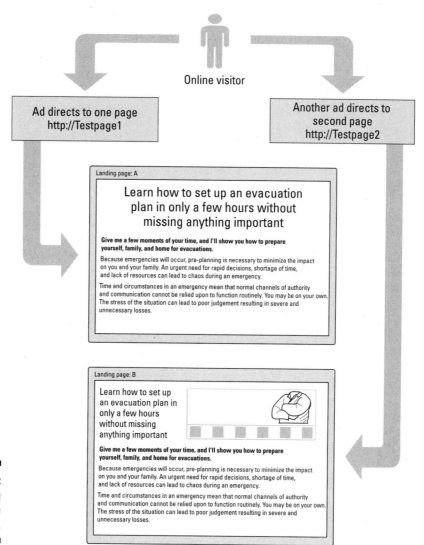

Figure 9-5:
Using
direct page
addresses.

Advantages of Creating Multiple Landing Pages

Creating multiple landing pages can occur in a number of ways, depending on your knowledge level and how much you really want to find out about Web site construction. You have two paths you can go by when it comes to landing page creation — manual or automated setup. No matter what style of landing page system you go with, the ultimate goal is to split test your result. (*Split-testing* is simply pitting one page against another to see which one converts the best; it's like a cage match for landing pages.)

For instance, you might test two different headings on a landing page. If one outperforms the other, you'd know which headings to use.

Sounds pretty straightforward, but it turns out split-testing can accomplish even more for you:

- ✔ **You can use split-testing to determine how people behave when they visit your site.** Split-testing can help determine what elements attract visitors compared to those that don't.

- ✔ **Split-testing can be used to isolate a problem you have.** Specifically, you can use split-testing to check which element on your landing page caused the problem by systematically swapping out and replacing elements to verify their effectiveness. For example, try one heading on one landing page then a different one on another.

- ✔ **Split-testing allows you to test your assumptions.** Is the heading really working? Is your text actually readable?

The power of testing is to test repeatedly, not just once. Keep on split-testing and you'll get answers to questions you didn't even know you had. It's your experimental opportunity. (You can find more information on split-testing in Chapter 12.)

Building techniques for multiple landing pages

Your two paths to multiple landing page creation — manual versus automated — each come with its own learning curve. Unless you plan on hiring a marketing firm to do the work for you, you're going to have to figure out some of the skills.

For those in a rush, selecting the automated version — which involves designing automated scripts — may be a good place to start. However, if you already have a landing page in action and have a basic knowledge of HTML, you may wish to take the manual approach. In any event, to find out more about the two approaches, check out the following sections.

Automated landing pages

The automated method involves using software to manipulate the results and information displayed on the page. The depth of what can be changed and at what frequency depends on the software you use. As an example, automated landing pages can change according to the keywords that are being searched for. If someone searches for Adidas running shoes, the heading and content can be specific to Adidas. If someone searches for running shoes, they are taken to a landing page with a more generic heading and content. In a way, the search dictates the images, headings and content of the landing page. Of course, this is more work but imagine the possibilities.

What's the benefit of automated software? Say you're testing three different headings, three call to actions, and three price points. That's a lot of testing.

With automated software, you can automatically test these combinations and report back over time which one is the best to use. You can then repeat the process again and again until you get your desired conversion rate.

When you work with many page variations, don't expect groundbreaking results quickly on any kind of testing because it takes lots of visitors to see what they like.

Automated systems require you to follow instructions to set up your page to work with the software. Programming code must be inserted into your pages for the testing software to work. That can be a bit of work, but to save time, Prepare your page variable information in advance. You can streamline the setup process substantially by knowing your different headings, price points, and so on before you begin.

So what program can you use for automated testing?

> ✔ **Google Analytics:** No surprise here, Google Analytics is a good starting point for beginners. Offered by, you guessed it, Google, Google Analytics offers many tools, including a Website Optimizer, which allows you to determine which headings, graphics, and so on convert the most visitors. For a majority of landing page beginners and intermediates, this program is more than enough to work with.
>
> Google Analytics is pretty straightforward to set up, but expect your first run-through to take several hours.

✔ **Custom software:** This approach isn't for the faint of heart, but if you have the skill set and the time, you might want to consider creating your own custom software. Due to the time and financial investment required, we advise this route only if you're planning it as a business or plan to do a long-term project.

Reasons for using your own custom software include

- Total privacy of your information and the results generated

- The ability to develop your own keyword testing and marketing methods

- No limits or restrictions on testing capability — except for your knowledge level and budget

Creating manual landing pages

Manually creating multiple landing pages is an option for you if you want to do the work and prefer to have more control on your testing. Manual is the way to go if you feel boxed solutions, such as Google Analytics, may not permit you to test what you want to in a way that satisfies your needs.

If you plan to do your own manual pages, you need to know (at a minimum) the following:

✔ **Basic HTML:** HTML (HyperText Markup Language) makes up the structure of Web pages. HTML tells the computer browser what the page is supposed to look like and what's supposed to be shown.

✔ **Page layout:** If you know advanced HTML, you can create your pages from scratch, use a preformatted template, or use a Web page-editing program, such as Dreamweaver, to streamline the learning curve.

✔ **FTP:** FTP (File Transfer Protocol) is how you deliver the pages and images you've created to the Internet. You need to know how to upload your files from your computer to your hosting account with an FTP program, such as CuteFTP, or free programs, such as FileZilla.

✔ **Tracking code:** You need to be able to install all the code for tracking purposes if your work is going to be even remotely useful. If you don't know which pages (or elements of those pages) help and which hinder, all the pages in the world won't show you what you need. Step-by-step guides on how to install tracking codes should come with your Web site tracking software.

Building landing pages manually is a great choice for those who have a basic understanding of Web page design. Use the following process:

1. **Create the landing page you want to consider as your baseline or average page.**

The page you currently have as your landing page is generally your baseline page. A good idea is to save this baseline page in a safe spot so you can always return to that point in your landing page development. Multiple pages are used to adjust and improve your baseline page after the results of what works and what doesn't are in.

2. **When changes are made to your baseline page, save them under a different filename.**

This makes a copy of your landing page, thus allowing you to change only parts of the page — such as the heading or an image — without affecting the original page.

3. **Repeat Step 2 as many times as necessary.**

Make as many pages as you have the time to monitor or need the results for. You can stick with testing only two headings at any one time, or you can be ambitious and split test images on one set of pages and headings on another, and so on.

4. **Upload your pages.**

After you've designed your different pages, upload them to your Web site. With each having different filenames, they'll have different Web site addresses allowing you to track the pages specifically.

5. **Direct your advertising.**

For each of the ads that you run, be sure that they land equally on the various landing pages you've developed. After all this work, the last things you want are skewed results!

By using the manual process, you can test new looks, promotions, or group your products with free bonus offers to see what's grabbing your visitor the most persuasively and consistently.

Whether you choose an automatic or manual approach, both are effective in improving your landing page results. In the end, your choice should be driven by how comfortable you are with the building process.

Strategies for matching multiple landing pages to your advertising

The number one thing online marketers can improve upon is making sure that their ads and landing pages match — not only in text but also in what the customer is really thinking.

Getting inside the mind of the prospective client and matching your ad to your landing page is sure to increase your conversions and reduce your bounce rate significantly.

Matching your ad content to your landing page can be accomplished by following a few simple rules. Some basic strategies you can use to ensure a better match include

✔ **Matching keywords:** Make sure that the main keywords that attracted the visitor to search for your site in the first place are also something she sees right away on your landing page.

✔ **Matching phrases:** If you're using phrases in your ads, such as Get Free Advice Now, use Get Free Advice Now on your landing page. Phrase matching allows the visitors' eyes and brains to conclude quickly that they're in the right place.

✔ **Running multiple landing pages:** Running multiple versions of a landing page, each matching a different ad, is a great way of not only testing which ads work best, but also a way to speak directly to the consumer the ad was designed for.

✔ **Matching image ads:** Be sure to match keywords not only with the text on your landing page, but also with the images used. Be careful not to use colors in your ads that don't match your landing page. You want customers to have a seamless transition between your ad and page.

✔ **Testing your ads and landing pages with friends, family, or a focus group:** See how they interpret the ad compared to the landing page. Ask questions like

    • Does the ad match the landing page?

    • Are you seeing what you need to see?

Be sure to show them only the fold area (discussed in Chapter 4). Make sure your message gets across right away.

If you say it, show it. Make sure what you say and what you show on your ads matches what visitors see right away. They're ready to hit that browser back button if they feel they're on the wrong page or if it's not what they expected.

Chapter 10

Improving Customer Communications

· ·

· ·

Communication is an important part of both your landing page and your customer service. As you'd expect of something that can have serious consequences for the success of your online enterprise, you have a number of communication options you can use on your landing page, if you so desire. Some are quite effective; some not so much.

In this chapter, we look at your communication options, including features you can easily incorporate into your landing page, such as customer feedback forms, e-mail, phone, and visitor forums. Each of these elements increase the communication you have with your visitors (and potential customers). Incorporating these features and others into your landing page can significantly change how well your online business is perceived and then ultimately change your conversion rates in a positive direction.

Communicating with Your Visitors

Right off the bat, for the most part, less is (sometimes) best when it comes to communication. Why? Too much communicating can take lots of time (and money) and distract you from other tasks you need to do. The goal, when you design a landing page, is to keep communication to a minimum. Basically, the goal is to design a landing page where visitors arrive, buy something, and that's the end of it. There's no back and forth communication. You don't need to answer customer questions or respond to comments. Visitors just arrive, buy, and leave. Such a dream site can be achieved only when you know your visitors well and take the time to create a landing page that's clear, concise, and gives visitors what they need without having to contact you for additional information.

Three levels of communication are used with landing pages: one-way, limited two-way, and full two-way, to use our own coinages here. Whether each level is required depends on your product, your service, or what conversions you're looking for. Read on to get the details on each level.

One-way communication

One-way communication is the simplest level of all. You use your landing page to communicate with visitors; that is, you tell them why your product's the best, why they need to buy it today, how it will change the world, and so on. You control the dialog — no back and forth communication. Visitors simply read what you have to say, and if you relay your information clearly enough and effectively enough, you have your conversion.

This type of communication is often best for your landing page. Why? Simply because two-way types of communication are time-consuming and often costly. Answering e-mails and phone calls as well as responding to queries can take up a lot of time. We prefer logging onto the Internet every morning and reviewing the sales for the day, rather than setting aside time to answer calls and e-mails. So, how can you customize your site to help reduce the need for lots of back and forth communication?

We recommend several strategies that you can incorporate on your landing page to help reduce some of the back and forth communications that can eat up your time:

- ✔ **Develop a comprehensive frequently asked questions (FAQ) section.** Most of the questions customers have can be answered in your FAQ section. Policies, shipping questions, product questions, and more can all be answered without any further communication. FAQs are developed over time; the questions you receive from customers can be answered and added to the FAQ to make it more comprehensive.

- ✔ **Make sure your page layout is clear and displays your content well.** A well-designed landing page makes a big difference. The easier your information and details are to find, the less people need to contact you.

- ✔ **Make the checkout procedures easy.** If visitors have trouble making their way through the checkout procedure, they simply stop altogether or contact you with questions on the checkout procedures.

- ✔ **Make a sample product available.** If potential customers have a chance to try your product, it can answer a lot of the questions they may have.

A little more on FAQs

Many landing pages make use of an FAQ section but don't take the time to really develop it to its full potential. Here are several advantages of creating a comprehensive FAQ section: It provides another avenue for you to get keywords onto your page, the question and answer format provides easy reading for those who don't like to read blocks of text, and it's great for giving visitors answers without relying on back and forth communication. This is why many sites encourage people to read the FAQ section before actually trying to contact the site with a query. Most of the questions asked have already been asked before by other visitors, so putting these questions in an FAQ just makes your life easier.

But how do you know what exactly to put into your FAQ section? Here are seven tips to consider when developing your FAQ section:

✔ **Brainstorm:** Sit down by yourself or with friends and make a list of all the questions you think you may be asked. Provide a detailed answer for those questions. The more questions you can think of now, the less you'll need to modify your FAQ section later.

✔ **Add visitor queries:** Every time you receive a question from an online visitor, add it to the FAQ. Chances are if a question is asked once, others will have the same question.

✔ **Review the competition:** Take the time to review FAQs from competitors' Web sites.

What questions are they being asked? This can help ensure that you're on the right track with your question and answer section.

✔ **Organize the FAQ:** Over time, your FAQ section can grow to be quite large. A good practice is to divide your FAQ section into categories. This organization can make it way easier for your visitors to find the answer they're looking for.

✔ **Make it visible:** Keep links to your FAQ section visible and easy to navigate. You really want people to review the FAQ, so make it convenient to find and access.

✔ **Use keywords:** Don't be afraid to pepper the FAQ section with a few keywords here and there. This can help with your SEO (search engine optimization) efforts, but it also keeps the visitor focused on the theme of the site.

✔ **Encourage feedback:** A good idea is to seek feedback on the FAQ section or questions within it. Just asking "Was this question helpful?" is all that it takes. The feedback provided can be used to create a new question or modify the answer to the current question.

Remember, your FAQ section isn't a static element of your landing page; rather, it's quite dynamic. Your FAQ section needs to change over time, with new questions added and older ones removed. Keep this document active and updated for the best results.

Ideally, you want a site that requires the least amount of back and forth communication as possible. Admittedly, creating a site that requires minimal communication can be a lot of work. You need to do a lot of stuff upfront, most of which has to do with getting the right information from your customer. Your visitors let you know what they like about the site (and what they don't), and you need to put that feedback to work to customize your site for easier use. After you know exactly what your customers are looking for, you have less need for ongoing back and forth communication. To find out what visitors think about your site and customize it for less communication, you're probably going to need to incorporate limited two-way communication elements into your landing page.

Customer reviews

One element that works great for a one-way communication element is customer reviews. We strongly recommend you use them. Not only do customer reviews offer an online version of word-of-mouth and give you a quick gauge of how you and your product are doing in your customer's eyes, but also can be used to answer questions before they come to you. Online shoppers *read* customers reviews; for example, sites, such as Amazon, rely heavily on customer reviews for book sales.

So just how important are customer reviews? A Nielson online survey (2008) revealed that 81 percent of online holiday shoppers read online customer reviews. That 81 percent of visitors are less likely to call you in order to check you out or ask a query if they read positive customer reviews that comfort them and answer questions.

Customer reviews are a gold mine of information. Because reviews are unsolicited and relatively anonymous, customers are more likely to be candid with their comments. You may not know your product dents easily or that it fits perfectly under a car seat for storage. You can build the positive comments into your sales pitch and on the flip side, fix those things that need it.

Every customer looks for reassurance that they need the product and that they're making a good choice in the product they buy. Offering customer reviews gives them the reassurance that they're buying the right item and will be satisfied. A review, such as in Figure 10-1, explains the products' features and what makes it a great buy, all in common, everyday language.

Getting reviews ahead of time

You can get reviews before your landing page goes live — and no, we don't suggest you just make up your own reviews, which clearly is as far away from best practices as you can get. There are two effective ways to obtain customer reviews before going live with the landing page.

- ✔ Giving out free product samples and asking people to write a review
- ✔ Running a focus group and collecting opinions and comments

Getting reviews ahead of time can be very beneficial. It allows you to modify your product and your site before going live to the world. Additionally, you can design your landing page with positive customer reviews right from the start and not wait to add them later.

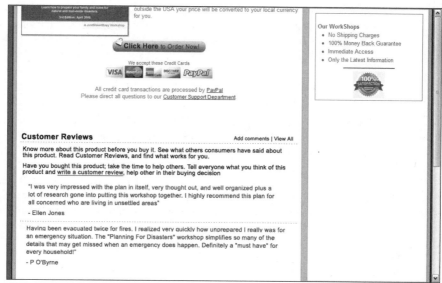

Another consideration when you use customer reviews involves where to place them on your page. Pay attention to how you display them, what they say, and how effective they are. (For more on how to track an element's effectiveness, see Chapter 12.) Keep the following in mind:

- ✔ **Prominently display your reviews.** Don't hide your review on separate pages, but instead have at least one or two right on your landing page.

- ✔ **Keep your reviews fresh.** If you keep the same reviews up for extended periods of time, the reviews get stale and it may look like your product is out of date or not selling.

- ✔ **Keep the most recent review on the top of the page**. Earlier reviews can be placed farther down the page.

- ✔ **Keep it real.** Don't artificially add to the comments. *Salting* reviews with your own additions/emendations only promotes inaccurate responses and doesn't help in the end. Reviews are most effective in the voice of the author; letting that voice come through unvarnished lends authenticity to your site.

Limited two-way communication

Most of the landing pages you see on your Internet ramblings incorporate a limited two-way communication strategy. Whereas the one-way style is just you and your landing page, limited two-way communication requires feedback from the visitor. Basically, you communicate with your landing page and then incorporate methods for the visitor to let you know her thoughts on the site or product. This is purely an information-gathering exercise for you, and you're free to use the information you receive from visitors as you like, although we of course recommend that some of the information you gather be incorporated back into your site. In this section, we review two of the most common strategies you can use to gather information from your visitors: surveys and feedback forms.

Surveys

We realize that not everyone wants to take the time to fill out an online survey, but the information you can obtain with surveys can greatly impact the effectiveness of your entire landing page. And although it's definitely true that many of your visitors don't want to take the time to fill out lengthy surveys, they might be willing to take the time for a short survey. To be useful, your questions should be very focused and written specifically to get the information you require. As for the format, you have a couple of options available:

- ✔ **Yes/no questions:** Yes/no questions are commonly used on online surveys. These questions can be answered with a simple yes or no; thus, they're easy for visitors to answer but don't always provide great insight. Yes/no questions are *dichotomous* questions because your visitor can choose between two *(di)* possible answers, either yes or no. Sometimes a third option — *maybe* or *unsure* — is added to the yes/no question.

  Here's a typical yes/no question:

  > Have you ever purchased a product from a Web site before?
  >
  > Yes
  >
  > No

  Yes/no questions have thousands of uses. You could, for example, use them to separate your demographic into those who use Internet Explorer or another Web browser, or those who make more than $60,000 compared to those who don't currently. In the sample question earlier, you can use the answer to the question to separate those who've purchased from a Web site before compared to those who haven't.

- ✔ **Multiple choice questions:** You've all probably seen multiple choice questions before and know that they contain a question and three or more answer options. In your survey, you can use multiple choice questions to gather important information from your visitors. The trick is to include very carefully written multiple choice questions and answers. Be clear about the type of information you're trying to obtain. Here are a few multiple choice questions that show what we mean:

What type of Web browser do you use? (Choose all that apply.)

> IE
>
> Firefox
>
> Chrome
>
> Other_____

How did you hear about our landing page? (Choose all that apply.)

> Internet affiliates
>
> Radio ads
>
> TV ad
>
> Google AdWords
>
> Other_____

In these examples, the questions and answer options are very specific. Multiple choice questions are used to ensure your site meets the needs of your visitors, to determine whether you use the right technologies with your site, to figure out whether your advertising dollars are well spent, and more. You can also use the information you obtain from multiple choice surveys to create a graph or pie chart of the responses. You can then use the pie chart to track visitor trends over time — say, the percentage of visitors that arrive at your landing page from radio ads compared to online advertising. Comparing the pie charts over time gives you a snapshot of how your site is performing. The more information you have, the better equipped you'll be to get those all important conversions. Figure 10-2 shows how a pie chart may look from the responses from the question earlier.

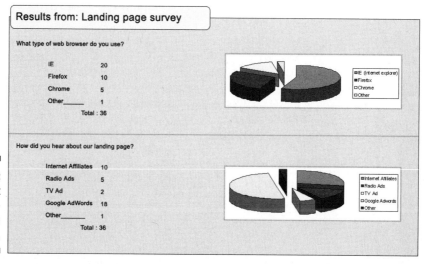

Figure 10-2: A pie chart for multiple choice responses.

✔ **Level-rating questions:** Level-rating questions aren't as common as multiple choice and yes/no questions. The goal of level-rating questions is to have your visitor choose among a range of responses. A level-rating question may look like:

> When you visit our Web site, how would you best describe the site's navigation:
>
> > Very difficult
> >
> > Somewhat difficult
> >
> > Below average compared to other Web pages
> >
> > Above average compared to other Web pages
> >
> > Somewhat easy
> >
> > Easy to navigate

Notice that in the above example, the first and final options are opposites. Typically, use an even number of choices so that your visitor can't respond with middle of the road answers. He has to be on one side or the other.

Level-rating questions work well with a large number of survey responses. The data can be analyzed and then charted to give a real idea of where you stand. With the earlier question as an example, Figure 10-3 shows a sample graph for the level-rated responses.

LEVELED SURVEY RESPONSES

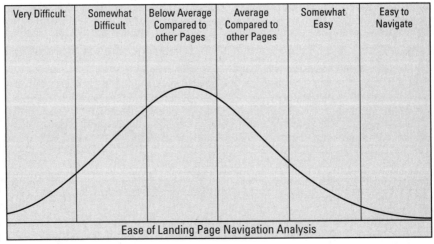

Figure 10-3:
A sample
chart for
survey
responses.

Eight tips for survey questions

The information you can obtain from a well-written survey can be an important part of your landing pages success or failure. With that in mind, here are eight tips to consider when you create your landing page survey:

1. **Limit the number of questions.** The attention span of most visitors is short, and you don't want to overwhelm them with too many questions. No specific rules exist on how many questions to actually include in a survey, but the fewer you use while still getting the information you need is a good rule of thumb. Bottom line: Your online survey completion rate will be higher if the survey is short.

2. **Watch grammar and punctuation.** You definitely don't want your survey to look amateurish. Your visitors won't want to fill out a survey that appears put together by kids from the local elementary school.

3. **Watch personal questions.** Some surveys are going to ask personal questions, such as salary information, relationship status, and so on. If you really need to ask questions of a personal nature, let the visitor know what you intend to do with the answers and that they're kept anonymous. Getting too personal is a great way to have people avoid your survey.

4. **Keep the survey neutral.** You can easily write questions that lead survey takers to a certain response. The purpose of the survey is to obtain information that can be analyzed. To do this, the questions can't be leading and must be neutral. Remember, don't take the results personally; good surveys undoubtedly show weaknesses in your landing page. This is exactly what you're looking for.

5. **Watch question length.** Most survey takers prefer short question and answer options. Short questions aren't always easy to write but will get a better response.

6. **State the purpose of your survey.** As a courtesy, let visitors know why you're conducting the survey. If the survey is intended to optimize the landing page for ease of use, let the visitor know this. The more she knows about the survey and why you're conducting it, the better chance you have of someone filling it out to completion.

7. **Test your survey questions.** Before you let your survey out into the world, try out the questions and answer options on a few friends or colleagues. This helps you determine whether your questions are going to get the answers you want and that the questions and answers make sense. After it's tested, it can go live.

8. **Create a visual representation of the results.** As mentioned earlier in this chapter, creating charts and graphs from responses gives you a quick look at how you're doing and quickly highlights areas of concern. Such visual representations are great for pinpointing areas for landing page optimization. The charts can be collected and kept for future reference.

Charting is an important part of the survey process; it gives you a visual representation of your visitor responses. In Figure 10-3, for example, when all responses are combined, most visitors feel that the navigation is below average compared to other Web sites — which is good to know if you really want your site to succeed. You have lots of options when it comes to creating your own charts and graphs, including applications, such as Microsoft Visio and Excel, as well as several online companies which take survey results and provide comprehensive analysis of the responses. Such analysis can be pricey, but the results can be invaluable for your optimization efforts.

Tracking survey responses and putting them in some form of visual representation is an important part of landing page optimization. Doing so gives you a better idea of what needs fine-tuning on your landing page.

Using feedback forms

Feedback forms are one of the quickest and reliable methods of gathering visitor information on your site. Feedback forms give you insight into your visitor's mind and at the same time, make the visitor feel that his opinion matters. Feedback forms are a win/win situation.

Feedback forms come in all shapes and sizes and have different requirements based on the needs of the company. They can be used to obtain specific information about your landing page, your demographic, and potentially new markets to expand to. Feedback forms can appear in many areas on your landing page, such as

- **Contact Us form:** The Contact Us form (see Figure 10-4) is commonly used on most landing pages and Web sites. This form is often a box in which visitors can type comments, questions, or suggestions. The Contact Us form is great for getting feedback on the site that can be used for optimization, and any questions you may end up receiving can be added to the FAQ section.

  The Contact Us form can either be a limited two-way communication process or a full two-way communication process. If the expectation is that you'll reply to the form, it's a full two-way communication element. Many forms are designed to be a limited two-way communication style, allowing visitors to comment on the site but not to expect return correspondence.

  You may not realize this, but Contact Us and About pages have become important pages that search engines now look for to verify that you're a real business. Use your Contact Us page wisely; make it easy to find and user-friendly.

- **Customer Support form:** Not all companies require a separate Customer Support form; however, a dedicated form is ideal if you've noticed recurring issues. You can use the Customer Support form to take complaints or questions from visitors. The input you receive from the Customer Support form can be used to increase the effectiveness of your landing page. Over time, you'll find that the Customer Support link is rarely used if you take the time to address each issue when it arises.

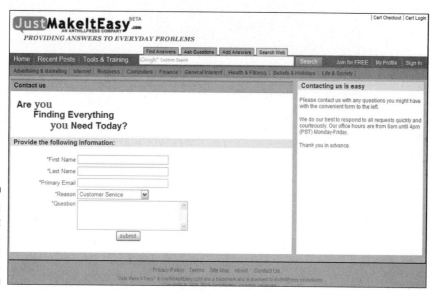

Figure 10-4:
A Contact
Us form with
operating
hours.

The information you obtain from a Customer Support link ranges from product-related issues such as shipping, hard to follow instructions, poor navigation, confusing checkout procedures, and more. Customer Support forms help identify whether and where a problem occurs.

If you plan to use two-way customer support communication, the form is usually directed to a person on staff who's responsible specifically for customer problems. You can design forms to direct requests to different people or departments inside your organization, such as accounting, shipping, or sales.

Even if you don't have different departments inside your organization, you can take advantage of using different e-mail headings, allowing you to filter your incoming e-mail to different inboxes.

✓ **Sign-up for more information:** This form style is used to collect e-mail addresses and some basic information from your visitors with the promise of giving them something in return, such as more information or a coupon. This technique allows you to tell how many people are interested in your topic or product while also providing you a way to contact the interested parties later. This is often an automated process; visitors sign up with an e-mail address, and the information is shipped. The idea here is that the process doesn't add anything to your workload.

The most common Sign-Up forms include joining a newsletter (see Figure 10-5) or providing ways of receiving more detailed information. The trick is to offer the customer something she wants so she'll be persuaded to join.

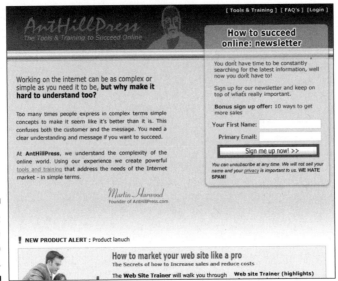

Figure 10-5:
An example
of a Sign-Up
form.

Placing form elements in your landing page

Where your links are located isn't as important as offering the ability to contact you in the first place. However, it's important that the forms you use are visible. Customers, on first glance, may never use your contact form or other informational links, but for the sake of comfort and trust, they need to know that they *can* use them if they need to.

The typical landing page has four primary spots where you can place informational links for your visitors:

- ✔ **Side menu:** Left or right positioned menus are often used to display links to important information. These types of menus might contain small links to the information or share space with a small ad spot. These links are often kept short and to the point.

- ✔ **Top menu:** Similar to a side menu in functionality, the top navigation of the page usually limits the communication to short links to the information. Very little detail is provided.

- ✔ **Top fold area:** The top fold is the mother load of navigation space. Generally not restricted by link size, you'll often find more elaborate options for visitors. A newsletter sign-up is a good example. Not only is there room for a Sign Up Today link, but you have the room to explain why they should sign up.

✔ **Footer:** The bottom of the page usually holds the legalese, such as policies and short links to contact pages. Using the bottom of the Web site this way is a standard in the industry. Very few sites don't provide extra informational links located in the footer of the page. As we mention earlier, not everyone is going to use these links, but visitors often notice their absence if they aren't there.

Pop-ins and pop-ups

You've likely seen pop-ins and pop-ups used in a variety of different ways on landing pages. Pop-ups are a form of advertising where an ad is displayed, or *pops up*, when you visit a site. Similar to the pop-up ad is the pop-under ad, which appears behind the Browser when visiting a specific site. The pop-in variation has ads "fly-in" the view of the browser. They are similar to the pop-ups for appearing right in front of the user.

Besides advertising, you can use the pop-ups for surveys with the survey request appearing right on the screen of the user. These communication elements are often on the more annoying side of the spectrum — to the point where some sites shy away from this type of feedback form completely. A *pop-in* or *pop-up form* literally jumps in front of the visitor's eyes. They can be very effective in bringing attention to a survey or a critical announcement; however, a fine line exists between grabbing your customers' attention because it's important and irritating them enough that they run to click the Close button.

The difference between a pop-in and pop-up form is subtle. Neither has a title bar, and both appear on top of the current content the visitor is viewing. Pop-in forms, however, are programmed in such a way that they often get past ad blocker software. They're less obtrusive than the conventional pop-up window.

A practical use for pop-ins is to add a deal to sweeten the pot when people try to leave a site. This attention grabber gives you one more shot at selling an item or getting a newsletter sign-up with an extra deal. Although not great for providing or gathering a large amount of information, the pop-in example in Figure 10-6 gives the visitor an unbeatable deal before he leaves.

Full two-way communication

Time to face facts: Full two-way communications can be costly and time-consuming. Why? Because it costs you time and money to answer all the phone calls, faxes, and e-mails you could potentially get from your site visitors. Imagine your landing page has 2,000 visitors a day, half of those visitors send an e-mail query, and 50 more place a phone call. This is fine if you're running a larger operation, but if you're just starting out with your landing page, these communication requirements are too much.

Figure 10-6:
A pop-in displaying an unbeat-able deal for sign-up.

The good news is that with a well-designed landing page, you're not going to have as much contact as what could happen if your page was less polished. We've found that when a landing page first goes live, you're going to get significant contact and queries. Over time, as you incorporate feedback into your site, the communication requirement lessens.

You may use several types of two-way communication elements on your landing page, with phone, e-mail, and feedback forms being the most common. The following sections give all the details.

Phone support

We don't like getting lots of phone calls or fax queries from our landing pages. If you write your landing page correctly and all the elements are there, you shouldn't be getting lots of phone calls or faxes. That just isn't an efficient use of your time — unless of course, you use your landing page for sales leads and then close sales on the phone.

Any small business dedicates a significant amount of time to answering calls, returning calls, transferring calls, checking messages, and so on. One of the supposed benefits of having an online business is that you're not supposed to be strapped to the phone. If your landing page does promote phone numbers and you're getting lots calls, it goes without saying that you're going to have to take these calls. Listed here are a few ideas to turn these phone calls to your advantage:

- ✔ **Testimonials:** If you're speaking to a satisfied customer, try to get him to give you a testimonial. You may not need a testimonial right away, but collecting them for future use is a good idea. Great phone skills can get you wonderful customer reviews.

- ✔ **Surveys:** Have a survey ready. While she's on the phone, try to hit her up with a quick survey. Questions may include why she decided to phone and whether she could find the FAQ section.

- ✔ **Critiques:** Write down any criticisms. Is he angry on the phone? Take the time to find out why and make modifications on the landing page as needed.

- ✔ **Sales:** Depending on your product, you can use the opportunity to upsell. Do you have new products coming out? New features? If someone takes the time to phone, try to close the sale she's calling about and see whether you can make any more conversions over the phone.

E-mail communication

You can't get around answering e-mails. They cost visitors nothing, and they're easy to write and send. A well-designed landing page can stop many e-mails before they get to you, however, especially if you have a well-developed FAQ section in place so visitors' questions get answered without them resorting to the ol' e-mail client — and clogging your inbox.

Although one of the most informal types of communication, e-mail is potentially the most important type of writing you'll do on a daily basis. The key, however, is to reduce the number of e-mails received in the first place so that your workday isn't held captive by it. Each e-mail you write is an opportunity to build your client base and ultimately, your business.

Not that we want to put any pressure on you. Far from it. But seriously, e-mail can be a powerful component of anyone's online marketing strategy, so powerful that it makes sense to take a look at what makes or breaks an e-mail — which is what we do in the following section.

Writing professional e-mails

Before computers revolutionized the international business world, memoranda were written from employees to other fellow employees within the same organization. If an employee needed to correspond with a client, however, she'd write a business letter. In today's computerized world, the need to write to fellow employees and clients has stayed the same; what's different now is that the media has changed to make communication faster. Speed makes e-mail the most popular form for communicating with fellow employees and clients, but speed also makes certain rules evolve to safeguard the writer from making an unprofessional impression upon the reader. The following list highlights some of the more important guidelines for writing professional e-mail:

- **Addresses:** Write the reader's name in the To field as opposed to the actual e-mail address whenever possible (if your e-mail account settings allow you do this.) This helps to personalize the message. (Usually you can do this by adjusting your e-mail address book settings so that the recipient's name appears in the "TO" line instead of an impersonal e-mail address.)

- **CC versus BC:** If you have more than one recipient, list each of them in the CC field only if you're absolutely sure that these recipients don't mind sharing their e-mail address with each other. To protect multiple people's privacy, it's probably better to use the *BC* option instead, meaning *blind copy.* This option doesn't allow a reader to see the names or e-mail addresses of other readers receiving the same message.

- **Informative Subject lines:** In the Subject line, ask "What's this message about?" The answer takes the form of a fragment; a title, in other words, that sets up your reader's expectations of what's to follow. This helps your reader prioritize which messages he needs to read first, second, third, or not at all.

- **Organization:** Think of the message as having three parts: an overview of the message, the details of the message, and the next action that needs to take place.

  Overview: Determine the level of familiarity you have with your reader. If you know him or her well, you can use the greeting "Hi, Bill," or "Hey, Paula!" If you don't know your reader at all, keep your salutation polite and formal: Use "Hello, Mr. Chips," — but save the more old-fashioned "Dear John," for those situations when you're breaking up with someone. Then refer to your last correspondence with him or her, dubbed *bridging,* which helps to orient your reader to your message and your relationship. Finally, if you have good or even just neutral news, state it immediately. If you have bad news, buffer the message so that you protect the reader's feelings as much as you can. This helps to preserve your relationship with the reader. Business communication today is all about building and preserving positive relationships.

  Body: The paragraph following the overview needs to contain the details of the main message that you've just identified in the overview. Anticipate what kinds of questions your reader will have about that main message and then provide those details. For example, if the main message is "You've won $100 for being our 100th customer!," the second paragraph answers questions, such as "How did that happen?," "Is it taxable income?," "Is this for real?," "When will I receive the check?," and so on. These questions help you to generate the necessary details for this body paragraph.

Conclusion: The last paragraph is the closing paragraph. Here you can restate the message, if necessary, before you state what action needs to be taken by the reader or what action you'll take next. For example, you might write, "Please send a self-addressed and stamped envelope" or "For being our 100th customer, please find attached your coupon for $100 off your next purchase" That is the *exhortation* or *call to action.* After that, you may write an additional positive statement about continuing the company-customer relationship before you move into the final sentence, which is the *feedback loop* — state how to contact you if the reader has any questions, comments, or concerns. An example of the feedback loop is a sentence like this: "If you need further information about any of our Widget products, please call our toll-free number 1-888-1234, ext. 567."

Most writers feel the need to end with a kind of signature block that characterizes the business letter. The traditional signature block includes the closing "Yours truly," followed by an actual signature, and then the writer's name, job title, and contact information under that, but this is optional for e-mail. If you know your reader and what he expects in terms of formality, choose a signature block, an initial, or nothing at all to close the e-mail.

✔ **Polishing:** Don't hit Send yet! Your rough draft may be complete, but the most important step still remains: polishing the style for professionalism and depending on the purpose of your message, for persuasion as well. Here are a few pointers:

Readers love to see their names in print, so for example, type **Mike** into the overview paragraph, the body, and especially the conclusion, particularly if you want Mike to respond favorably to your call to action.

Read your message aloud so that you can hear any errors in grammar or punctuation — the *clunky* sentences. Such errors paint an unprofessional image of you and your company in the reader's mind. Essentially, write how you speak but then go back and clean it as needed.

Avoid anything potentially embarrassing, such as using slang or revealing anything too personal. Never use profanity or risqué jokes. The company owns all that you write on its time and on its computers, and it can use it as evidence for your dismissal!

E-mail isn't as secure and private as you may think. Managers can tap into your e-mail account and flag certain key words, such as *management,* to see what you're saying to others about them. As a result, re-read your message in light of the fact that your managers may potentially be reading it. If that happened, would you be in some hot water?

Persuasion works best when you create a trustworthy impression with your reader (an appeal to ethics), when you support your claims with credible evidence (an appeal to reason), and when you keep a human face on the issue and the relationship (an appeal to emotion).

✔ **Topic:** Make sure that each e-mail covers just one main topic; this makes it easier for the reader to file it appropriately.

✔ **Conciseness:** Keep the message short without sacrificing the integrity of the message. Brevity and personalization facilitate not only the reader's comprehension of the message but also the continued positive feeling toward you.

✔ **Relationship-building:** Every contact with clients is an opportunity to build a positive relationship with them, which contributes to making the sale or maintaining continued sales. Knowing this, you can attach sales material, such as a brochure, a technical sheet, or a Word document with different fonts or colors, to your e-mail. Keep the e-mail message's font in the standard 10- or 12-point font size and in Times New Roman. If you really want to doll up the message, write it in a Word document and send it as an attachment. Don't forget to refer to the attachment in the message, however.

Never e-mail while angry. You may get nasty e-mails from customers; you don't need to respond in the same fashion. Take the time to cool off before you reply.

Tips when returning e-mails

Returning e-mails can be very time-consuming, but you can turn the situation to your advantage. We list a few things to consider when you return customer e-mails:

✔ **If someone sends you an e-mail, you have her e-mail address.** Feel free to ask her whether she wants to sign up for your newsletter or be informed about new products or services. Keep track of the e-mail addresses when you receive them. You can create a huge database of e-mail addresses and use them as part of your marketing campaign.

✔ **If you're asked an e-mail question, do more than just answer it.** Get information about why he had that question or comment. Ask what elements of the site didn't work for him and what *he* might do to improve the site. Keep track of this feedback — create a chart or a graph from the results and use the input to optimize your site.

✔ **Use your e-mail surveys.** When you have a chance, develop a survey that can be included with an e-mail.

✔ **In your e-mail, give information about upcoming offers and promotions.** If you receive a complaint e-mail, respond with a coupon or another offer. This is a great way to turn a complaint into a customer.

Using Forums

Forums are another name for *discussion boards.* Essentially, forums function as a space on your site where people can chat. Forums are unique in that the conversation isn't between you and the customer, but among the customers themselves. Here word of mouth can spread quickly, both the good and the bad.

There are both pros and cons to having a forum on your site. Time to review a few of the cons. Monitoring and maintaining forum discussions can be time-consuming. If your goal is to reduce the amount of communication, forums seem to be a step in the wrong direction. You need to monitor for language, bad reviews, inappropriate behavior, and more. Forums add a level of complexity to your site, so why would anyone want to include them?

Well, we have a simple answer for you. Despite their drawbacks, online forums can have a very positive impact on your site when used correctly. Here's what we mean:

- **Forums make for repeat visitors.** Visitors who post questions, answers, or other statements are going to return (and return often) to see whether anyone has responded to their questions or comments. If things go right, you can build a community of people who come to your forum to post questions, answer questions, and look around. You have repeat traffic.

- **Forums lead to greater keyword exposure.** The discussions on the forum can hold many of your keywords and themes. Search engines see the keyword in the forums and increase your SEO.

- **Forums enable you to track e-mail addresses and other information.** Forums can require that participants enter their e-mail addresses. When this happens, you begin to build a database of visitor e-mail addresses. You can use these addresses to announce new products or offers.

- **Forums allow you to trace demographic data.** With the help of software, you can identify where visitors come from and thus, identify the demographic that's actually visiting your site. This allows you to optimize your site for the visitors who view it.

- **Forums allow you to build relationships.** By participating in the online discussions, you can build relationships with your visitors. This builds trust and goes a long way to getting conversions.

- **Forums allow you to show your expertise.** If you take the time and respond to your online discussions, you can show your knowledge, which in turn makes visitors confident in your ability and more likely to buy from you.

No doubt about it, forums can really be a benefit, so then why doesn't every site use one? Simply because forums take a lot of work to make and maintain — not to mention the effort involved in setting up a forum to begin with. Forums are not a build-it-and-they-will-come type of landing page element. You need to seed the discussions and try hard to get people to participate in the forum and visit it regularly. A long time may pass before enough visitors arrive to make the forum float. Even when things take off, your work on the forum is just beginning. Despite all the work, though, a well-run forum can really produce great results. So, what we're really saying here is don't be afraid to use the forums but be prepared for a lot of work. (Figure 10-7 shows a standard forum interface.)

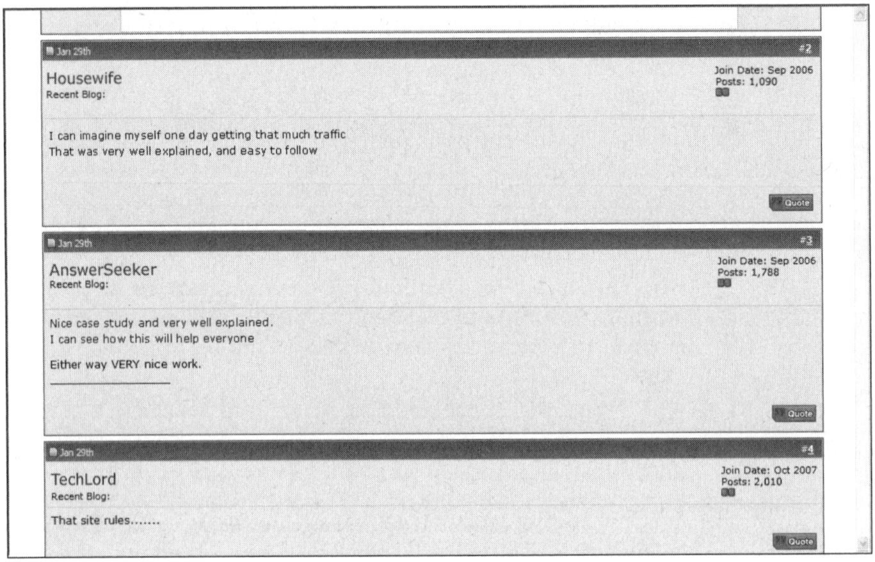

Figure 10-7: A standard forum interface.

Part IV
Increasing Your Sales

The 5th Wave   By Rich Tennant

"So far our web presence has been pretty good. We've gotten some orders, a few inquiries, and nine guys who want to date our logo."

In this part . . .

Face it, one of the most common purposes of landing pages is to make online sales. Chapter 11 deals with the aspects of closing these sales. Here you'll find everything you need to know about e-commerce, including a few common e-commerce mistakes, tips on your shopping cart, and help with a merchant account.

If you're having trouble closing your online sales, you need to fine-tune your landing page, which we cover in Chapter 12. This includes using focus groups, tracking software, and usability studies. Look to this chapter to isolate problems with your landing page and make the correct changes.

Chapter 11

Understanding E-Commerce and Closing Online Sales

In This Chapter

▶ Understanding the key elements of e-commerce

▶ Identifying common e-commerce mistakes

▶ Closing online sales

*I*magine for a minute that you've created what seems to be the perfect landing page. The page attracts lots of traffic, and visitors are just clicking and clicking their way through your page. This is a major accomplishment. However, if all this traffic isn't converting to sales, your landing page really isn't that successful. That's where your e-commerce elements need to come into play.

The Internet is full of e-commerce sites that try to sell everything from boomerangs, to glass eyes, to cars, and everything in between. Some of these e-commerce sites are designed well, whereas others are simply terrible and drive away customers.

This chapter focuses on the key elements and concepts of your e-commerce strategy, in an attempt to help you push your e-commerce to the Well Designed side of the spectrum. We help you get the basics of e-commerce, master the design and placement of e-commerce elements within your landing page, choose the best online payment methods and merchant accounts, and pick up a few tips for successful e-commerce landing page integration for good measure. All these strategies combine to ensure that you can do Job #1: Close your online sales.

Understanding E-Commerce Basics

So what exactly does e-commerce mean? *E-commerce (electronic commerce)* refers to buying and selling goods over a computer network. Most often today, e-commerce refers to purchasing, selling, and doing business over the Internet. E-commerce can be divided up into four distinct categories:

✔ **Business to Business (B2B):** With B2B, e-commerce solutions are designed specifically for one business to another. End consumers aren't part of the picture, so buying, ordering, and shipping methods are designed with companies in mind.

✔ **Business to Customer (B2C):** B2C e-commerce sites are designed for businesses to sell directly to the end consumer. The strategies used — payment methods, shipping, packaging, and what have you — are all designed with the consumer in mind. As shown in Figure 11-1, some significant differences are apparent in pages designed for B2B sales and those designed for B2C sales.

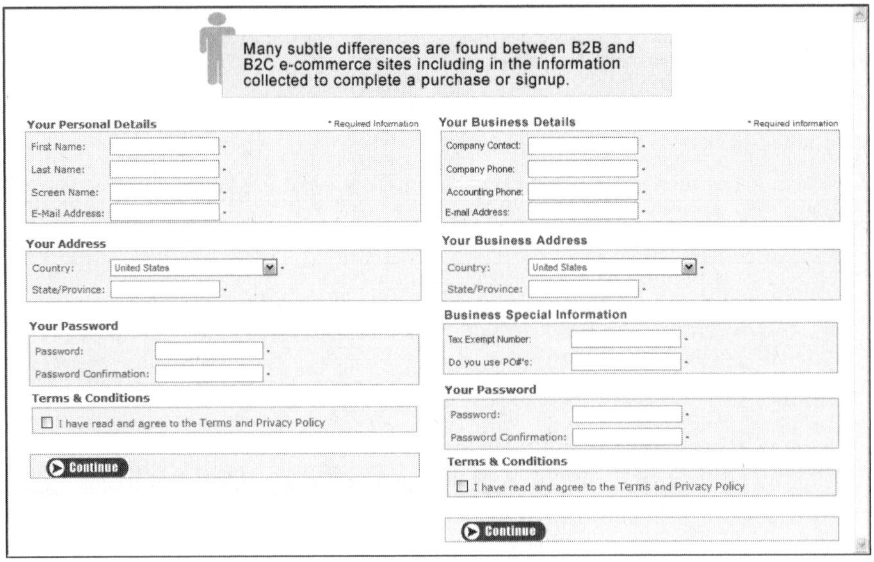

Figure 11-1:
Comparing
B2C (left)
and B2B
(right)
checkout
pages.

✔ **Consumer to Consumer (C2C):** Many e-commerce sites focus on C2C purchasing in which two consumers sell to/purchase from one another (think eBay).

✔ **Consumer to Business (C2B):** In C2B, consumers sell directly to businesses.

Reviewing e-commerce components

E-commerce isn't a single piece of software; rather, e-commerce is the interaction among several key components. For online sales to take place, all these components must work together on your site. In this section, we briefly describe the various elements of e-commerce and show how they all fit together within your landing page.

Landing page

Naturally, your landing page is an important part of your e-commerce solution. As we discuss throughout this book, the landing page is your storefront; it provides visitors with a look at you and your products. If the landing page has done its job, visitors are going to want to buy your product or service and therefore, follow the necessary links through the landing page to the checkout.

The landing page is arguably the most important part of your e-commerce strategy. Your landing page leads visitors gently through each click until they arrive at the checkout. No matter how strong the rest of your e-commerce solutions are, if the landing page isn't working, it doesn't matter how well the rest of your e-commerce strategy works.

Shopping cart

You won't get too far talking e-commerce before you hear the term *shopping cart,* which refers to an e-commerce software that allows a user to add items to buy while he browses through your online catalogue. Shopping cart software enables customers to place items into a virtual cart where all desired items are listed, and the software then calculates the total cost for the order, including all taxes and shipping and handling. (Check out Figure 11-2 to see how this works.)

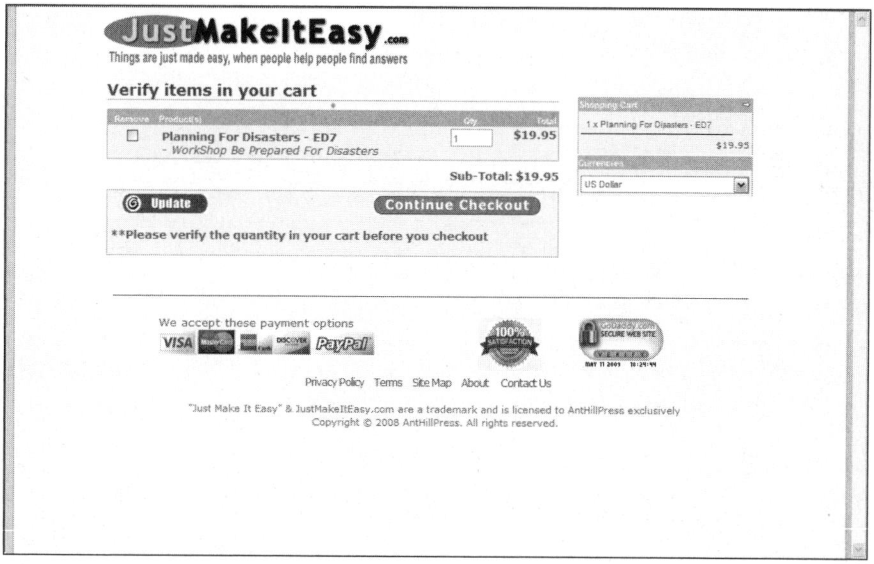

Figure 11-2: An example of an online shopping cart.

Shopping cart software tracks items a visitor chooses while on your site and lists them for your customer at checkout. Note, though, that such software doesn't manage the entire financial transaction; it's actually just the front end. The payment gateway and the protocols that secure the transaction work behind the scenes. We discuss both later in this section.

Another term you're likely to see — though you may not want to — is *cart abandonment,* which represents incomplete transactions. This is the equivalent of seeing an abandoned grocery cart in a store. This happens when your customer exits before she completes the transaction.

If you experience high cart-abandonment rates on your site, you have a problem. The trick is knowing you have an abandonment issue. For this, you need your tracking software, such as Google Analytics. You can use analytic software to review your site's performance, to see where visitors are going, to determine for how long they stay on your site, and to figure out where they leave the site. Analytic software quickly shows whether your shopping cart is letting you down. We provide a discussion of analytic software and how it's used in Chapter 12. Something is spooking your customers, and you're left holding the cart. The sections later discuss closing online sales and common e-commerce mistakes. These sections help explain why you may have a high percentage of incomplete transactions.

You can choose from many different shopping carts. In fact, the choices are almost overwhelming. The software you purchase for your shopping cart depends largely on personal preference. Table 11-1 outlines some of the shopping cart software available.

Table 11-1	Shopping Cart Software	
Shopping Cart	**URL**	**Cost**
CartzLink	www.cartzlink.com	$59 basic cart and $395 for comprehensive cart features
ShopCMS	http://shopcmssoft.com	$80 for basic shopping cart. Has free demo offer
CS-Cart	www.cs-cart.com	$265
CubeCart	www.cubecart.com	$179.95
Pinnacle Cart	www.pinnaclecart.com	$54.95 basic and $597 complete cart package

The list of shopping carts in Table 11-1 just scratches the surface of what's available for shopping cart software. You'll have to take some time to track down the one that offers the look, price, and features you need for your landing page. Still, we bet it's nice to know that you have plenty of options.

Despite all the options, shopping carts tend to follow the same set of check-out processes and also tend to flow essentially the same way. In Figure 11-3, you can see how a typical purchase process with a shopping cart takes place.

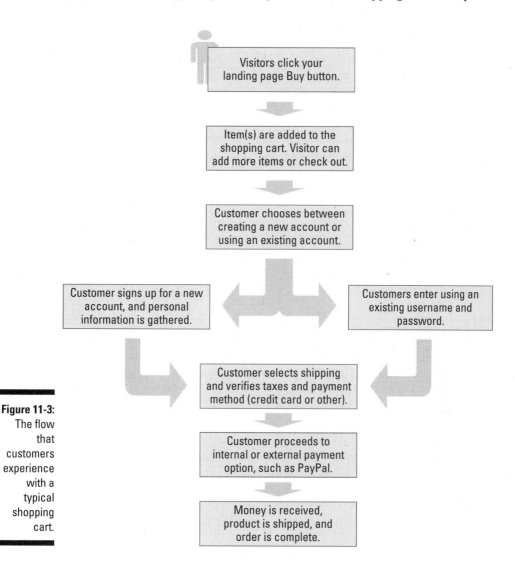

Figure 11-3:
The flow that customers experience with a typical shopping cart.

Merchant account

To accept online payments, you need a merchant account. The merchant account allows you (as a vendor) to accept credit card payments from purchasers. The funds are transferred from the merchant account directly to your bank account. Banks and other private institutions provide e-commerce merchant accounts. Table 11-2 lists a few of the more popular merchant-account–granting institutions.

Table 11-2	Getting Your Merchant Account
Institution	*URL*
Merchant Warehouse	`http://merchantwarehouse.com`
InstaMerchant	`www.instamerchant.com`
Merchant Express	`www.merchantexpress.com`
Durango Merchant Services	`www.durangomerchantservices.com`

Whichever merchant account provider you decide to go with, be on the lookout for hidden fees, high setup fees, and other surprises. Although these fees may not be crippling, they can be a shock if you aren't expecting them. The fees vary from bank to bank, but some fees may include

- ✔ **Statement fees:** Monthly statements are a good way to keep track of sales. Still, be sure you know whether you're charged each month for statements on transactions.

- ✔ **Setup fee:** Be sure you know how much you have to pay to set up your account.

- ✔ **Transaction fee:** Will you be charged for each transaction? If so, how much?

- ✔ **Monthly minimum:** Imagine a month in which you make no sales. Will you still be charged a monthly minimum fee for service?

- ✔ **Chargeback fees:** Chargeback fees occur when an online transaction is debited against a merchant account in cases of fraud or product returns. Chargebacks typically require a fee charged against the merchant. You want to know what the chargeback fees are for your merchant account.

- ✔ **Reserve:** Whenever someone returns a product, you may be subjected to a chargeback fee. To make sure you have funds to pay this, money is kept in *reserve* for payment. Chargeback fees can be significant. This is why some merchant account providers require a minimum reserve to be kept in the account in order to cover any chargeback fees.

This list details just a few of the hidden fees and surprises you may find along the way. These little surprises make it important to research your merchant account provider carefully. Although further discussion of merchant accounts isn't the focus of this book, we strongly encourage you to do your homework to find a merchant account that works for you.

Payment gateway

Shopping cart software is great for taking and organizing orders from your customers, and hopefully your merchant account does a good job of depositing the money you accept on your Web site into your bank account. That's all great, but one more important piece fits neatly in between these two services that we still need to discuss — the payment gateway.

How safe is all that money flying around?

Most have probably seen HTTPS in front of the URLs on secure Web pages. So what is HTTPS, and why do you need it? First, you need to know a little about HTTP proper. *HTTP (Hypertext Transfer Protocol)* allows text, graphics, multimedia, and other materials to be downloaded from an HTTP server to your computer. In a practical implementation, HTTP clients (that is, Web browsers) make requests in an HTTP format to servers running HTTP server applications (that is, Web servers). Files created in a language, such as HyperText Markup Language (HTML), are returned to the client, and the connection is closed.

Everyone uses HTTP to communicate on the Internet, which is all great; but there's one problem — HTTP requests are sent in clear text, meaning they're legible to everyone who can peek into Internet traffic while it flashes by. (And yes, some disreputable folks have managed to figure out precisely how to peek at such traffic en route.) For some applications — e-commerce being the most obvious example — this method of exchanging information isn't suitable. A more secure method was needed, so technology types came up with HTTPS. HTTPS uses a Secure Socket Layer (SSL) security protocol, which encrypts the information sent between the client and the host so that anyone trying to peek at the contents just sees gobbledygook.

For HTTPS to be used, both the client and server must support it. All popular browsers now support HTTPS, as do Web server products, such as Microsoft Internet Information Server (IIS), Apache, and almost all other Web server applications that provide sensitive applications.

The *payment gateway* is the system that connects the shopping cart to the merchant account. The payment gateway is the intermediary between your shopping cart and the merchant account you've chosen. This gateway is responsible for encrypting transaction details, getting the transaction details to their destination, decrypting the data, and returning it to the shopping cart. This process is invisible to your customers.

Fitting it all together

Okay, if you've had a chance to review all the important components of your e-commerce site, it's time to see how they all fit together to make your landing page a success. The following is how the process works:

1. A visitor arrives at your site, drawn by your online ad efforts or as a result of Google or another online search.

2. Your landing page is so well written and engaging that she can't help but buy something.

   Maybe she scrolls through your catalog and decides she can't live without your advertised wooden clogs.

3. She clicks your Buy Now button.

The coveted wooden clogs are added to the shopping cart, which calculates the total cost, including shipping and taxes. You think that $100 is a bargain for clogs. (Wouldn't anyone?)

4. She's taken to the checkout, where she enters her credit card information or other method of payment.

5. The information given, including credit card information, is transmitted to a payment gateway, which secures the data and transmits it to your merchant account provider.

   In this case, the merchant account is Visa.

6. If the credit card is approved (and you hope it is), the customer card is debited the $100 for the clogs and your Visa merchant account is credited the very same $100.

7. After all funds clear, you can transfer money to your own business checking account.

8. If she's happy with the clogs, you're done. If she returns the shoes because she realizes that wooden clogs are the most uncomfortable shoes on earth, you owe a chargeback fee.

So, there you have it: a bird's-eye view of how online transactions occur. Anywhere in this scenario, the customer may drop out (shopping cart abandonment), and you lose the sale. Not a good result, but you can take steps to lessen the possibility of the customer skedaddling, which the following section makes clear.

Getting paid

Although a comprehensive discussion of online payment methods falls outside the scope of this book, it's important to have an idea of how you can be paid. Part of your e-commerce solution is deciding which payment methods you accept. This can sometimes be determined by your clientele, but you still need to be able to accommodate your customers.

We think credit cards are the best way to go. Many Web surfers have access to a MasterCard or a Visa, and setting up your site to accept these cards isn't difficult. All cards have fees for transactions, and each have a fee for chargeback. These fees, especially charge-back fees, can add up, so be aware before taking payments.

Credit cards aren't the only payment option. Many regular Internet surfers choose to use PayPal, which is an online-based application for the secure transfer of funds between member accounts. With PayPal, you don't need to have a merchant account and customers can put money directly into your bank account. For a look at PayPal and its fees, check out their Web site at www.paypal.com.

Depending on your product and clientele, you may wish to provide your visitors with an offline purchasing option. This includes phone, fax, and snail mail sales. This is by no means an option we're crazy about, but plenty of people are uncomfortable putting credit card information online, which means offline payment methods will be your only chance to make the sale.

E-Commerce Mistakes: Ten Ways to Lose a Sale

After you know how e-commerce works on your landing page, we identify some of the common e-commerce mistakes. (Truth be told, you can make way more than just ten mistakes, but if you avoid these ten, you're at least moving in the right direction:

1. **Poor product choice:** Okay, maybe you love pound cake, but not everyone wants to buy it online and have it shipped across the country. Choosing a wrong or completely impractical shipping product will certainly sink your e-commerce efforts. The bottom line is, not every product sells well online. Choose your product carefully so as to not sabotage your efforts before you even begin.

So what products sell the best online? That's the million dollar question. We've seen products sell online that we would've bet against, and others that really should have sold and didn't. In general, products that can be downloaded and easily distributed make great products. Also, information-based products typically sell well. You can create them easily, distribute them widely, and update them as needed — the perfect online product.

2. **Awful landing page design:** Many people don't take the time to plan and design their landing pages for optimum sales. In fact, landing pages are often created in an afternoon and put on the Internet in hours. In reality, landing pages are hard work and take hours to create. Your e-commerce success hinges on your ability to create a quality landing page.

3. **Not keeping up with trends and technology:** Landing pages that prove successful both short- and long-term are *dynamic* — the content changes and reflects current trends and technologies. If your landing page appears stagnant and out of touch, you may lose visitors to more dynamic sites that pride themselves on being up-to-date. This includes having the latest e-commerce tools available. Although newer isn't always better, newer e-commerce solutions may have easy-to-use tools as well as other features.

4. **Bad checkout procedures:** Imagine you're standing in line to buy lunch, but at the last minute, the cashier tells you that you need to fill out a form with personal information on it before you could chow down. Or maybe the cashier asks you to fill out a survey or cough up a few names of friends that the restaurant can add to their menu subscription list. You wouldn't be happy, right? Well, this is what it's like for online customers who simply want to buy a product but are greeted with barriers on their way to the purchase. The idea here is to make the checkout procedures as easy and as quick as possible.

A few more takes on customer service

Poor customer service can quickly undermine all your e-commerce efforts. So what exactly constitutes poor customer service? You probably already know what poor customer service is, but here are a few things to keep in mind that add to customer frustration:

✔ **Site failure:** Poor customer service includes any site malfunctions, such as slow loading pages, broken links, or broken images. Good customer service requires that all site elements are tested and working.

✔ **Poor response times:** Maybe you can't respond to phone calls or e-mails immediately, but they can't be left too long. An expected courtesy is to respond to customers promptly and professionally.

✔ **Ignoring customer comments:** If you have a customer comment section on your e-commerce site, customers expect that you reply to any comments and complaints that they post on the site. Replying to customer complaints is important for customer service, but it also gives you valuable feedback on the site.

✔ **Sending the wrong product:** Sometimes, orders can get confused. Customers can get frustrated if they ordered a kite and received a pair of shoes. Keeping your orders straight, organized, and shipped on time is expected.

✔ **Not abiding by your Return Policy:** Having a Return Policy is one thing, sticking to it is another.

This list is just an example of the kinds of things that can impact your reputation as an online merchant. The point is you can spend lots of time and money on an e-commerce site, only to have it rendered ineffective by poor customer service.

Keep in mind that having a comprehensive FAQ section goes a long way to meeting customer expectation. The FAQ section can reduce customer frustration by answering questions they may have. How long should shipping take? What's the Return Policy? How can you be contacted? It may take some time, but developing an FAQ section is well worth the effort.

5. **Bad links and slow loads:** Few things make your visitors more frustrated than slow loading Web pages and bad links. Take the time to ensure that your page loads quickly and test periodically for dead links.

6. **Asking for too much:** Okay, here's a pet peeve: We know it's important to get information from visitors for marketing purposes — we make that point often enough in the book you're holding right now — but people are easily turned off when you ask *too* many questions. And it's not just the Asking Too Much Too Soon bit that's a problem but also the Asking Seemingly Irrelevant Questions part: a one-two combination that's sure to drive away traffic. Stick to getting just what you need to know to complete the purchase and keep things as simple as possible.

7. **Not updating product information:** Many sites continue to display out of stock or no longer available products. This makes the site look unprofessional and poorly maintained. If you're all out of wooden clogs, take them off your site.

8. **Poor customer service:** Just because your business is online, doesn't mean that you don't need to focus on customer service. Word of mouth is very important for online business. Any bad experiences with your online business can find their way onto blogs or other online forums, and that will certainly damage your reputation. Keeping your customers happy is an important part of a successful e-commerce site.

9. **Not preparing for growth:** Suppose you create a great landing page and sell an outstanding product, but you didn't put the proper elements in place to accommodate growth. Have a plan for growth: Know what to do if you need more bandwidth to accommodate traffic, more office space, more staff, or a new Web hosting plan. Be prepared for growth so that when it comes, you can take full advantage of it.

Not every landing page is a success, but you need to plan with success in mind. Sales can come quickly on the Internet, and you don't want to be unprepared because you didn't plan for success.

10. **Poor order fulfillment:** Does your download work with Mac and PC platforms? Can you ship on time? It's important for repeat business that you fill your orders on time and as promised.

Strategies for Closing Online Sales

If your e-commerce site and landing page are successful, visitors are going to end up at your shopping cart and may become customers. Remember, though, a visitor doesn't become a customer until the final sale is made. Web surfers can be a fickle bunch, which is why you need to use specific strategies to close your online sales and get those customers to commit. To help you get your customers to take that final step, check out the following few sections for ideas we've used effectively.

Create urgency

After a visitor leaves your site, he may never be back. This is why — throughout the site and especially in the checkout area — you create elements that suggest a sense of urgency. This includes phrases, such as

Buy now and receive a second at half price.

Order now and get a free coupon.

Half price, today only.

Free shipping included for the first 100 customers.

Order now, and we pay the tax.

The sense of urgency gets your visitors to buy now and not put off the purchase. Using these types of urgent messages is a great way to get a sale to close because they make the customer feel he'll lose out if he doesn't buy now. Fear of losing a good deal is a powerful motivator.

Show confidence

Okay, do you really want to buy a product from someone who seems unsure about its merits? If you present mediocrity, that will be seen by your visitors. You've taken the time to develop a product, build a landing page, and set up an e-commerce site. All this suggests that you have a strong belief in the merits of your product. This message needs to be conveyed.

Confidence is tied in with landing page show-and-tell, which involves:

- Placing product demos on the site
- Using pictures to clearly show the product
- Using pictures to show how the product is used to benefit your customers
- Using testimonials from satisfied customers
- Making clear guarantees for the product
- Offering an easy Return Policy

All these types of elements show that you're confident in the product and stand behind it. This is critical for closing the sale. Your site needs to display such elements prominently as a way of showcasing your confidence in the product and the company.

Remove obstacles to sales

Online shopping has many obstacles to overcome — rumors of security problems, fraud, and unknown companies, to name just a few. You're going to have to deal with these obstacles if you want to close the sale. After you remove the obstacles, your visitor is going to feel more comfortable in buying online from you. The following list features several strategies you can use to make your visitors feel more comfortable so you can close sales.

One of the most important things you can do to close a sale is to remove the obstacles to sales. Without removing them, your customers aren't going to buy.

✔ **Using a clean and efficient page design:** Before you can get most visitors to reach for their credit card, they need to see your professionalism. This includes the design of your landing page. Closing a sale is difficult if your site is hard to navigate, looks unprofessional, or seems unnecessarily complex. An easy-to-navigate page that focuses on the customer is going to be an asset when it comes to closing sales.

✔ **Making your sales intentions clear:** Many Internet users are leery about e-commerce and rightly so. Many unscrupulous merchants try to take advantage of people online. To combat this, you need to clearly display the total cost of products, including shipping and taxes. When it comes to your sales intentions and costs, be above board and open. If customers suspect you've hidden something, you're going to have a real time closing the sale.

✔ **Getting rid of your anonymity:** Let your visitors know about you, your business, and your product. Clear communication about who you are and how you can be contacted goes a long way to closing sales.

✔ **Keeping the shopping cart process uncluttered:** When your visitors are close to buying and at the checkout, they tend to become a little nervous. Here you need to keep the process simple. Many people think this is the time to ask for customer information — either through surveys or other means — but we think it may not be. Don't put anything in the way between the customer and the final sale.

✔ **Ensuring that personal information is secure:** Credit card security is still a main impediment to online shopping. You need to consider the threat of electronic theft and fraud when you design your online business. Security is a top priority even before your site goes live.

✔ **Overcoming distrust:** Many visitors will be distrustful of you, your product, and even buying on the Internet. Maybe the visitors have purchased things in the past that didn't work out or heard horror stories from friends or family. Two common methods used to combat these concerns are to eliminate the customer's risk of loss (with money back guarantees) and to establish your sales practices and record (with testimonials).

Chapter 12

Fine-Tuning Your Landing Page

. . . .

. . . .

Most won't get their landing page right the first time out. Like everyone, you're going to create the site to the best of your ability and then post it live. If you're really lucky, that will be all you need to do, but it's more likely that you'll need to tune and fine-tune your page until it gets the conversions you expect.

Fine-tuning is a systematic process, meaning it's probably best not to just make modifications to your site without a plan. Instead, you need a strategy that involves finding elements on your site that may not be working, researching how to make those areas better, and testing your solutions. The key to fine-tuning your landing page is getting information from two sources: your demographic and your statistics.

In this chapter, we look at how to get that information, so you can make clear and accurate changes to your landing page.

Locating Five Problem Areas with Your Landing Page

In order to know where your problems are with your landing page, you need to set up a good tracking system. When it comes to your landing page, Web site visitor statistics and feedback from your demographic are critical in fine-tuning your efforts. But before we begin with all the tracking and statistics stuff, we need to break the landing page into parts to help you isolate specific areas to fine-tune.

Landing page tuning can be a tricky process. One small change may have a significant impact on conversions, whereas several big changes may have little or no impact. Sometimes your changes even make your conversion rate fall. To help you isolate the areas to fine-tune, your landing page can be broken down into the following five distinct troubleshooting areas: checkout, page presentation, page information, technology, and navigation. The following few sections take a look at each problem area in some detail.

Imitation is the sincerest form of flattery, but this doesn't necessarily hold true for landing pages. You're sure to be making changes over time to your site, but so, too, will your competition. You may be tempted to watch your competitors' Web sites and copy their changes — the technologies added, images used, text layout, navigation style, checkout procedure, whatever. Although a good practice is to keep an eye on what the competition is doing, it's not prudent to assume they have the edge on you. Stick to a methodical and calculated approach to your landing page fine-tuning, and you may find your competition following your lead!

Checkout procedures

The checkout area is *the* make or break area of the landing page. Imagine that you're using Web traffic-tracking software and you see that 40 percent of visitors duly read your landing page and follow through to the checkout. However, of that 40 percent, only 1 percent follows through with the purchase. If that's the case, you definitely have a checkout problem, which could be anything from cost, layout, technologies used, or even spelling mistakes.

A certain percentage of visitors naturally drop out of the purchase at the last minute. This type of cold feet is absolutely normal, but having only a few visitors follow through to the actual purchase or conversion just isn't acceptable. If your stats tell you that your checkout needs a little fine-tuning, here are a few common troubleshooting tips you can try:

- ✓ **Stamp out spelling errors.** This may not seem like a huge deal, but when people see spelling errors, they may be more hesitant to enter their credit card information. Numerous spelling errors give the feeling that the site isn't professional and perhaps not trustworthy.

- ✓ **Make sure your contact information is prominently displayed.** Your customers want to see your contact info on the checkout page. They most certainly want to know how to contact you if they have a problem with a checkout procedure, shipping, or another checkout-related area.

- ✓ **Insist on secure checkout procedures.** If you're taking credit card or personal information, visitors want to be reassured that the communication link is secure.

✔ **Have the best checkout navigation possible.** Make sure your checkout is clean and clear. Keep the navigation simple with as few clicks as possible. Get rid of any distractions between the visitor and the conversion.

✔ **Use trust elements and icons.** The checkout can be a great place to include *trust elements* — those testimonials or icons showing your affiliations. You can't afford to lose your visitors trust at the checkout. (For more on trust elements, see Chapter 7.)

✔ **Test the checkout procedures.** Every now and then, you or someone you know needs to go through the checkout. Test it to make sure it flows easily and that no dead links or other dead ends exist.

Streamlining the checkout and ensuring it looks and functions perfectly is very important. As shown in Figure 12-1, a good checkout page is uncluttered, informative, and builds confidence.

Figure 12-1:
A well-designed checkout page.

Page presentation

Page presentation is the overall look of the page and how your content is organized. You can have the best content, and it can all be undone if the layout is cluttered and difficult to read. Fine-tuning the page presentation is an ongoing process, and unfortunately, you have tons of page presentation elements to consider, including

✔ Page header size and contents

✔ Background color choice

✔ Text color and size

✔ Font choice

✔ Page element (such as trust logos, testimonials, or contact info) placement

✔ Size, location, and color of call to action features

✔ Choices used for visitor input (drop-down lists or radio, for example)

✔ Page white space

✔ Graphic size and placement

✔ Heading size and placement

As this list makes clear, you have lots of elements involved in the page layout — and fine-tuning just a few of them can have very positive results. And yet, which few are we talking about? If left completely up to you, it'd be very difficult to know what elements of your page presentation work and which ones turn away visitors. In most cases, you're going to need to gather lots of information to troubleshoot your page presentation. This information comes from two key sources: your visitors and your tracking software. We discuss both of these later in this chapter.

You can find plenty of Web sites and articles online that offer help and solutions for troubleshooting page presentation. Some of these hints and tips are helpful, whereas others are counterproductive. Go ahead and read as much as possible from others, but keep in mind that your site is unique, with its own challenges and demographic. You can't always rely on the advice of others; you need to figure out the strategies to gather the right information and fine-tune the page.

With that in mind, we know a few common trouble spots to keep an eye on with your landing page layout. Here's our handy list:

✔ **Place trust elements in a clearly visible location on the landing page.** Trust elements include your trust logos, testimonials, and contact information.

✔ **Allow your calls to action to stick out.** Tell your visitors what you want them to do with a call to action, such as Click Here to Order or Download Your Copy Here. Use colors and shapes to distinguish the call to action from other elements on your landing page and use urgent language encouraging your visitors to click.

✔ **Do not use a distracting background.** Backgrounds with too many colors or distracting graphics can be more problematic than helpful. Content that's truly professional doesn't need such elements to get across the point.

✔ **Keep the layout clean and uncluttered.** Most visitors respond well to an uncluttered look — one that makes your information easy to find, as shown in Figure 12-2. Tips for keeping things uncluttered include

- Keep your paragraphs short.

- Use a few well-chosen pictures.

- Keep the font size not too small and not too big. Certainly, no hard and fast rule exists regarding what's too small or too big. If seniors are your demographic, your font size may be larger. Split-testing or using a focus group can help determine whether elements, such as font size, work for you.

- Stick with a traditional font style, such as Times New Roman or Arial.

✔ **Avoid flashy and distracting elements.** Flashing colors, rotating graphics, and similar features can complicate your landing page, making the critical information difficult to find.

Remember that with your page layout, you're not trying to impress you. Your landing page isn't for you; it's for your visitors, so keep your demographic in mind when you design and fine-tune your site layout.

Figure 12-2:
A clean,
uncluttered
landing
page.

Page information

The information you include on your landing page is, of course, critical to making conversions. The information has to be presented and organized in such a way that it appeals to and informs your visitors. All important content has to flow logically and relate to your demographic. The following list gives you some best practices when it comes to page information:

- ✓ **Present your information in short paragraphs as well as bullets and numbered lists.** This keeps information accessible to scanners.

- ✓ **Choose your page titles carefully, making sure they entice the visitor to read the following text.**

- ✓ **Include just the information necessary to define the product or service.** The information you include needs to focus on the product/ service and nothing extra.

- ✓ **Look out for poor grammar and spelling mistakes, which may cause visitors to lose your message.** These mistakes stop the flow if visitors are distracted by errors on the page. Have others read your page to help spot errors.

- ✓ **Keep an eye on the tone and style of your writing.** Getting down the right information is one thing, but if it isn't relayed correctly, the best information can be lost. Word choice, your syntax, and the sentence length determine your tone, which is in turn, determined by your demographic.

- ✓ **Make sure you use only original work.** You don't have to be online long before you see plagiarism, and it probably won't take your potential customers long to find out whether you're cribbing from other sources. Ensure your content is your own work.

Landing page technology

Another area on your landing page that may need fine-tuning involves the technology used. This includes everything from your HTML programming to your browser compatibility to technologies that enhance your page, such as JavaScript and Flash. Using the wrong technology or not keeping the technology in line with what your visitors use and expect negatively impacts your conversion rates. Here are a few things to consider:

- ✓ **Are you ready for the mobile world?** If your tracking software shows people visit via mobile, such as PDAs and cellphones, you may have to build a mobile version of your pages to display as well. We list screen sizes for various portable devices in Chapter 4.

✔ **Having browser problems?** View your site in all main browsers. Does your landing page view properly in Windows Explorer, Firefox, Chrome, and so on. If your landing page works well in one, that doesn't mean it works well in all browsers.

✔ **Trouble playing landing page videos?** Technologies change, which means new video players can't always play older videos. Make sure that your file formats are up to date.

✔ **Do you have the right plug-ins/readers to view documents?** Offering a PDF (Portable Document Format) or another online document format for customers as a sample page or other feature is a great idea, but newer software versions can render older versions unusable or cause problems with customers viewing the information. Keep an eye on reader and/or plug-in software and be sure your PDFs and documents remain accessible to your site visitors.

✔ **Do you use Flash?** Like other special features, you need to monitor your Flash plug-in to make sure it's working properly. You may also have compatibility issues because some cellphones don't run Flash properly.

Site navigation

Navigation is a key component to landing page success, so you'd better expect a bit of troubleshooting and fine-tuning of your navigation strategy from time to time. For your landing page, the navigation has to flow in a logical order without too many areas to navigate to before visitors actually get to the checkout page. For that to happen, you need to be aware of three key elements of effective navigation strategy:

✔ **Don't place _external_ links (which lead to another site) on your landing page.** External links are rarely a good idea because they give visitors the option to navigate away from your page, plain and simple. Navigation needs to guide visitors gently to the checkout page for the conversion. If external links are used, have them open in a new window and keep your site in the background.

✔ **Watch for dead links.** Dead links stop navigation in its tracks and leave the visitor frustrated. Test your links periodically to ensure they all work as they should.

✔ **Have a well-designed navigational structure.** If visitors click a contact form, can they easily navigate back? Testing your navigation for logical flows and dead ends is critical when it comes to usability.

Even if you know that five separate areas of your landing page can pose potential problems — remember, checkout, page presentation, page information, technology, and navigation? — how do you know which ones are working and which ones are letting you down? If your conversion rate is low, is your technology to blame? Your language? The page design? You can't really tell without more information at your fingertips. The key to your landing page fine-tuning and to your overall conversions success, therefore, lies in your ability to get the information you need. Without the right information, fine-tuning your landing page comes down to hunches and best guesses — and who wants to build a business on guesswork?

Getting the Information to Fine-Tune Your Landing Page

We stress that you have five areas to consider when fine-tuning your landing page: checkout, page presentation, page information, technology, and navigation. The question is how do you know which area to focus on and what to tweak in that area? Picture this: You've already created the site and took your best shot in terms of making it the best it could be, but you're missing something. You need more information.

When it comes to fine-tuning your landing page, you need as much information as possible. Without info, you really are blindly making changes to the site that may help or may even make things worse. We recommend that you don't make any changes to your site before you gather information on the problem. You have two primary sources for such information: You can interview people who fit within your demographic or you can use software that analyzes the behavioral patterns of the people who visit the site. (Okay, you can also do both, which we suppose would be strategy #3.) Getting information directly from your demographic includes usability studies, focus groups, surveys, forms, and blogs. (More on those in the following sections.)

Spending the time to find areas to fine-tune on your site is critical to your overall success. Many landing page ventures that fail do so for one simple reason: No one took the time to review the site for errors or shortfalls.

Usability testing

The function of a usability study is to have your landing page tested under real world conditions. With a usability study, you locate elements of your page that hamper the, well, *usability* of the site. This can be anything from the technology used on the site to the load times to the checkout procedures. Here are the three ways to conduct a usability study:

✔ **You can employ a company to work through your site.** This can be very costly because professionals testing your site know not only how to find potential problems but also how to charge. These companies do provide, however, a soup to nuts report of your site's usability. If you have the money, it's not a bad way to go.

✔ **You can arrange to have people go through the site and comment on their experiences.** This is a focus group of sorts. Get the gang together over pizza and have them all test the site for usability. Watch their efforts, and you can spot holdups along the way.

✔ **You can use usability questionnaires, which you circulate to folks representing your demographic.**

All approaches yield fantastic results.

To begin a usability study, locate people who represent your demographic and are willing to take part in the study. This isn't as difficult as it sounds. For example, if you promote footwear for seniors, gather at least six to ten seniors to take part in the study. We've performed these usability studies a number of times, and if you can really target your demographic in the study, you'll get invaluable insight on potential problems and you can isolate areas that need fine-tuning.

After you gather people who will be involved in the usability study, give them the link to your landing page and a copy of the usability study to fill out. We use a simple questionnaire to obtain the usability information. You can create a usability questionnaire in many different ways, but typically it includes your study goals, questions, and outcomes. The following is a sample template for a usability study. Yours will be different, but this gives you an idea of how they work:

Overall objectives for the usability study

This usability study is designed to assess the overall effectiveness of `mylandingpage.com`. Three identifiable objectives of the study include

- Identifying obstacles preventing visitor conversion
- Reviewing overall site functionality for the intended demographic
- Revealing navigational bottlenecks

Sample study questions

This study asks the following questions related to usability:

- Was any technology used on the site that was incompatible with your computer system?
- Could you navigate effectively through the landing page?
- Could you complete the checkout procedures?
- Were the landing page load times an issue for you?

- Could you sign up for the newsletter? If not, what problems did you encounter?

- What areas of the site do you recommend changing and why?

Overall outcomes

At the end of the sessions, the results show

- **Errors in completing checkout procedures:** The study should identify any areas of the checkout procedures that need to be modified and improved.

- **Errors in navigational structure:** This study pinpoints any errors or bottlenecks in navigation. With the usability feedback, the navigation can be fine-tuned to meet the demographics' needs.

- **Which elements may have adversely impacted conversions:** We can pinpoint conversion issues, even if participants make errors on the way to the conversion.

You can set up the questionnaire and report any way you want, but we recommend keeping it short and to the point. People tend to put off any chore when it involves large amounts of paperwork. (Taxes, anyone?)

Focus groups

Focus groups are much like a usability study in that they use a representative cross-section of your demographic, but the overall outcomes are somewhat different. A focus group provides specific feedback on the entire look and feel of your landing page. We've run several focus groups for various landing page ventures and can assure you that they make a huge difference when locating areas on your landing page that need tweaked. A well-designed and managed focus group increases your chances for conversions. As an example, the first focus group we conducted used ten participants to review our landing page. A one-hour session revealed 18 very specific areas on the landing page that weren't working for our demographic. After corrected, the conversion rate jumped significantly. We may or may not have found these trouble spots on our own, but the focus group sure made it easy.

The truth is that many landing page developers would rather not take the time and effort to run a focus group, opting instead to tweak the site with their own best-guess efforts. Running usability studies and focus groups sometimes can separate the weekend landing page designer from those who really want to take their pages to the next level and make consistent (and income-earning) conversions.

Here are several advantages to using a focus group:

- ✔ **You don't need to hire a company to conduct a focus group.** You can arrange and organize it. It's a cheap and effective method to get quality feedback.

- ✔ **Focus groups go under the surface.** They give you deep insight into your landing page from those who matter, your targeted demographic.

- ✔ **Focus groups provide a grassroots marketing campaign.** If the members of the focus group like what they see, that's great word of mouth. A little free advertising never hurts. Conversely, if they don't like what they see, you may get some bad press. Better to find out now with a limited sample, however, before going live to the Internet.

- ✔ **Focus groups provide solutions.** Not only are focus groups one of your best sources for identifying current shortcomings, but they also give you direction where to move your landing page in the future. The focus group helps identify what you need to improve now but also helps you identify positive steps you can take in the future to improve your product and business.

 When you run a focus group, you get lots of input and suggestions on your landing page. Some of the feedback may be conflicting. Consider the information as a helpful guideline and in the end, know that you may have to go with your gut feeling. However, don't become defensive and try to protect your page from negative feedback. If your demographic doesn't like something on your page, don't take it personally. After all, the page is for them, not for you.

Preparing for focus groups

To make your focus group a success, you have to do a little planning beforehand. Your focus group should contain about eight to ten people, if possible, and you should all meet together so you can present your landing page to them all at the same time.

In your focus group, you want open discussion and feedback from everyone. Here are a few tips to consider when preparing for your focus group:

- ✔ **Be clear on the purpose of your focus group:** Are they reviewing your entire site? Just your checkout procedures? Before you can get the results you need, you must be very clear on what information you want from the members of your focus group. This guides your discussions and (ultimately) your outcomes.

- ✔ **Keep your questions focused (no pun intended):** After you're clear on the information you want to obtain, develop your questions. Don't overwhelm the focus group, so limit to perhaps 10–15 well-written questions. Questions should be targeted and open-ended.

✔ **Develop your session plan:** The people in your focus group are giving up a bit of their time to be a part of your study, so you'd better ensure that you're organized and ready to go. Being unprepared and wasting your participants' time is inconsiderate. Planning your session includes preparing a written agenda so all participants know what to expect, offering refreshments, establishing the ground rules for the discussions, and having clearly identified goals that are reviewed by all participants before the session begins.

✔ **Make a courtesy reminder call:** Call your participants a few days before the study begins. Your turnout rate will be much higher if you invest in a simple phone call.

✔ **Record your session:** You may think you'll remember everything said in the group, but much can be forgotten. Using a small tape recorder helps you to capture all the feedback from your focus group. Of course, if you plan to do this, make sure you get the permission of everyone in the focus group.

Running a focus group really isn't that complicated, and for the most part, they're social and fun. Think about it: A group of people in a room, eating snacks and talking about your landing page — what's not to like?

Surveys, forums, and blogs

In terms of fine-tuning your landing page, surveys, forums, and blogs can be a great source of information. Surveys can be sent via e-mail to potential respondents or given on the Web site as a pop-up. In the best-case scenario, your survey will be completed by members of your target population — surveys filled out by people who don't fit your demographic probably aren't going to yield the best information.

Establishing online discussion forums and blogs can also get input from your demographic. Both can often provide details on the concerns and problems of your target audience. Both blogs and forums offer communal avenues to discuss both pros and cons of your landing page, your product, online technology, and more. (We discuss surveys and forums in more detail in Chapter 10.)

Tracking software

Surveys, forums, usability studies, and focus groups all provide methods to identify areas on your landing page that may need to be tweaked. In addition to these methods, you can use one more great strategy to gather information: tracking or analytic software.

You'll find it's next to impossible to fine-tune a landing page without gathering very specific information, and Web statistics are invaluable for identifying landing page trouble spots. All statistics of your landing page can be identified with software such as *Google Analytics,* Google's Web tracking software, as shown in Figure 12-3. In addition, you can employ companies to analyze your landing page and provide you with all types of statistics about it.

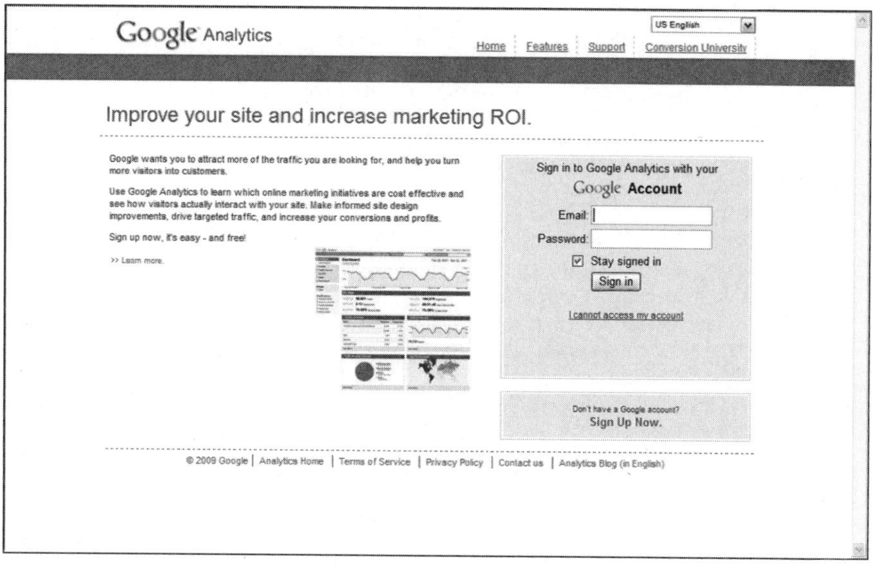

Figure 12-3:
Google
Analytics.

With applications like Google Analytics, you can track a range of landing page related statistics. In general, track elements, such as

- **Bounce rate:** This is the percentage of people who arrive at your site and then leave (or *bounce*) quickly without hanging around to really check out your site. Tracking the bounce rate lets you discover how long people stay on your site, what they view on your site, and where they choose to exit your site. For example, your tracking software can determine if your visitors are going through your site but then leaving when they hit your checkout. This could indicate that your checkout procedures need some fine-tuning.

- **Visitors:** Your tracking efforts can also determine where the bulk of your visitors come from. You can track by a broad area, such as country, state, or city. This helps you pinpoint where the bulk of your traffic comes from, which then enables you to fine-tune your page in terms of location.

✔ **Traffic sources:** Visitors don't just show up at your site — they need to find it. Tracking software allows you to see where your traffic comes from. Also, you can see if the traffic comes to your site directly by typing in the URL (perhaps due to offline marketing efforts) or as a result of online marketing (such as that done by pay per click [PPC] campaigns).

✔ **Visitor type:** Your tracking software can help you determine whether your visitors are unique or whether they're returning visitors. Returning visitors who don't buy indicate some hesitation. If you can get a survey to these returning visitors, they may be able to tell you *why* they're hesitating: It could be a navigation issue, not enough contact information, poor checkout procedures, or more.

✔ **Network capabilities:** You can track how fast your page loads on various Internet connections. If the page is taking too long to load, you see visitors bounce almost immediately.

✔ **Visitor paths:** Tracking software lets you know precisely where people visit on your page — their footprints, as it were. This can help you identify navigation issues and determine where people visit before they bounce off the site. If visitors are commonly bouncing from the same page, it may be that the page needs tuning.

✔ **Cart abandonment:** If they're not finishing the sales cycle, you're not making any money, so you need to know whether your cart is causing people to drop the notion of buying from you.

Google Analytics

Several types of Web analytic software are available online — including the aptly named Google Analytics, which remains one of the more commonly used. Web analytic software helps you understand how visitors interact with your landing page and assists you in driving targeted traffic to your site. In this section, we provide you with an overview of Google Analytics, using a practical approach. A complete tutorial of Google Analytics falls outside the scope of this book; however, to give you a taste, we include a few analytic reports in this section. Take a look at how Google Analytics can be used to create reports, starting with one dealing with bounce rates.

Visitor bounce occurs when a visitor comes to the site and then leaves almost instantly, without really exploring the site. Visitors bounce for many reasons and some bounce is expected, but too much bounce indicates a problem with your site or a particular page in your site. With Google Analytics, you can easily track your bounce rates for the entire site, as shown in Figure 12-4, and the bounce rates for individual pages within your site.

Figure 12-4:
Reviewing bounce rates in Google Analytics.

Notice in Figure 12-5, that there were 784 page views and a 51.87 percent bounce rate. Nearly 50 percent of visitors bouncing may sound like a lot, but in landing page terms, this is great. You'd be quite content with a 50-percent bounce rate.

You can look a lot deeper into your bounce rates with Google Analytics. For example, Figure 12-5 shows the bounce rates by individual page. The pages with the highest bounce rates may need some fine-tuning.

To read more on bounce rates and Google Analytics, check out `http://googleblog.blogspot.com/2009/02/stop-bouncing-tips-for-website-success.html`.

The second type of Google Analytics report includes goals and funnels. In Google terms, *goals* measure your overall business goals and your progress. The *goal funnel* is a sequence of steps that lead to the successful completion of a goal, which is likely a conversion. Figure 12-6 shows an example of a goal funnel.

Figure 12-6 shows an example of a goal funnel in which 788 visitors arrive to the site, 296 (38 percent) proceed to the checkout, and 10 (3 percent) proceed to the checkout *and* buy the product. This type of report lets you clearly see your success or failure at each step in the process. In terms of fine-tuning your page, a goal funnel gives you a great look at where you may need to focus your efforts.

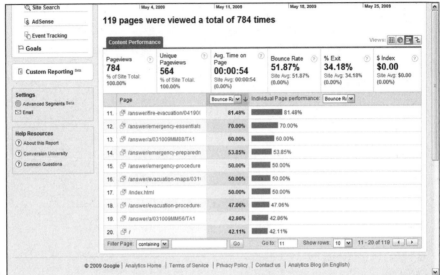

Figure 12-5:
Reviewing
bounce
rates by
individual
page in
Google
Analytics.

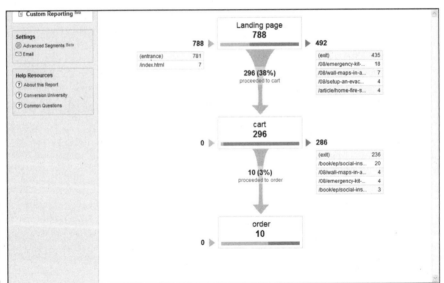

Figure 12-6:
A goal
funnel
example.

For more information on Google's goals and funnels, check out the tutorial at
http://analytics.blogspot.com/2009/05/how-to-setup-goals-
in-google-analytics.html.

Another report you can try has to do with traffic segmentation. (A *segment* refers to a subset of your traffic.) You can break down your traffic into segments according to the type of traffic you want to monitor. You can view traffic by browser used, by unique visitors, by languages, by locations, and more. Comparing segments helps you fine-tune your marketing efforts by targeting the types of traffic that are actually accessing your site. The Google Analytics segmentation report, as shown in Figure 12-7, provides great insight into all types of traffic and different ways to view that traffic.

Notice in Figure 12-7, you have a total of 273 visits. Of those visits, 251 are new visitors, and 22 are returning visitors. This shows that this particular site attracts new visitors, but few return to the site. Your fine-tuning efforts may include strategies placing elements on your site that will work to attract more returning visitors.

More information on the segmentation report and how to use it can be found at http://analytics.blogspot.com/2008/11/deeper-look-at-advanced-segmentation.html.

Another report makes use of the e-commerce tracking tool, which reports on all aspects of the actual transaction online. The report includes information on

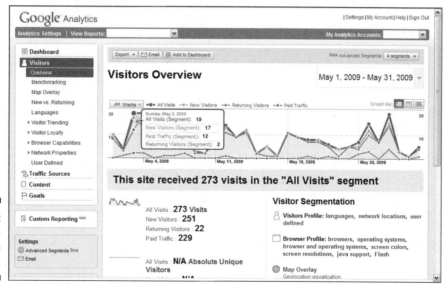

Figure 12-7: Google segmentation report.

✔ Total sale cost

✔ Purchase tax

✔ Shipping costs

✔ Purchase location

✔ Item data

✔ Number of units sold

With the e-commerce tracking tool, you can nail down where people buy from, how they buy, how much they buy, and more. This can help you determine where best to market and how to fine-tune purchasing for your demographic.

Figure 12-8 shows an example of a report built by the e-commerce tracking tool. Notice that this report lists 53 products sold, generating $5,200 in sales. Figure 12-8 shows the initial screen of the e-commerce tool. More screens delve deeper into the transaction process.

Figure 12-8: Google e-commerce report.

For more information on the Google e-commerce tool and how it's used, check out the tutorial at `http://analytics.blogspot.com/2009/05/how-to-use-ecommerce-tracking-in-google.html`.

Making and Evaluating Changes to Your Landing Page

After you have your five landing page areas to focus on and you know how to isolate areas that may need fine-tuning with surveys, analytic software, focus groups, usability tests, and more, time to actually make the changes to your site. Making changes actually isn't difficult after you gather information on the potentially weak areas of your landing page. Here are the three best practices to keep in mind when you make changes to your site:

✔ **Don't change everything at once:** It's difficult to evaluate whether a change was effective if too many changes were made simultaneously. The best idea is to make a few changes (one or two) and then evaluate the impact.

✔ **If it ain't broke, don't fix it:** Make changes when you have the information to back it up. That is, don't just make changes for the sake of change. In a way, Web developers are tinkerers that love to get in there and modify and tweak. The information, however, guides the changes you make. When you gather information from surveys, focus groups, or other sources, you can feel confident that you need to fine-tune something — and you'll have a pretty good idea what that "something" is.

✔ **Document your changes:** You really need to have a reference point for the changes you make. Keep a running log of your changes and note whether the change was successful.

Using split-testing

After you've made changes to your site, what's an easy way to know if the change was successful? One way, of course, is to use your tracking software to identify whether the statistics have improved. Do visitors stay longer? Are conversion rates higher? Another way, however, goes by the name of split-testing or as some experts call it, *multivariate testing* or *A-B testing.*

Split-testing involves running multiple landing pages to test the results of your changes. In this scenario, you have two versions of your page, *A* (the original) and *B* (the edited version). The traffic is *split* — some goes to the current page (A) while other traffic goes to the page with the changes (B).

In some ways, split-testing is a contest in which you pit the champion (version A) against the challenger (version B). The one that wins becomes your primary landing page. The two landing pages can be vastly different from one another, or (more commonly) small changes are made between the two. Perhaps you try modifying the heading (or maybe the font choice or background color) on one page.

Here are several advantages to split-testing your landing page:

- **Easy way to quickly test changes to your site:** Perhaps your focus group thinks your heading is ineffective, but you think it is great. Running a split-test campaign allows you to easily test who's right. The landing page can be exactly the same except for the heading, and you get to see which one visitors respond to more favorably.

- **Easy to put into practice:** Unlike other more difficult test types, split-testing is relatively easy to put into action. Within minutes you can make a change to your primary site and post it online.

- **Easy result interpretation:** If you have two identical pages except for one small change, you can easily easy tell which one is the better option. You don't have to interpret graphs. A chart or a log file is all you need to identify which of the two pages performs better.

Split-testing with Google Analytics

You're not on your own when it comes to split-testing your site. Google Analytics can do it for you. Google Analytics provides a Website Optimizer, which is basically a tool that allows you to test different versions of your landing page to identify which one works better.

For more information on split-testing with the Google Website Optimizer, check out www.google.com/support/websiteoptimizer.

Part V
Driving More Visitors to Your Site

The 5th Wave
By Rich Tennant

"Maybe it would help our Web site if we showed our products in action."

In this part . . .

Part V is all about driving the correct traffic to your landing page to make a lot of conversions. Chapter 13 starts with a discussion of keywords — choosing and placing them on your page. In Chapter 14, we look at the basics of search engine marketing and search engine optimization.

Search engine optimization is just one avenue to drive traffic to your landing page; you can also drive traffic with online ads, which we discuss in Chapter 15. Not only that, but you can use ads in which you pay for clicks. In Chapter 16, we discuss just that — pay per click (PPC) ads. After you know a bit about PPC, Chapter 17 adds to the discussion by looking at how to run a Google PPC ad test campaign. By the end of this part, you can drive qualified traffic to your landing page.

Chapter 13

Using Keywords Effectively

*W*hy can't the search engines find my landing page? Why aren't my ads working? Why isn't my traffic increasing? Why are my bounce rates so high? These are some of the more common questions we hear all the time from people who struggle with their landing pages. Although all these troubles seem ominous and diverse, they can all have the same solution: keywords.

Knowing how, when, where, and which keywords to use is critical for landing page success. Choosing the wrong keywords and placing them in the wrong areas are sure to sink your efforts. This chapter is all about keywords — where they're used, why, how, and when. If you want your landing page to succeed, take the time to read and re-read this chapter until you're sure you have down the basics of keywords.

Reviewing Keyword Basics

You won't get very far in your Internet business if you don't have a thorough understanding of keywords — what they are, how they're used, and when they're used. Choosing great keywords and placing them correctly on your landing page is critical for your success. Working with keywords isn't as complicated as some may have you believe, but it does take some work and knowledge of online keyword resources.

So what exactly are keywords? You can compare keywords to the ads you find in the phonebook's Yellow Pages. In the Yellow Pages, each profession or service is divided into categories, such as plumbers, real estate, hairdressers, and so on. Keywords divide the Internet world in much the same way. With search engines, search for *plumbers* and get the results associated with that keyword, similar to flipping through pages.

The trick is you need to choose the correct keywords for the search engines to place you in the right category for searchers to find you. This doesn't always happen. For example, you can do a search for *plumbers* and get results for sugar plumb fairies, plumb pudding, apple plumb, and more. Tuning your keywords so that search engines find you and your product can be a real undertaking.

Whether you know it, keywords are integrated into every part of your online experiences, from the time you look up a site to when you actually buy a product. Landing pages are full of keywords; strategically placed to maximize search engine effectiveness. Keywords are what attract the right visitors to your Web site — those visitors who are most likely going to be buyers.

Time for a few keyword-related definitions you need under your belt before going further. The distinction between them can sometimes be difficult to identify. *Keywords* typically refer to the words used when a user performs a search. So, for instance, if you used a search engine and typed in **plumbers**, your keyword is obviously *plumbers*. The search engine can then display those sites that match this keyword. The problem is how many results are returned for the broad search *plumbers?* Thousands? Millions? To break down this monolith into more manageable chunks, folks came up with two subcategories — and two new terms:

- ✔ *Short-tail keywords:* Short tail refers to using several distinct words with your search engine. So, instead of searching for *plumbers,* search for *Seattle plumbers* or *cheap plumbers.* The search engine tries to match the keyword phrase with Web sites associated with the keyword phrase. The more specific the keyword phrase, the more focused the search results.

- ✔ *Long-tail keyword:* One step beyond the keyword phrase is the long-tail keywords. Long-tail keywords involve longer phrases, with as many as five or six words. Long-tail keywords can be quite specific — as in *Seattle plumbers using green technologies.* That specificity can be used to your advantage because if your site consistently ends up being a match for a long-tail search, it might not mean tons of traffic, but you'll draw focused and qualified traffic, which can, of course, lead to more conversions. Additionally, long-tail keywords can be cheaper in terms of advertising because you may have lots of competition for the words but less competition for the long-tail keyword phrase. You can find more information on advertising in Chapter 16.

Benefiting from long-tail keywords

While on the topic of short- and long-tail keywords, we should clearly highlight the benefits of using them. Essentially, the long-tail keyword expands upon a core — a more general keyword or short-tail keyword — and as a result becomes more specific. But how does this help?

First off, long-tail keywords aren't as competitive as general keywords. By *competitive,* we mean the longer the phrase, the less people are typically bidding on that keyword phrase. For example, lots of people may be using the *digital cameras* short-tail keywords, but far less are using *Nikon D90 Black SLR Digital Camera.* Those using the long-tail keyword have likely already done their research and are looking to buy, so if a search on *Nikon D90 Black SLR Digital Camera* leads to your site, you have a good chance at a conversion. You can see a few more examples in Table 13-1.

Table 13-1	Search Engine Options
Short-Tail Keyword	*Long-Tail Keyword*
Antique guns	Buying antique guns in California
Snowshoes	Repairing Arctic X snowshoes
Travel maps	Free detailed travel maps
MP3 players	Apple iPods under $200
Flower shows	Flower shows in Western Idaho

You get the idea. The more you focus your keywords, the less searches result in your site but those that do result are more specific. This means that visitors aren't coming to your landing page to shop but to buy. Long-tail keywords may bring in less traffic, but they can have a very positive impact on your conversions with less traffic. This is the second key advantage of long-tail keywords. Folks who search with long-tail keywords are more likely to know exactly what they want. Your landing page can respond if you can match the keywords.

Understanding the connection between keywords and search engines

To understand how keywords work, you need a basic understanding of how search engines typically work. In this section, we give you an overview of how search engines do their stuff. Admittedly, this is only a quick summary, but it gives you a good idea of the connection between keywords and search engines.

The inner workings of search engines can be pretty complicated, but because we're keeping things simple, think of search engines as consisting of three constituent parts: the seeking software (often termed *spiders* or *bots*), the indexing component, and the searching software:

- ✔ **Seeking software:** Search engines use seeking software to collect information about Web sites it finds on the Internet. This seeking software, known as *spiders* or *bots,* looks for keywords on your landing page and indexes your page with others with the same keywords. This is why your keywords have to be dead on. You need the search engine spiders to find your keywords to index you correctly. If don't use the right keywords for your site, searchers will have a hard time finding you.

- ✔ **Indexing component:** Search engine indexes are huge collections of associated Web sites. That is, spiders send the content they find to the indexes, and the search engines categorize it with keywords.

- ✔ **Searching software:** The spiders and the search engine index are invisible to the Internet searcher, but the searching software isn't. The searching software refers to the actual interface of the search engine; it's where you type the search to be performed. The search goes to the index where results are returned based on the keyword search.

When you conduct a search, the search engine doesn't go out and search the Internet. Rather, it goes to the index and returns results from there. This is why making sure you're in the search engine index is so important. Read Chapter 14 for more information on the workings of search engines and indexing.

Searching basics

Internet users search in different ways. For some, a simple search is enough, but others often use advanced search features to get desired search results. When you're choosing keywords, which we discuss in the following section, it's often necessary to understand the different ways in which users can search. Table 13-2 discusses some of the different search types.

Table 13-2	Search Engine Options
Search Option	*Description*
Basic search	Common search where no parameters are used. Keywords can be any of the words used in a basic search. An example is *drum lessons.* Results are returned for both words.

Search Option	Description
Excluding words in searches with −	Using the − sign right before a word excludes that word from the search results. This is sometimes done if you need to exclude pages that include a specific word. Any word in your search query followed by − option is ignored.
Exact searches with +	The + symbol identifies a search for the exact keyword as it's typed into the search engine. The + sign is put directly before the word so the engine looks exactly for that word. For example, in a Google search, several words are ignored, such as *and, or, the, how, I,* and similar words. These are considered *stop* words and are ignored by a Google search because they slow the search results. Maybe you need an entire phrase looked up, including the stop words. Maybe you're searching for a book called *How I Saved Money.* Without the + operator, Google sees this as *saved money,* but with the + sign before the phrase, the entire phrase is included in the query.
Phrase search using double quotations ("")	By placing a keyword phrase within quotations, the entire long-tail keyword phrase is in the search. Whereas the phrase *green solutions for business* looks for all words contained in the string regardless of order, the phrase *"green solutions for business"* looks only for sites that use that exact phrase.

As we mention in Table 13-2, certain words are commonly excluded in a basic search. *Stop words,* such as *a, the, at,* or *for,* in phrases are often ignored, and each search engine has a list of them. If you use stop words in your keywords, be sure they're being recognized. If you sell a product that has a title with stop words, be aware that it may impact your SEO traffic. Try using more keywords to attract a wider clientele.

Getting on the Right Keyword Track

Before you can place keywords all over your landing page or include them in your ad campaigns, you must first choose your keywords carefully. Your keywords have to be specific and representative of your landing page. When choosing your keywords, keep the following tips in mind:

✔ **Always choose your keywords with your potential customers in mind.** What are they searching for? What words are they using? What phrases? You have to know what keywords they're searching for to match them to those found on your landing page. You don't want to spend time using keywords that aren't being used by your potential customers because they'll never find you. Think like your visitors!

✔ **Use focused keywords and long-tail keywords.** The more focused your keywords, the more likely your site will receive focused and interested visitors — and the more likely your landing page will be a success. General keywords don't work on any level because they make it difficult to get a high search ranking and they don't tend to drive qualified traffic to your site. Long-tail keywords that become the targets for quite specific searches are key in attracting such qualified traffic.

✔ **Track down the keywords your potential customers are using.** When we talk about landing page optimization, part of the process is knowing the words and phrases people use when they search. The keywords that searchers really use form the basis of your landing page marketing strategy. *These* keywords attract qualified visitors to your site rather than the words you tend to use or the words you surmise others use. If you don't find the words your potential customers actually use when thinking of your product, all your keyword-building efforts will be for naught.

With that out of the way, you can start choosing the best keywords for you. That's to say, choosing precisely those words as keywords that your potential customers use.

Picking the Right Keywords for Your Landing Page

Okay, you're finally ready to choose your keywords. Work through the process in a methodical fashion, and as such, we've come up with a five-part exercise to help you choose the best keywords. (No need to thank us; we're just naturally nice guys.) As an example, assume you're creating a landing page to sell that perennial favorite — the better mouse trap.

Step 1: Identifying a general short-tail keyword (and then expanding it)

For the sake of this example, imagine that you have a truly better mouse trap and you want as many folks as possible to come to your mouse trap-selling Web site and buy your amazing new product. You've determined, however, that using the keyword *mouse trap* as part of your marketing strategy is a non-starter, simply because *mouse trap* is far too general and does absolutely nothing to help you get on that highly desired first page of search engine results.

After you've made a list of short keywords that you think apply to your landing page, expand on those keywords. Using a keyword tool is a great way to do this. Although several keyword tools are available online — easily findable with any search engine — we use the Google Keyword Tool, as shown in Figure 13-1, to create a comprehensive keyword list.

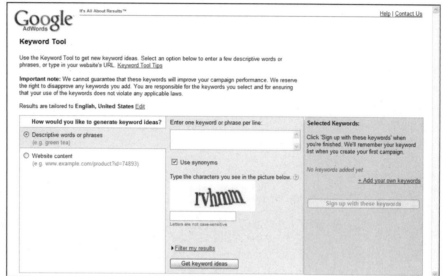

Figure 13-1:
The Google
Keyword
Tool.

Using the Google Keyword Tool is a snap. All you need to do is point your Web browser to `https://adwords.google.com/select/ KeywordToolExternal` and type in the keyword you want use as the basis for a generated listing. Continuing with the mouse trap example, you'd type **mouse trap** into the Google Keyword Tool and then click the Get Keyword Ideas button. The results of the search display additional keyword phrases, _competition level_ (how many others are using that keyword), and search volume around _mouse trap,_ as shown in Figure 13-2.

By using the Keyword Tool, you've identified several other keywords associated with the phrase _mouse trap — make mouse traps, live mouse traps, humane mouse traps,_ and many more. By using the Google Keyword Tool, you've identified many other keywords from which you can choose.

Notice in Figure 13-2, the difference between the search volume figures for _mouse trap_ as opposed to _mouse traps._ In one month, _mouse trap_ was searched over 300,000 times, whereas _mouse traps_ was searched just over 40,000. That's a huge difference. Deciding whether keywords should be plural or singular can have a huge impact on your keywords.

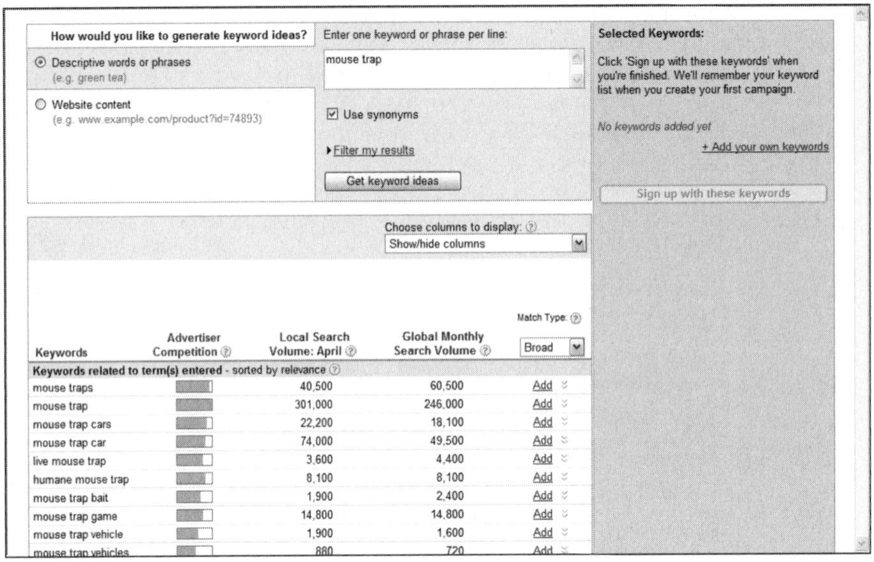

Figure 13-2:
The Google
Keyword
Tool results
for *mouse
trap.*

Step 2: Identifying associated keywords

Even though you've managed to expand your original keyword pool, your research is far from complete. Time to find relevant keywords one would associate with *mouse trap* but wouldn't necessarily contain *mouse* and/or *trap*. Most keyword tools allow you to search for other relevant keywords. The Google Keyword Tool adds an Additional Keywords to Consider section, which is performed automatically with your initial search. Figure 13-3 shows the additional keyword results with the Google Keyword Tool.

So, you started with a general *mouse trap* keyword term. You expanded your keyword pool with the Google Keyword Tool and then you broadened your keyword scope further to include keywords related to *mouse trap* but not necessarily using those exact words. *Pest control, rodent traps, mice traps,* and *rodent control* are all somewhat related to *mouse trap*. You're well on your way to a vibrant, muscular keyword set.

Step 3: Researching your related keywords

If you've followed along so far, you have a pretty robust list of related keywords scoped out for you. Time to crank up the Google Keyword Tool one more time, so you can research all the related terms you dug up in Step 2. If you plugged in, say, *rodent,* you'd get the results shown in Figure 13-4.

Perform a keyword search using each of your related keyword terms. This includes, *pest control, humane trap, live trap,* and so on. After that, compile all this information into one handy listing.

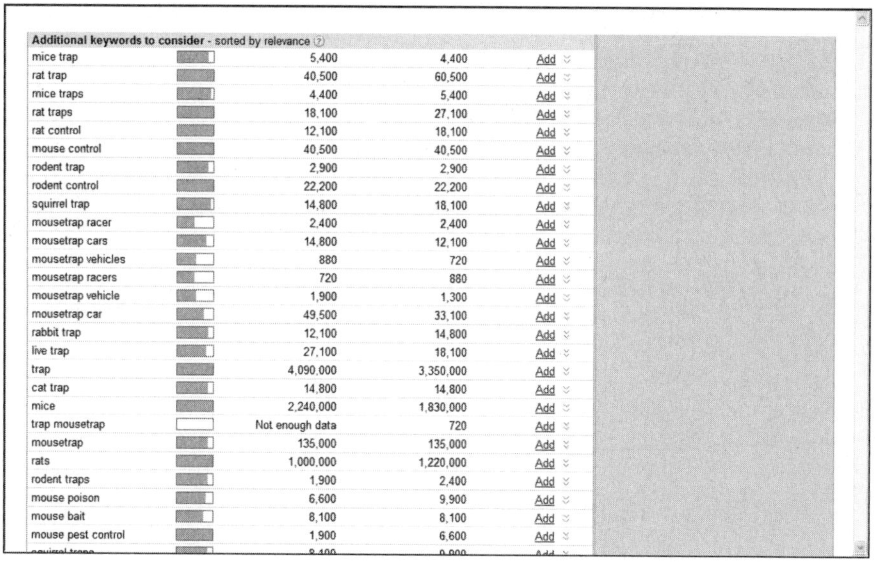

Figure 13-3:
Related keywords for *mouse trap.*

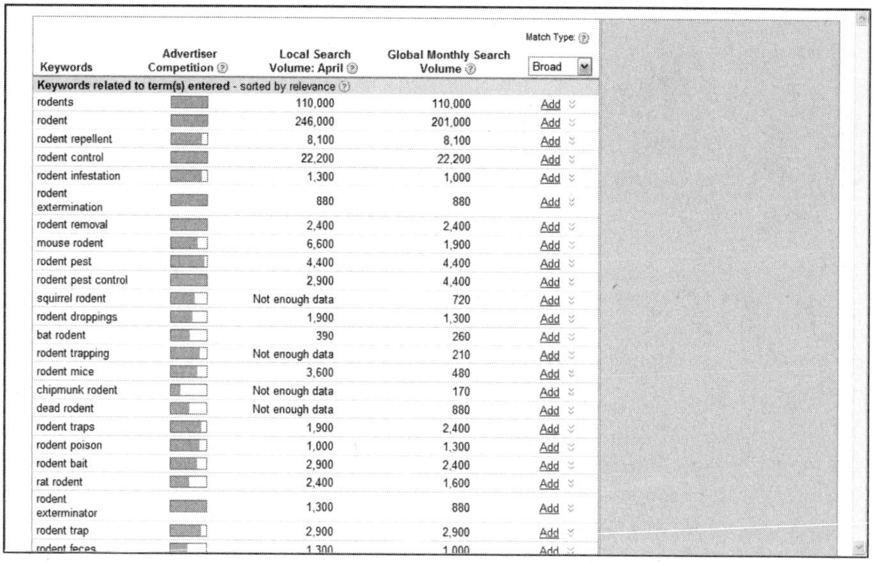

Figure 13-4:
Google keywords search for *rodent.*

Step 4: Putting it all together

After all this research, you're finally ready to put your work into a table or index, such as the one shown in Table 13-3. Essentially, all your research is gathered and displayed in an easy-to-read table.

Spreadsheets also work well for displaying your results.

Table 13-3	Keyword Index for Mouse Trap		
Mouse Trap	*Rodent*	*Rat*	*Mice*
Live mouse trap	Rodent extermination	Rat trap	Mice poison
Humane mouse trap	Rodent repellant	Humane rat traps	Mice repellant
Humane mouse traps	Humane rodent control	Live rat trap	Mice traps
Mouse rat trap	Rodent traps	Electronic rat trap	Mice control
Best mouse trap	Rodent bait	Mouse rat trap	Kill mice
Make mouse trap	Rodent infestation	Rat trap glue	Mice extermination

Ideally, you want a keyword with high searches and low competition. We discuss the reasons for this in Chapter 16. Basically, the less competition for a keyword, the better chance you have at a great ranking and the less it'll cost you for marketing.

Step 5: Choosing your best keywords

After you make your table or index, you can begin to pick your keywords. The ones you choose to focus on are based on many factors, including search relevance, search volume, and competition. You may find that while creating your keyword index table, you notice a trend or two. In Table 13-3, for example, *humane* and *live* sometime crop up in searches that involve trapping rodents. If you have a mouse trap that's humane and doesn't harm the rodents, this can be emphasized with your keywords, which could mean more visitors coming to your site.

If you don't take the time to complete a keyword index similar to what you see in Table 13-3, you'll have no idea what your potential visitors are searching for. With the table and research you've put together, you can pinpoint which keywords would be most effective as part of your landing page text and your ads in order to draw people to your site.

Still, how do you choose the keywords to go with? For the answer to that, we have a variant to Table 13-3 — one that adds in the statistics for monthly search volume advertiser competition. The stats, as shown in Table 13-4, are conveniently provided by the Google Keyword Tool.

Table 13-4	Keyword Search Volume for Mouse Trap	
Mouse Trap	*Monthly Search Volume*	*Competition*
Live mouse trap	3,600	High
Humane mouse trap	8,100	Medium
Humane mouse traps	2,400	High
Mouse rat trap	880	Medium
Best mouse trap	3,600	Medium
Make mouse trap	3,000	Medium

In Table 13-4, you can see perhaps the keywords to focus on. The keyword phrase *humane mouse trap* has the highest search volume and a medium level of advertiser competition. If you were designing an online ad to drive traffic to your landing page based on this information, your ad copy should include the phrase *humane mouse trap*. This phrase should also appear in the landing page in the heading or definitely in the fold area.

Search volumes are dynamic; they change over time. This means that to be really on top of your game, you need to review the keywords you're using every month or every other month. Rebuild your table to see whether they still apply.

Placing Keywords in Your Landing Page

After you decide on your optimized set of keywords, you still need to decide where they go on your landing page. In this section, we provide a quick overview of where to put those keywords on your page. Your choices are as follows:

✔ **Your URL:** It's great to have keywords in your URL. Using the example from earlier, www.humanemousetrap.com would be excellent indeed. This, of course, isn't always possible, but if you can squeeze keywords into the URL, it can make a big difference in terms of indexing for search engines and appealing to potential visitors.

✔ **Your landing page headings:** You're sure to have headings throughout your landing page. You probably won't use the keywords in all secondary headings, but your main heading within the fold should contain the keywords. The search engines are going to notice it, and having the right keywords in your main headings lets your visitors know right away that they're on the right site. Main headings for your mouse trap landing page may look like:

> Introducing the New *Humane Mouse Trap* 5000

> Finally, an Effective *Humane Mouse Trap*

✔ **In your initial paragraph:** The first paragraph on your landing page is typically shorter text, but it should display your keywords prominently. For instance:

> Getting rid of *mice* and *rats* safely and humanely has never been easier than with the *Humane Mouse Trap* 5000, the ultimate *mouse and rat trap*. The *Humane Mouse Trap* 5000 is designed for *live rodent* extermination that uses sound waves to knock out *mice* and *rats* when they attempt to retrieve the *bait* inside.

Compare this example to the keywords presented in Table 13-3. We managed to use 16 keywords found in that table in our little paragraph. (We've italicized the keywords here to make them stand out a bit more.)

When you write your body copy, headings, and other content for your landing page, keep an eye on the table index of keywords you created. These are the words and phrases you want peppered throughout your site. Having a detailed keyword table makes it easy to write your copy because you already know the language you need to use.

✔ **Keywords in body text:** In addition to the opening paragraph, your landing page is sure to have body text. Your keyword phrases need to find their way into this text as well. The trick is to include the keywords without saturating the page with them. Always remember, you're writing for the readers first and the search engines second, so make your text readable. Don't make the mistake of just making your text a keyword mess to appeal to search engines. An example of keywords being used (judiciously) in the body text is provided below. Keywords are again in italics.

> The *Humane Mouse Trap* 5000 is the last *mouse trap* you'll ever need. It's a safe *rodent extermination* device that ensures your home will be free from *mice, rats,* and other *rodents*. The *Humane Mouse Trap* 5000 operates as both a *live trap* allowing you to *trap rodents* and relocate them or as an effective *extermination* device. The choice is yours. The *Humane Mouse Trap* 5000 is the number one *mouse trap* recommended by exterminators for its ease of use, low cost, and effectiveness at ridding your environment of *mice,*

rats, and other pests. The *Humane Mouse Trap* 5000 is perhaps the most *humane trap* on the market, not relying on *glue,* electric shock, *poison,* or other painful methods of *extermination.* With the *Humane Mouse Trap* 5000, you won't need to see or handle dead or potentially diseased *rodents.*

As you can see in this example, the keywords identified in Table 13-3 are well represented. Search engines and visitors will love this.

✔ **Keywords in testimonials:** The purpose of testimonials is to be a voice that potential customers can relate to. This makes the testimonial area an ideal place for keywords. Now, don't think we're saying that it's okay to come up with fake testimonials that feature your favorite keywords because we're not. Fake testimonials are sleazy, pure and simple. But you can encourage those giving you a testimonial to include some of your keywords. We include a sample here:

> "Three months ago we had *mice* and *rats* all over the house. We tried many different *mouse traps* for *mice control,* but nothing worked. That is until we found the *Humane Mouse Trap* 5000 advertised online. Not only was the *Humane Mouse Trap* 5000 effective and a fraction of the cost of other traps, but also the option to allow *live* capture and release made our children feel better. We highly recommend the *Humane Mouse Trap* 5000."

> — Mickey Mouse

Doesn't that make you feel like buying the Humane Mouse Trap 5000? It's effective, kids love it, it's cheap, and it promises to make your life rodent-free.

✔ **Keywords in your HTML:** So far, we've outlined strategies that place keywords in front of visitors on your landing page, but keywords can also work quietly for you in the background of your site. Keywords are often placed in *meta tags,* which are special parts of your HTML code that can be used to carry information that can be read by browsers or other applications. Three meta tags of note for keywords include the TITLE tags, DESCRIPTION tags, and ALT tags. Placing keywords in these areas of your HTML code allows the search engines to crawl through your code looking for relevant keywords that they can use to index you and your product. We cover working with meta tags and HTML in Chapter 14.

Placing Keywords in Your Advertising

Placing keywords in your landing page is one thing, but you can't forget about keywords in your online advertising. Google, Yahoo!, and MSN Bing each have online advertising opportunities. Each of these companies have its own rules, guidelines, and payment schedules for online ads (see Chapter 16), but one thing in common is that the ads work best when keywords are used when writing your ad.

Your campaign is up and running with your ads showing on the search and/ or content network for people to see. (The *search network* is when ads are displayed on the search engine results pages, whereas the *content network* has your ads displayed on other Web sites.) Both networks are effective but attract a different type of visitor.

In your Internet browsing, you have more than likely noticed those online ads that appear on the page of any search results screen. If performing a Google search, you'd notice advertising on the right side of the page. The ads that appear with search engine results are part of the search network online marketing strategy. *Search network* refers to ads that appear with browser results, which is in contrast to the *content network* marketing strategy in which your ads are placed directly on Web sites. You've likely seen both content and search network online ads in your surfing; you've also more than likely noticed that the ads are related (or at least should be) to the search that you conducted. For example, Figure 13-5 shows the ad results from a Google search for *mouse trap.* You can also use Yahoo! or MSN to get an idea of how the search performed is related to the ad results displayed on a page.

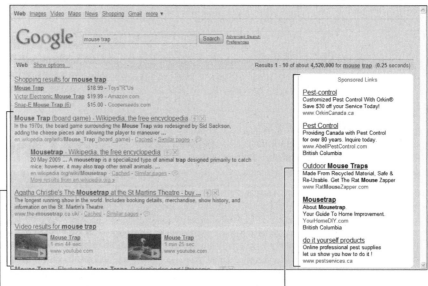

Figure 13-5:
Google ad results for a *mouse trap* search.

Search results   Ad results

Each ad listed in Figure 13-5 is written slightly different. If you plan to include online advertising in you landing page optimization strategy, and we encourage you to do just that, take the time to have a critical look over other competitive ads. How are they written? What words are used? What font is used? All this information can help you craft your online ad. Table 13-5 compares and contrasts the ad results for *mouse trap* with the results from a Google search engine. (Note that not all ad types appear in Figure 13-5.)

Table 13-5	Competitive Analysis for Mouse Trap Ads	
Ad	*Pros*	*Cons*
Pest Control Make the switch from pesticides. It's safe and easy for everyone `spcpweb.org/ yards`	*Pest control* is a related keyword to *mouse trap*.	No strong keywords, such as *mouse, mice,* or *rodent,* used in title or description.
Mouse Trap About Mouse trap. Your Guide To Home Improvement. `YourHomeDIY.com`	Uses the keyword *mouse trap* in the title and the description.	Links keyword *mouse trap* with home improvement. Home improvement is not a related keyword to mouse trap. The URL is a DIY and not related to mouse traps.
Live Mouse Trap Find Shopping Deals at Yahoo! Low Prices On Live Mouse trap `shopping.yahoo. com`	Great title; attracts people looking for mouse traps or rodent control.	Seems to be a bait and switch. Title is related, but description talks about a Yahoo! shopping site.
Do It Yourself Products Online professional pest supplies Let us show you how to do it! `www.pest services.ca`	Pretty good URL, `www. pestservices.ca`; could have something to do with mouse traps.	Horrible title and description. Seemingly unrelated to the keyword search.
Mouse Trap Find Mouse traps! Household Rodent Control Info. `pestcontrol. statusclean.com`	Great title, description, and URL. Easily identifiable keywords that are likely matched on their landing page.	No real obvious downside to the ad.
Super-Trap.com (pest) Offering different kinds of traps; control bird, pigeon, mouse, mole, and rat. `www.super-trap. com`	Great title and description. URL uses product name. Great use of keywords.	No real obvious downside to the ad.

Now that you have reviewed some ads for mouse traps, you can write your own, trying to incorporate what was good about some ads while making sure you don't duplicate the mistakes in other ads. Once again refer to Table 13-3 when you identify your keywords for your ad. Here's an example of a potential ad:

Humane Mouse traps

Trap live or *exterminate*

Effective household *rodent control*

`www.HumaneMousetrap5000.com`

As you can see from this ad example, many of the keywords found in the keyword index from Table 13-3 are represented. Because the ad focuses on the keywords and related keywords, it has a better chance of driving qualified traffic to your landing page. The ad leaves no doubt about where the link will take them, which can do a lot to increase conversions.

Reviewing Online Keyword Tools

Several online tools can help make your keyword research a little easier. You may find that one tool doesn't do everything you need, and you require a combination of tools.

We strongly recommend that you take the time to review each of the tools discussed here. The more versatile you are with the tools, the better you'll be to work with your keywords. In no particular order, some of the tools include

- ✔ **Google Keyword Tool:** The Google Keyword Tool is great for finding niche keywords. The results of the tool include search volumes and competitive analysis for keywords. The Google Keyword Tool is widely used for both PPC (pay per click) campaigns and SEO (search engine optimization).

    `https://adwords.google.com/select/KeywordToolExternal`

- ✔ **Wordtracker:** Wordtracker has been around for over ten years and is a proven keyword tool. Wordtracker isn't a free utility, but it does offer a 7-day free trial. Wordtracker provides keyword suggestions and competition on keywords.

    `www.wordtracker.com`

- ✔ **goRank SEO tools:** goRank analyzes sites for keyword density. You place your URL in the search area, and it returns details on word usage and keyword phrases. You can use this to examine your site or a competitor's site to see which keywords they're using. Figure 13-6 shows the results of search with goRank.

    `www.gorank.com/analyze.php`

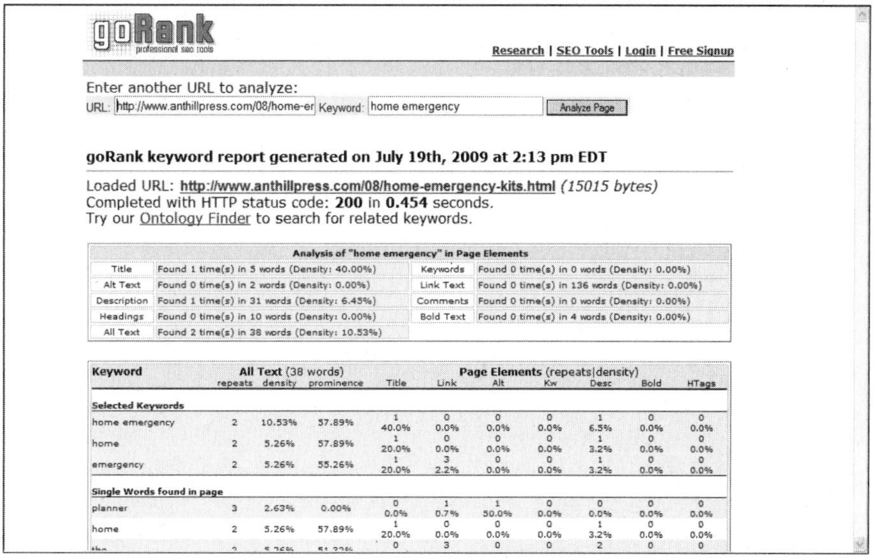

Figure 13-6:
Keyword query using goRank.

> ✔ **SEO Chat Keyword Density Tool:** Another useful tool used to test the keyword density of your site against that of a competitor's site.

```
www.seochat.com/seo-tools/keyword-density
```

These are just a few of the tools you can find online. Do a search and you can find many others. Bookmark a few of them and figure out to use them. They'll be your best friends.

Chapter 14

Understanding Search Engine Marketing

*Y*ou have lots of choices when it comes to getting the word out about your landing page. You can use ad campaigns, blogs, social networking sites, and many offline methods, including radio and magazine ads. Still, when all is said and done, search engine marketing is one of the most effective methods of advertising and visitor recruitment.

Search engines can be a powerful tool for attracting new visitors to your landing page, but search engine marketing isn't always easy and, quite honestly, it doesn't always attract the types of visitors you want. For now — and for a good while to come — search engines are going to remain an important part of your landing page marketing strategy. As such, you're going to need to understand a little of how search engines work and what it takes to get ranked high in search results.

This chapter's all about search engine marketing and optimizing your search engine marketing efforts. Here, you get an overview of search engines — how they work and how you can apply that knowledge to optimizing your landing page.

Understanding Search Engine Marketing

You're probably familiar with online search engines and — directly or indirectly — with search engine marketing (SEM). SEM refers to the various techniques you can use to drive traffic to your web site from search engines. Three common strategies include Pay Per Click advertising (PPC), Search Engine Optimization (SEO), and search engine submission.

Most successful online businesses incorporate these three strategies into their overall online business plans. This only makes sense because search engines are an important component to your online marketing efforts. However, many companies use SEM as their only real online marketing effort, erroneously assuming that high search engine ranking is the holy grail of online marketing. We can't stress enough that search engines are only one avenue for you to draw traffic to your landing page — and sometimes that traffic isn't even the best traffic to draw to your landing page. In fact, relying solely on SEM may be your downfall.

So why spend so much of this chapter on SEM? Without question, SEM represents an important source for new visitors to arrive at your landing page. If you sell baseball cards, you're probably going to think it's great when someone searches online for *baseball cards,* sees your landing page in the search engine results, and visits your site. However, one of the myths that surrounds search engine marketing is that most new Web site visits begin and end with SEM. This simply isn't true. To use the baseball card example, a good amount of new visitors are probably arriving at the landing page by typing the URL directly into the browser, by using online ad links such as Google AdWords, or by following links from other sites rather than by using online search engines. So, what does all this mean? You have to keep SEM in perspective; it's one element to your marketing campaign and not your entire marketing plan.

However, we can think of a number of reasons why SEM continues to play an important role in your landing page marketing strategy. The following list includes a few of these reasons:

- According to comScore, an organization that measures behavior in a digital environment, nearly 15 billion core searches were conducted per month in 2009. That's a lot of people looking online.

- SEM remains one of the cheapest forms of marketing. Other marketing avenues (such as click and offline ads) cost, and sometimes, they cost big.

- Repeat business and visitors is one thing, but SEM provides a strong strategy for bringing new visitors to your site. SEM provides access to a worldwide market from which you can pull visitors to your site.

✔ For many people, researching products, gathering information, or comparison shopping begins with the search engine. That simple fact of online life underscores the importance of SEM more than anything else.

Crawling, indexing, and sitemaps

Have you ever wondered how search engines find out about your site? They do so through an automated process in which software programs — known as *spiders* or *bots* — constantly survey the Internet, on the lookout for fresh data. This data is then analyzed and used to create a search engine index. So, when you search for something, the search engine looks to its index — rather than to the vast Internet as such — to retrieve the information. The search engine returns the best results from this index.

Although the concept of these roving information-gathering spiders is quite ingenious, they aren't without flaws. Knowing these flaws enables you to create a landing page that has a better chance of being identified in the index and therefore, displayed in the search results.

Spiders and bots are limited by what they've been programmed to do; they expect a certain kind of landing page, and when they come up against something unexpected, they might have trouble gathering the correct information. When this happens, certain parts of a landing page are essentially skipped over and don't get indexed. In the following section, we review how to verify whether your landing page is being properly indexed.

So, what areas cause spiders and bots to skip a beat? Two that instantly come to mind are Flash animation and JavaScript. Flash animation is commonly used on landing pages to attract visitors because it tends to be eye-catching and sometimes edgy. In our studied opinion, Flash animation really isn't all it's cracked up to be, and its ability to throw a monkey wrench in the indexing process is just another example of why you shouldn't use it on landing pages. Okay, we admit, some improvements have been made in Flash technology that make Flash content a bit more visible to indexing software, but when push comes to shove, spiders and bots still don't reliably index it. The same is true for JavaScript; when you use JavaScript drop-down lists or other features, the text isn't necessarily indexed. The obvious solution to these cases is to add actual text links somewhere on the page to accommodate the spiders.

Those spiders and bots have undoubtedly visited your landing page at some point in the past, but do you know how well your site is being indexed? You may not be appearing high in search results simply because something on your landing page isn't working with the index crawlers. To test with Google, type **site:yourdomainname.com** in the Google search bar.

The results from this query correspond to the index results from your domain. For example, Figure 14-1 shows the Google results screen when you run the `site: justmakeiteasy.com` search.

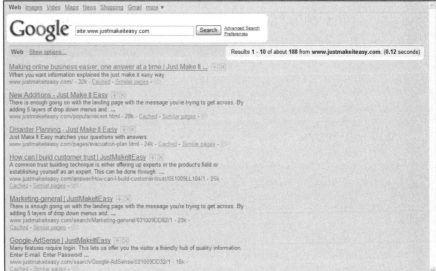

Figure 14-1:
Indexed results from the Google search engine.

In Figure 14-1, the search returned 188 index references from `justmake iteasy.com`. (Of course, this number may change by the time you read this book.) From this result, it seems that the Google engine has done a pretty good job of creating an index for this particular site. But does Yahoo!? Figure 14-2 shows the results from a Yahoo! index search with `site: justmakeiteasy.com`. In case you get a different result, there are two ways to enter the command: `site: justmakeiteasy.com` and `site:justmakeiteasy.com`. Notice one has a space after site: and one doesn't; each gets a different screen to view. Figure 14-2 was taken with the space in there.

Notice in Figure 14-2, Yahoo! displays fewer than half of the index pages than the Google search — 67 compared to 180. Why is this? This can happen for many reasons, but it may be that the type of indexing Yahoo! does isn't as friendly to this site as the Google indexing. (Yes, sorry to say, each search engine uses its own proprietary indexing scheme, and no, they'll never spill the beans about how they've programmed their own indexing software.) Worse still are the results from the MSN search engine, which returned a mere 16 indexed pages.

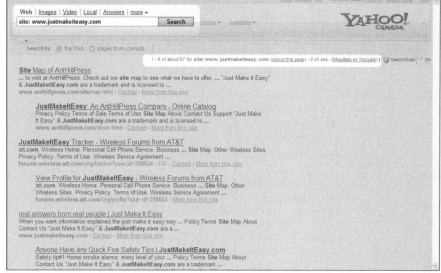

So what can you do if most of your pages aren't being indexed with the various search engines? Clean up your landing page and wait for the spiders and bots to find you. This approach may seem passive, but trust us — it does work. Later in this chapter, we talk about specific strategies for fine-tuning your landing page so that it's more search engine friendly.

Deciding on your search engine focus

Google, Yahoo!, MSN, AOL — we don't need to tell you that a lot of Internet search engines are out there. Do you need to focus your attentions on them all? If not, which ones are the most important?

Figures 14-1 and 14-2 show what's at stake here. Different search engines search differently, and some search engines may love your landing page, whereas others may seem decidedly disinterested. (The figures show a big difference in one particular performed search — `site: justmakeiteasy.com` — between Google and Yahoo!.)

Which leads us to a hard truth: You can't please everyone all the time but you should please the ones that matter. Each month, comScore identifies top search engine usage for the month on its Web site. For March and April of 2009, we provide the stats in Table 14-1.

Table 14-1	Search Engine Usage Percentages	
Search Engine	*March 2009 Usage (%)*	*April 2009 Usage (%)*
Google	63.7	64.2
Yahoo!	20.5	20.4
Microsoft search sites (MSN)	8.3	8.2
Ask.com Network	3.8	3.8
AOL	3.7	3.4

In Table 14-1, Google is far and away the most used search engine, with Yahoo! a distant second. The rest trickle down from there. These statistics clearly show that you need to be indexed well in both Google and Yahoo! to be successful in acquiring search engine traffic. The question then becomes, how do you get your pages into the Google and Yahoo! search engine systems? For that, you need to know a little bit about submitting an XML sitemap — which, curiously enough, we discuss in the following section.

Submitting an XML sitemap

Okay, say you've created a brilliant landing page, but unfortunately, no one knows about it. You need to make your site more visible to search engines. One way of doing this is with the help of a sitemap. The *sitemap* is an XML (Extensible Markup Language) file that allows you to get the word out about your Web site to search engines and (hopefully) increase your indexing.

There is often confusion about sitemaps, mainly because most Web sites have two of them:

✔ **The visible sitemap:** This sitemap can be found in the footer or bottom of most sites and acts as a shortcut to important links in the Web site such as Policies, Contact, and About Us pages.

✔ **The XML sitemap:** The second is the hidden sitemap specifically designed for search engines. This hidden sitemap is not accessible to regular Web site viewers, as it is an XML file that is uploaded to your Web server, where your actual Web site is hosted. The sitemap works behind the scenes, letting the search engines know where your Web pages are found. (Locating the sitemap is discussed later in the chapter.)

Why are sitemaps so important? Traditionally, when a search engine visits your site it follows the clickable links within your Web site. If you do not use an XML sitemap your special pages, such as independent landing pages, can be missed.

Using XML sitemaps is essential if you want search engines to index your site properly, especially if your landing page is heavy with JavaScript or Flash animations, as this adds a level of navigational difficulty for search engines.

The sitemap file becomes a roadmap that the search bots can follow to navigate your site. Fortunately, XML sitemaps aren't too difficult to create but keep in mind that site maps are not something you can just throw together. The major search engines have combined their efforts in the matter of sitemaps to set up a consistent format, having established rules and formatting that must be adhered to. For example, Google adheres to sitemap Protocol 0.9 (shown in the code sample that follows). Visit `www.sitemaps.org/` to learn about the organization that oversees the protocols.

The sitemap can be broken into four parts:

- ✔ **The** `<urlset>` **and** `</urlset>` **tags:** These tags are used to define the start and end of the sitemap file and to indicate what Web site sitemap protocol you are using.

- ✔ **The** `<url>` **and** `</url>` **tags:** These tags are where the individual page information goes, including the tags holding the Web address, how often the page gets changed, and when it was last changed.

- ✔ **The** `<loc>` **and** `</loc>`**:** These tags represent where you place your Web page address. This address can be your main home page URL or a specific page destination.

- ✔ **Variables:** The remaining tags on the page are more flexible. They are the specific tags that indicate how often you change the page, when you changed it last and what priority you place on the page importance over others in your site.

These tags are unique to every page on your site. For example, if you have a blog, your home page gets updated regularly therefore you might want to change the <changefreq> tag to daily instead of weekly. This tells the search engine where to find new information on your site — so instead of looking everywhere, it checks that page out first.

Check out how all the tags look in action:

```
<urlset xmlns="http://www.justmakeiteasy.com/schemas/sitemap/0.9">

<url>
      <loc> http://www.justmakeiteasy.com</loc>
      <changefreq>Weekly</changefreq>
      <priority>0.5</priority>
</url>
<url>
      <loc>http://www.justmakeiteasy.com/answer/What-does-it-mean-by-above-the-
              fold-when-someone-is-talking-about-a-web-page/020909LL1/1</loc>
      <lastmod>2009-03-06T12:16:27-07:00</lastmod>
      <changefreq>Weekly</changefreq>
      <priority>0.5</priority>
</url>

  </urlset>
```

Search engines are smart. If you try to trick them into returning to your site more often by setting your modify date as "changing daily" or other cheats like changing the `<lastmod>` (last modify date) tag every day, they catch on quickly that the content doesn't really change. Table 14-2 reviews the tags used in an XML sitemap.

Table 14-2	Common Sitemap Tags
Sitemap Tags	*Function*
`<urlset>` `</urlset>`	Sitemap tags are confined with the `<urlset>` and `</urlset>`. They represent the beginning and ending of the sitemap.
`<url></url>`	The `<url>` tag is placed inside the `<urlset>` and holds all the information about each URL in your document. See preceding sample code.
`<loc></loc>`	This tag specifies the URL of the page. The format uses the complete URL address, including protocol, such as `http://www.justmakeiteasy.com`.
`<lastmod>` `</lastmod>`	Specifies the date when the file was last modified. The date format used is typically, YYYY-MM-DD.

Sitemap Tags	Function

`<changefreq>`
`</changefreq>`
	This tag identifies how frequently you'll have changes to your landing page. Your options for this parameter include
	`always`
	`hourly`
	`daily`
	`weekly`
	`monthly`
	`yearly`
	`never.`

`<priority>` `</priority>`	The `<priority>` tag identifies the priority level of URL pages on your landing page. Valid values range from 0.0 to 1.0.

Third-party sitemap creators

Okay, so maybe you don't want to take the time to create your own sitemap. The good news is you don't have to. Plenty of third-party XML sitemap creators are just dying to help you. Table 14-3 lists a few just to get you started, but a quick search online is sure to reveal many more.

Table 14-3   Sample of Third-Party XML Sitemap Creators

Vendor	URL Address
XML Sitemap Generator	`www.xml-sitemaps.com`
Google Sitemap Generator	`http://code.google.com/p/google sitemapgenerator/`
SiteMapBuilder.NET	`www.sitemapbuilder.net`
Coffee Cup Google SiteMapper	`www.coffeecup.com/google-sitemapper`
SitemapDoc	`http://sitemapdoc.com`
SitemapGenerators: A collection of sitemap tools	`http://code.google.com/p/sitemap-generators/wiki/SitemapGenerators`

Submitting XML sitemaps with Webmaster tools

By giving search engines more information on your pages, they know when they should come back and check your pages again. The major search engines have Webmaster tools that you can either use online or download to monitor what the search engines see and index. Webmaster tools, in essence, are really just a group of programs to help Web site owners get more out of the search engines; one of these tools is a sitemap submission tool. However, what tools you get differ from search engine to search engine.

You will have to signup and submit the sitemap web address to every search engine you use. This allows the search engines to know where to access the XML files. To reduce XML sitemap cheating, you may be required to place special code that the search engine provides on your site as well to verify that you're in fact the site owner. Table 14-4 shows where you can access the various Webmaster tools.

Table 14-4	Webmaster Tools
Vendor	*URL Address*
Google Webmaster Tools	`www.google.ca/webmasters/tour/tour1.html`
Yahoo! Site Explorer	`http://siteexplorer.search.yahoo.com`
bing Webmaster Center	`http://www.bing.com/webmaster`

After you have access to your Webmaster tools, you can submit your sitemap. From time to time, the search engines check your sitemap for new and exciting content that you've added.

Since the first question we're always asked is, "How do I place my sitemap in Google?" so here is a quick run through. You'd begin by registering for the Webmaster tools by following these steps.

1. **Sign into your Google account and then visit: `https://www.google.com/webmasters/tools/` to access your Google Webmaster tools.**

2. **Click the + Add a Site button located in the center of the page.**

3. **Type your Web site URL into the text box and click the Continue button.**

4. Verify you are the site owner.

Google provides the HTML code needed to verify your page. They also provide an example of how you would cut and paste the code into your home page.

After you have verified your account, your Webmaster tool account is now set up. While the next step is using the Sitemap tool, it's important to point out that you now have access to all the Webmaster tools,

Take the time to go through all the Webmaster tools now at your fingertips. Exciting tools like Pages Index, Crawl Errors, and Pages Not Found are great tools to help any Web site owner.

To use the Sitemap tool, follow these steps.

1. **Login to your Google Webmaster account at** `https://www.google.com/webmasters/tools/`.

2. **Click the name of the site you want to create a map for.**

3. **In the menu on the left, click the + Site Configuration button.**

   New menu options appear below the Site Configuration heading.

4. **Click the Sitemaps menu link.**

5. **Click the site + Submit a Sitemap button.**

6. **Enter the URL to your Sitemap file in the text box that appears.**

7. **Click the Submit Sitemap button.**

You're done! At some point, a Google search bot will visit your site and start indexing your pages. You can log in from time to time to check the status of how Google is doing at indexing your pages.

If for some reason there is an error with your sitemap, Google will indicate on this page of your Webmaster tools that there is a problem. Most problems are caused by poorly formatted XML content or by the fact that the site address you entered to where the sitemap is located is incorrect.

When using Webmaster tools, you can view valuable information on your site, including how often the bot checks your site, any broken links, short meta tags, or duplicate title tags. This is a great way to double-check your site for hidden problems.

Ranking and Search Engine Optimization

So, both Google and Yahoo! have what they need to index your site appropriately, and things seem pretty good. Or do they? Having your site properly indexed is a great first step, but then comes the whole *search engine optimization (SEO)* aspect. Why? Because typically the earlier a site link appears in the search results, the more likely it is that it will be clicked. If all your pages appear in the 20th and lower results, a relatively small percent of your potential audience is actually in a position to visit your site.

SEO refers to the strategies you use to increase your position in search results. Assuming surfers don't typically look past the first ten search results, your landing page would work a heck of a lot better if it appears on the first page of search results. Unfortunately, appearing on the first page of search results isn't always easy and largely depends on what your products or services are. If you sell wooden clogs, gravy boats, or used footwear, you probably have less competition than those selling real estate, lawyer services, software, and the like — meaning you stand a better chance of getting a great search result position.

Most have products and services that do have some competition. Therefore, you need to spend a bit of time on SEO. In this section, we review several areas to focus on when trying to get your landing page to the top of the charts.

Creating search-friendly landing pages

Maybe you've already created a landing page and are having trouble getting its search ranking higher, or maybe you're about to create a landing page and want to explore SEO before you start. Whatever the case may be, this section is for you.

Despite what you may read on the Internet, SEO can be tough work, requiring hours of testing and fine-tuning. Be wary of those companies or individuals who promise quick results that will supposedly get you to the top of the search order. Many of these companies can help in your SEO efforts, but some aren't worth your money. Additionally, you also need to make sure that they're using accepted SEO techniques. Every search engine has acceptable SEO usage guidelines. Violation of these guidelines can result in your domain being penalized, which could mean being assigned a low ranking or even removed from the index altogether.

For those who aren't going to rely on outside help, the following describes several things you can do to increase your own search results. However, some of the tips require knowledge of HTML. Those who've designed and written their own sites will have little problem with the content. However, if you need a refresher on HTML, we suggest picking up *HTML, XHTML & CSS For Dummies,* by Ed Tittel and Jeff Noble (Wiley). They're great guys, and their book is a terrific reference.

Using <TITLE> tags

The function of the <TITLE> tags within your landing page's HTML is to identify what to display in the browser's title bar. If you are not familiar with the browser Title bar, you can see it along the top of your screen with the Title itself showing in the top- left corner every time you open a Web browser. The <TITLE> tag is placed between the <HEAD> tags within your HTML landing page code, using the <TITLE> (beginning) and </TITLE> (ending) syntax.

The <HEAD> and end </HEAD> tags are used to contain the general information about your Web page that search engines look for. This area is special and includes your Meta tags, title tags, and other specialized HTML tags. The information stored inside the tags are not displayed in your actual Web page.

The information within the <TITLE> tag is quite important in an SEO context because search engines view the text within the <TITLE> tag and assume (correctly or incorrectly) that whatever's in <TITLE> tag is directly related to the content of your page. The <TITLE> tag should therefore contain keywords associated with the content of your site.

To see how all this lines up in the HTML code of a typical page, check out the following:

```
<HTML>
<HEAD>
<TITLE>How can I build customer trust -JustMakeItEasy</title>
</HEAD>
<BODY>
```

What does all this code look like in the search engine? Figure 14-3 shows how this <TITLE> tag appears in the search results.

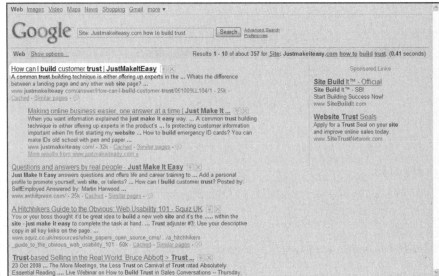

Figure 14-3:
The <TITLE>
tag in
search
results.

The following list brings together a few things to consider when you work with <TITLE> tags:

✔ **Make the content within the <TITLE> tags relevant to the content of the page.** If your page is about shoes, your <TITLE> tag better be shoe-related.

✔ **Test your <TITLE tag> by seeing what actually appears in the search engine.** The tag may not be formatted correctly within the HTML code and is therefore, not displayed.

✔ **Create a separate <TITLE> tag for each page within your site.** For landing pages with just a few pages, you may be tempted to use the same <TITLE> tag across all pages. Not a good choice. The title is the unique identifier for your Web page; it should indicate the information that is on the page. Also, search engines prefer unique identifiers for classifying your Web pages, so we recommend giving them what they want.

✔ **Don't use long <TITLE> tags.** Long tags aren't displayed in search results, and your text will be cut off. See what your tag looks like to surfers when they see it in the search engine.

Using <DESCRIPTION> tags

The <DESCRIPTION> tag informs search engines what the site is actually about. The <TITLE> tag is much shorter than the <DESCRIPTION> tag, with the <DESCRIPTION> tag often being several sentences or an entire paragraph. The <DESCRIPTION> tag is placed between the <HEAD> tags within your HTML landing page code using <DESCRIPTION> and </DESCRIPTION> syntax.

The <DESCRIPTION> tag is known as a <META> tag. The main goal of a meta description tag is to provide a brief description of a Web page. This information can be used by search engines or directories in cataloging your page.

A sample <DESCRIPTION> tag from a landing page is shown in the following code and in Figure 14-4, which shows how the HTML code appears in a search engine's results.

In Figure 14-4, you may have noticed that the description presented in the search is not an exact match to the one we have in our description. Google and other search engines display their *interpretation* of your description tags, often combining both description tags and content from your actual page. Does this mean you want to leave this tag out completely? Absolutely not. This is your opportunity to tell visitors what they will find when they visit your page.

```
<HEAD>
<TITLE>How can I build customer trust | JustMakeItEasy</title></HEAD>
<META name="description" content="A common trust building technique is either
           offering up experts in the product's field or establishing
           yourself as an expert. This can be done through: Blogging Writing
           articles Publishing a book Television YouTube ">
<BODY>
```

The following list highlights things to consider when you work with <DESCRIPTION> tags:

- ✔ **Make them relevant.** Search engines are going to respond far more positively to your site if the content in the <DESCRIPTION> tag is complete and relevant to the information within your landing page.

- ✔ **Ensure that you actually have a <DESCRIPTION> tag.** Commonly, you'll find pages with incomplete <DESCRIPTION> tags or lack them altogether.

✔ **Make them make sense.** Your <DESCRIPTION> tag is read by potential customers, so make the description they see interesting, accurate, and relevant to what they're searching for. Even if your content may be truncated by the search engines, it's best to be thorough to get as much of your message across as possible.

✔ **Create a separate <DESCRIPTION> tag for each page within your site.** This makes sense because the content for each page in your site is going to be different.

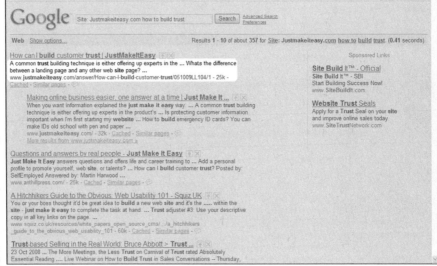

Figure 14-4:
A <DESCRIP
TION> tag
displayed
in Google
search
results.

Content, content, and a little more content

Search engines are big fans of actual content and so are your (human) visitors. The more content you have on your page, the more search engines can find — it's more likely that they can index you properly. How much content do you need? All pages need at least a few paragraphs, perhaps at least 250 words. Of course, there are always exceptions.

Additionally, be sure to keep your content highly focused. Visitors can get confused if you go off message, and if humans can get confused, you can bet that search engines can get confused as well. If your content is unfocused and all over the place, search engines are going to have more trouble understanding what the page is all about, which could lead to you ranking on a subject not related to your page at all. If this happens, you end up with traffic that's not really interested in the real thrust of your site, and uninterested traffic doesn't convert into paying customers.

Search engines love content as long as they can actually see it. We recently worked with a client who embedded much of his text in pictures and Flash presentations. This was pretty, no doubt, but the problem is that the search engines came by, shrugged their shoulders, and left. The content was largely invisible to them, hidden within the pictures and Flash.

Here are a few things to keep in mind when you use content on your landing page:

- **Update your site periodically with fresh content.** Fresh content makes your site appear active, which brings current visitors back for another look and attracts new visitors. Search engines love sites that update their content.

- **Wherever you put your content, try to periodically include keywords in your text.** However, you don't want to fall into the mindset in which you try to add content as if the search engine is your primary audience. In other words, don't just sprinkle keywords around that may appeal to the search engine but make the site less visitor friendly.

- **Search engines love to review the first few paragraphs of your page.** Make the first 25 or so words very targeted to your site; keywords and content should match.

- **Ensure that you don't have content hidden within Flash animations and images.** Such content can't be read by the search engine spiders and bots. Try as much as possible to eliminate Flash and replace images with readable text when appropriate.

- **Keep your content well-written and error-free.** Errors hamper readability for search engines and visitors.

After you have a better idea of how to display content on your page for search engines, we outline two things *not* to do with content. Both tactics — using hidden text and using duplicate content — are flagged by Google and Yahoo! as no-no's that shouldn't be incorporated on your page.

Hidden text is a strategy whereby text is included on your landing page that's visible only to the search engines. This is done by setting the font size to 0, hiding text behind images, or matching font color to the background. The technology works because the search engine definitely detects more relevant content for your indexing. However, Google and Yahoo! just aren't into Stupid SEO Tricks; if they detect hidden text, you may be removed from the Yahoo! and Google indexes altogether.

Using obvious duplicate content is also another dangerous area. All sites have duplicate content to some extent. For example, you may have printer-friendly versions of text on your sites articles. However, duplicate content can be used to trick search engines into thinking you have more content than there actually is. If Google or Yahoo! determine that you use repetitive and duplicate content to manipulate the search engines, you may be removed from their indexing.

Thanks to a new canonical tag introduced by Google, Yahoo!, and MSN this year, you can now tell the search engines which content you want them to mark as your primary content so that content such as the printer-friendly versions we mentioned above are not counted as primary content. SEO professionals everywhere have been waiting for a way to specify what URL the search engine should use and this new tag is the answer! The tag goes in the <HEAD> section of the page and looks like this:

```
<link rel="canonical" href="http://www.justmakeiteasy.com/
        index.php?Pageid=1232" />
```

Keywords

Keywords are an important part of SEO. Their job is to tie in the content from the landing page to the search and the search results. We cover developing correct keywords in detail in Chapter 13, so for now, we're concerned with keyword placement. You know they have to be on the page, but where should they go and how often should you use them?

Keyword placement doesn't have any real hard and fast rules, but always remember that you're writing for the visitor first and the search engine second. If placing keywords in certain areas works well for the search engine but makes the text awkward for the reader, we strongly suggest foregoing putting keywords in that area.

With that in mind, look at some other keyword considerations for SEO:

- ✔ Whenever possible, include the keyword in some of your <TITLE> tags.
- ✔ Whenever possible, include the keyword in some of your <DESCRIPTION> tags.
- ✔ Whenever possible, include a keyword in your page's URL.
- ✔ Whenever appropriate, use your keywords in your content, especially in the first few paragraphs.
- ✔ If possible, use the keywords in your <H1> to <H6> headings.
- ✔ Avoid *keyword-stuffing,* that is, placing keywords all over the page hoping to attract the attention of search engines.

Headings and sub-headings

Headings are an important part of your page, both for the visitor and for the search engine. Headings are great for organizing content, but they're also a great place to sneak in a keyword to help the search engine isolate the purpose and the content of a particular page.

Normally you get to use six sizes of headings, with <H1> being the largest and <H6> being the smallest. Again, you can use any and all types of headings throughout the landing page as a way to organize your content and highlight keywords. The following is an example of using keywords in the <H1> and <H2> headings. The keywords in this example are *landing page* and *conversion.*

```
</HEAD>
<BODY>
<H1>Building Landing Pages that Sell</h1>
<H2>5 tips to increasing landing page conversions</h2>
<p>Building landing pages that sell requires hard work and a methodical
          approach. Your online conversions do not happen by accident rather
          they follow a formula. In this section, we review five tips to
          increase your conversion rates. </p>
```

Monitoring your HTML file size

With the widespread deployment of broadband Internet, large amounts of HTML coding isn't the problem it once was. In terms of best practices, however, keep an eye on your HTML file size because it can impact load times for dialup or slow Internet connections. Giving an exact size limit for your HTML page is difficult, but a page somewhere between 100–150KB should be fine. Opening a 100KB page on a 56k dialup modem could take somewhere between 10–20 seconds.

You can see how big your HTML file is when you go to open the file in question. You can either hover over the filename for details or look at the File Size column for the size.

Plenty of users are still out there on dialup and slower Internet technologies. Keep these folks in mind when you create your HTML page.

Optimizing images

Images are an integral part of most landing pages today. You use them to show your product, to show people using the product, and so on. Having the image on your site is definitely important but remember that images aren't read by the spiders and bots of the search-indexing world. You have two strategies to increase the effectiveness of your images' *readability* when it comes to search engines. The first involves using image filenames, and the second technique involves using the alt attribute.

Always give images a descriptive filename. Image filenames, such as pic1 or image3, are *not* descriptive and will *not* help the search engines determine what's actually on the page. A short, concise, and accurate filename description, such as Landing Page Conversion Chart or Visitor Eye Map, lets search engines know what's what in terms of the images in your landing page, meaning that search engines can render a more accurate indexing of your site.

In addition to the descriptive filenames, you can use the `alt` attribute as part of your `<img>` tag, which normally allows you to assign text to an image that can't be displayed. The great thing about the `alt` attribute of the `<img>` tag is that even when the image displays properly, the text you use as part of the tag is visible to search engines, even if it isn't necessarily visible to site visitors.

Here's the syntax for the `alt` attribute:

```
<img src="http://www.justmakeiteasy.com/img/resumecoverletter.jpg" alt="2009
        Resume Cover Letter Template"/>
```

In this example, the text, `2009 Resume Cover Letter Template` appears when an image can't be shown, and the alt text can be identified by the search engine for referencing.

Link text

Your landing page no doubt has several links on it. *Link text,* or *anchor text,* is the text associated with a link. Many links you see on pages these days say something like Click Here, and that's about it. Needless to say, this is rather limited information for both your (human) visitors and the search engines. If you add link text that says Click Here to Find Out More about Asian Dogs, both search engines and visitors know what to expect next.

Link text lets the search engine know what the page links to and can then follow that navigation. This makes indexing your site easier. As a general rule, link text should be brief but descriptive of what you find when you follow the link.

For the actual link code, use the following syntax:

```
<a href="location">opening tag and </a>closing tag
```

Here's an example of this code in use:

```
<a href="http://www.mikessample.com">Pictures of Mike</a>
```

The link text accurately describes what you see when you click the link — in this particular case, pictures of Mike, one of the two authors of this tome.

SEO Checklist

Okay, it's crunch time. How does your site stand up to the SEO checklist and scorecard? If you're missing some of the elements in the checklist that we display in Table 14-5, consider updating, fine-tuning, and modifying your site where appropriate.

Table 14-5	SEO Checklist		
Criteria	*Yes*	*No*	*Score*
Do you use <TITLE> tags?			If yes, +1
Do you use <DESCRIPTION> tags?			If yes, +1
Do you use unique <TITLE> and <DESCRIPTION> tags for each separate page within your site?			If yes, +1
Do you represent keywords in your <TITLE> tag?			If yes, +1
Do you represent keywords in your URL?			If yes, +1
Do you represent keywords in your <H1> and <H2> headings?			If yes, +1
Do you keyword stuff your landing page?			If yes, −1
Do you mention your keywords in the beginning content of your landing page?			If yes, +1
Is there sufficient search engine–friendly content on your page?			If yes, +1
Is your content fresh and updated periodically?			If yes, +1
Do you use hidden text?			If yes, −1
Do you use duplicate content to fool search engines?			If yes, −1
Does your site use `<alt>` tags for images?			If yes, +1
Do you use a sitemap?			If yes, +1
Do you use lots of Flash content?			If yes, −1
Do you use link text?			If yes, +1

How does your landing page measure up? Just for fun, here's a grading scale:

- **12–14:** Great job; your site is optimized well. A little bit of fine-tuning, and you'll be there.

- **9–11:** Looks pretty good; you have a handle on the SEO thing. Touch up a few areas and you're on your way.

✔ **5–8:** You have some problems. Give your site a good review and clean up those loose ends where you may be neglecting optimization. Pay close attention to content and keyword usage.

✔ **1–4:** Oh dear, you may have created a site without optimization strategies in mind. Go back to the drawing board and this time think SEO.

Chapter 15

Driving Traffic with Ads, Articles, and Other Tricks

You can design the most amazing landing page imaginable, but if no one comes to it, you've missed your mark. In addition, if you're successful in driving traffic to your landing page, you still have to figure out how you optimize the page for conversions.

If you've been exploring how to drive more traffic to your site, you've probably already figured out that this can be accomplished in more than one way. In this chapter, we look at the different traffic drivers and the different strategies to optimize your landing page for conversions based on each type of traffic driver. To keep things exciting, we also explore some unique traffic drivers that could work for you.

Driving Traffic and Its Considerations

Driving online traffic is about being in a competition. Just like you, every site is trying to make money. You can't get caught up in thinking that by just doing a little, you're sure to get a lot. According to `http://royal.pingdom.com/` (June 2008), the online world is big — with over 1,463,632,361 users — you're essentially a very small fish in a very big pond. To succeed, you need strategies you can apply every day that work to put you before your potential customers.

Knowing your niche and cutting your slice of the market is sure to save you time, effort, and frustration. Attracting the wrong type of traffic, on the other hand, will have you sitting in front of your Web site, checking stats and scratching your head asking why people aren't buying. Before you drive any traffic, make sure you know who you're after.

To take advantage of your strengths, we suggest working with traffic-driving techniques you're comfortable with — use what works for the nature of your business and expand from there. Not all types of online traffic drivers are going to work for you or your business, so it maybe necessary to make some hard decisions on where to focus your marketing efforts.

The more you know, the better you can apply the principles of that knowledge. This relates not only to general knowledge but also in finding new trends and opportunities for more traffic. Don't be fooled into thinking that after you get up and running, your job is done. Actively driving traffic to your site is something you have to do every day. Why? Because *no traffic* equals *no conversions or sales.*

Always make time to review your site. Nothing says unprofessional faster than a broken link or image. It's sure to happen — that's just part of online life — but consistently double-checking your site helps to minimize the possibility. Test all your forms, e-commerce solutions, and pages *before* you launch and *after* every change. As you are creating your Web pages, you can avoid "Under Construction" pages by not uploading them live until they are complete. This will lessen the amount of partial information and "in progress pages" your visitors see.

Driving traffic comes at a cost

Online marketing is free — fact or fiction? Definitely fiction, so forget it if someone told you it is. Even if the investment you make is time and not money, it still comes at a cost.

All traffic that comes to your site costs you financially, whether in the effort to get them there in terms of your time, the hosting fees to cover their visit, the management fees to maintain your site, or the means to sell them a product. Because of this, each of these traffic-driving factors makes up part of your *ROI, return on investment,* which is the bottom line in determining whether all your efforts are worth it. All your efforts to market online not only have to reward you by covering the cost of your time, but you want it to successfully convert visitors as well.

Calculate the hourly wage you need to cover your costs. This helps you focus on putting your efforts in the right place.

Driving traffic precautions

Driving traffic to your landing page is a skill worth learning, but it takes an effort to avoid some of the problems that can arise. Click fraud and scams are two that come to mind and need to be considered if you want to avoid some unpleasant surprises.

When you're dealing with online advertising, it comes down to four players:

- ✔ **The advertiser:** The person who writes an ad to bring attention to their Web site or product.

- ✔ **The publisher:** The Web sites that display the ad written by the advertiser.

- ✔ **The distributor:** The ad company, such as Google AdWords, that works as a contact point between the advertiser and the publisher.

- ✔ **The customer:** The people who, in the process of visiting Web sites, click the ad.

Keeping these four players in mind, here's how you'd run your advertising campaign, pure and simple: You pay a small fee to Google (the distributor) who in turn pays a portion of that fee to the publisher. For your investment, you (the advertiser) get to pitch your product to the customer. While you want to keep your costs low with an effective advertising campaign, you can imagine that publishers are looking for ads that will generate as many clicks as possible, so they get a bit more money. This is where click fraud comes into play.

Click fraud costs companies millions of dollars a year. This occurs when a site owner, auto-script, or custom program clicks your ad with the sole intent of making advertising money. You can minimize this problem by keeping a close eye on your stats and stop dealing with publishers that underperform and do not generate healthy buying traffic from your ad.

Watch for length of visitor time at your site, higher than normal bounce rates, traffic that arrives at the same time every day, or groups of traffic. Your Web logs are a huge asset to help you detect odd traffic patterns or visitor problems.

Making money online is a very hot topic, with many places offering great deals that promise lots of traffic and guaranteed sales. However, it is very important that you take everything advertised with a grain of salt. Don't be caught up in the hype of great advertising-speak and be sure to use your common sense. The Internet has done great things for mankind, but it's safe to say that it's also the greatest source of scams this side of Alpha Centauri. One rule we live by goes as follows: If it seems too good to be true, it probably is.

Advertising scams can be tough to recognize even when you know what you're looking for. Consider this. You have found an online company that specializes in generating traffic; you're told an ad for your site will get placed on a network of sites, exposing your ad to 100,000 visitors. They take your ad and place it on 50 Web sites. Sounds great, right? What if we told you that a) this company actually owns all 50 of those Web site domains and b) the mass amount of visitors you were "promised" was not per day but a whole year's worth and c) the topics of those sites would not interest your ideal customer. Great use of resources or a scam?

We've found it comes down to how the business presents itself. Three possible warning signs include payment method, type of information gathered and service results.

It could be a scam if:

- ✔ **Only inflexible payment options are offered:** Overnight money order or "cash only" options as the sole source of payment are a red flag. While many businesses offer this type of payment method, if this is the *only* option, ask yourself why the company needs your money so fast and in an untraceable manner.

- ✔ **They request irrelevant information:** Especially where e-mail communication is concerned, be aware of fill-in-the-blank information as this is known as "phishing." (Someone asking for your bank information as part of a sign up for a newsletter would be a good example of asking for irrelevant information. Of course you will need to provide items such as your business name, contact information and even what your project budget goal may be, but be sure the information is relevant to the service you are requesting, especially where financial or banking details are concerned.

- ✔ **Not getting the results promised:** Are you getting the results promised or are you just paying and paying for something that never happens? If you are unable to improve the results by working with the company, it's probably time to find another service provider.

Watch for over-the-top claims and unclear Terms of Use Policies. Ask lots of questions. If they are unwilling to answer your questions, give vague answers, or you don't have access to where the traffic comes from or reports of how much your ad's been seen or clicked, ask why. What are they hiding? Is this real traffic or a scam?

Driving Traffic When You Have Writers Twitter

Okay, we could probably have done without the play on *twitter,* but if you can write understandable content, you *can* find a huge market on the Web. Online is all about content, so if you have the literary gift of gab or are willing to proofread your work a few times to refine it, you have a unique opportunity to drive traffic to your site.

Remember, you don't have to be an expert; people just want honest help and information that benefits them. Spelling and grammar are appreciated, but on the Web . . . well, I would hazard a guess that you've read enough online material by now to realize that a misspelled word now and then isn't exactly a deal breaker. Still, that being said, the better the writer, the more opportunities you have available to you.

Finding gold in Q&A sites and forums

Question and answer (Q&A) sites and forums allow people to post — you guessed it — questions and answers and even general comments on topics of interest. These sites lend themselves to tapping into pools of people who are experiencing similar problems and bring together people interested in the same things; this works particularly well for you if you supply the solution to their problem.

Imagine a forum for folks who love things organic or want to get back to the land. Then imagine that folks post queries in the forum about the best place to find "authentic" wooden clogs. If your business specializes in crafting clogs such as this, here is the perfect opportunity to join in the conversation. Not only can you tell people — people who have already shown and interest — about your clogs, but you can mention to your best or most faithful customers that you found a place discussing similar interests as their own and, as we all know, if we truly like something, we tell everyone around us.

Now, we'd like to take a minute and offer a bit of advice on forum etiquette. Forums encourage discussions on a wide range of topics, but that's not to say you're free to talk about *any* topic. In the clog example above, if your business sold all kinds of shoes, including those not so back to the earth and organic, this would *not* be the place to mention your other products. The main theme of any forum needs to be respected and that includes no spamming and no off-track discussion attempts. Remember, others are looking for help and advice, not a sales pitch, so be constructive and helpful, not pushy.

Forums were the first generation of this kind of site, with Q&As coming next, bringing with them a more mature feel and a different organization. Both Q&As and forums have the advantage of constant information being added to the site, so search engines tend to visit more often. More frequent visits put the content into the search engines faster, which allows your efforts to get noticed sooner.

Another advantage is the writing style used. Expert writers aren't essential because many posts are a casually written solution. This casual approach opens the floor to all levels of knowledge, often triggering extended discussions and informational exchanges.

Benefits of using forums and Q&A sites include

- ✔ **Being able to establish your expertise:** Users of Q&A sites and forums have ample opportunities to establish themselves as experts worth listening to.

- ✔ **Allowing for a casual writing style:** You don't have to be a Pulitzer Prize winner — or write like one — to get favorable notices.

- ✔ **Making a fast setup and minimal learning curve:** You can start in only minutes and add rich content to the Web.

- ✔ **Working according to your own timetable:** Answering people's questions can be done when you have time.

- ✔ **Often leading to repeat visitors:** One answer can lead to many visitors over the lifetime of your posts.

- ✔ **Expanding your content:** By supplying links on your site to your answers, you increase what you have to offer without doubling your work.

Not that everything to do with forums and Q&A sites is just hunky dory. Things to look out for include

- ✔ **Not knowing the answer:** Not good. And cutting and pasting an answer from someone else is probably the surest way possible to get you quickly labeled as a non-expert.

- ✔ **Not writing for the layman:** You need to write and answer the question simply, in terms the readers will understand. (Often harder than you'd think.)

- ✔ **Not keeping your own sales pitch subtle:** Customers want answers, not product plugs, so make sure any practical advice you give takes precedence over any product placement you might be able to accomplish.

Many Q&A and forum sites allow for links to your site or provide a profile page to talk about you and your business. Take advantage of them because they can provide other forum users direct access to your site.

Take for example, the Q&A site www.justmakeiteasy.com, as shown in Figure 15-1. This site allows you to set up a profile, ask or answer questions, and piggyback its traffic-driving efforts to get your own site known by having its visitors look at your answers and find out more about you.

Figure 15-1:
Member
profile area
of www.just
makeiteasy.
com.

The traffic that may get driven from this type of site often consists of information seekers, so your landing page might need to be tweaked to give the cross-traffic sound information — rather than just a sales pitch — when they visit.

Submitting articles

Online content providers are always looking for people to provide information. We suggest you scope out content Web sites that cover topics related to your product line or expertise and then check whether they allow article submission. (You can often find either their submissions process in the footer of their site or a contact link to their article submission policy.)

Depending on your writing know-how, you may have to start with smaller Web sites until you can improve your writing style and work your way up. Regardless, be it e-mails, landing pages, or your own articles, writing online needs to become part of your everyday routine. Improving your writing abilities never hurts.

Benefits of article submission include

- ✔ **Proving your bona fides:** Establish yourself as an expert in your field.

- ✔ **Promoting your primary product:** You can show how easy your product is to use and/or the advantages it holds.

- ✔ **Promoting an auxiliary product line:** Article content is great for e-books.

- ✔ **Targeting traffic:** Article readers are specifically interested in your topic.

- ✔ **Generating additional revenue:** Some Web sites will pay for article or content submissions.

- ✔ **Increasing your own traffic:** For every article you write or content you submit, you can mention your own Web site or have people look you up with your byline.

Things to watch out for when you consider article submissions include

- ✔ **Duplicate content problems:** Search engines hate duplicate content, meaning they're likely to give your site a low rank resulting in your page becoming lost at the bottom of the search results. In extreme cases, they may even remove your site entirely from their search results if they sniff it out. To avoid this problem, always use original, fresh copy — in other words, don't scoop it from someone else! We recommend that you don't even take your own articles word for word — change them up to keep the search engines happy.

- ✔ **Ownership of content issues:** Check terms and polices closely to find out who actually owns the content when it's submitted. You may have written it, but you may not be able to use it again for your own product.

- ✔ **Linking restrictions:** Some article sites don't allow linking to your site or landing page, which defeats the purpose.

Make sure that you can track where your traffic comes from and which article triggered it. You may need to offer different advice or information on your landing page in conjunction with the content you provided in the trigger article.

Take, for example, an article on buying baby products leading in to the selling of baby safety products. A perfect lead in from the article you posted might look like, "You need ten things to protect your baby in your home; click here to see the complete list." Now that you've snagged the reader's interest, make sure you have that information on your landing page as part of the sales pitch, thus providing the reader with information he wants and you with a potential sale.

Doing the blogging thing

Blogs are a form of an online diary that's become a big part of the Web. With over one hundred million blogs online (according to `http://royal.pingdom.com`), people talk about and express themselves on just about any topic you can imagine. Blogs are easy to run and as long as you keep blogging or adding relevant content, you can find readers all too willing to read your posts.

You have two approaches when it comes to blogs driving traffic to your landing page:

- ✔ **Create your own blog:** "If you build it, they will come," as the saying goes. Blogs are seen as a word-of-mouth site. You can use that to your advantage by using them as a testing ground and then providing a Web link to the parent site for items on sale.

- ✔ **Utilize an existing blog:** Some blogs offer opportunities for others to join the conversation, rather than keeping to a strict diary format. Adding comments or advertising to blogs that already have traffic in the demographic you're interested in increases your own traffic. Instead of building your own blog and maintaining it, you can find blogs that relate to your product, eliminating half the work!

Benefits of blogging include

- ✔ **Opportunities for market testing:** You can test separate marketing approaches simultaneously by using multiple blogs.

- ✔ **Ease of use:** Blogs are easy to set up, with lots of online templates and online help out there. It also doesn't hurt that, with blogware such as Google's Blogger.com, everything is ready and set up for you to start without delay.

- ✔ **A savvy use of others' blogs can lead to back links:** Back links — links from other Blog sites to your main site — are easy to do in a blog environment, as blogging software often has a built in way that allows you to add a link back to your site.

- ✔ **Great for audience testing:** You can test different demographics without altering your main site.

Things to watch out for when you consider blogging include

- ✔ **It's time-consuming:** You must weigh the cost and traffic benefits against the amount of time you spend blogging.

- ✔ **It's distracting:** Blogs have a tendency to take over your life, meaning you get off track of what you're trying to do or promote.

- ✔ **It's limited exposure, folks:** To be effective, blogs need to be marketed in addition to simple word of mouth.

- ✔ **You have traffic limitations:** Not all blogs have enough quality traffic to warrant advertising on them.

 Blogs give the benefit of word of mouth, allowing you to literally say, "Here's a great idea for solving the problem of . . ." and then directing the readers to a sales page, all without changing the tone of the sales pitch. The only change your site may need is a more powerful heading or opening paragraph that really talks to the demographic of the blog your visitor came from.

Tweeting and Twittering

In case you haven't heard about it, Twitter is a (relatively) new phenomenon, based on the notion that 140-character-text–only communication can actually say something substantive. Short and to the point, twittering can be used productively to drive traffic to your site.

In simple terms, twittering is microblogging. Designed in 2006 to allow friends, family, and co-workers to keep in touch with each other, sending *tweets,* as they're called, has become a huge trend.

This form of instant messaging can be linked to social networks, blogs, and Web sites, which is where your traffic-driving opportunity comes into play. The more people that sign up for your tweets, the more people that are aware of your business and promotions.

Benefits of twittering include

- ✔ **Elicits help easily:** If you need feedback on a product or help with market research, send out a tweet. Your Twitter followers will help.

- ✔ **Targets quality traffic:** Because tweets are so focused and to-the-point, followers are more inclined to actually read them and get the gist of what you share. If they're interested, they'll go to your site. If not, well, it isn't a waste of their time or your resources.

- ✔ **Facilitates networking:** Whether in your personal life or business, you can keep in touch with the people that improve your knowledge every day. This can be your business mentor or your favorite news network, anyone you gain knowledge and experience from can improve the quality of your business life.

Things to watch out for when considering Twitter include

- ✔ **It's not time-tested:** Twitter is a relatively new media, so it really hasn't stood the test of time. Twitter's a big unknown regarding whether it'll continue to be popular long term.

- ✔ **It's a time commitment:** Sending updated tweets takes time. Yes they're short, but you want to keep your followers interested.

- ✔ **Tweets can be brutally honest:** Twittering tends to foster a certain sense of freewheeling abandon among its users, which means you may come up against a level of frankness in tweets that visitors might not express directly on your site. The important thing is to not take comments personally, but to treat them as a learning experience and as an opportunity to improve.

The first step in taking advantage of Twitter is to sign up for an account at `www.twitter.com`, which is both free and easy to do. Twitter offers you the ability to keep in touch and to the point with your visitors — an ability that any site owner would value. Be sure to mention on your landing page that you Twitter and show how they can find you to become a follower.

Keep the new and exciting tweets you send out to manageable levels; you don't want to lose your followers by being annoying!

Social networking

Facebook, MySpace, or as we like to call it, in-your-face social networking is everywhere. *Social networking* is the gathering of friends, family, and acquaintances to talk about everything and everyone. Tapping into this online networking for traffic is gathering steam.

If you're one of the diehards that refuse to get caught up in the hubbub of Facebook or MySpace, here's what you need to know about it. Online social networking isn't that different from being a part of a neighborhood or club. Many people gather all in one place — in this case, online — to share their experiences with each other. That is the long and short of it — sharing.

As a business owner, you need to take advantage of all the sharing you can get. Letting free exposure like this get away would be like having an exclusive deal to sell souvenirs at the Olympics but turning it down because you don't like sports. You aren't there to watch the competition; you're there to sell your souvenirs!

Benefits of social networking include

- **Networking, networking, networking:** Tapping into a group that already trusts you is to your advantage if you're eventually going to suggest an item to buy or try; people are simply more likely to trust someone they know.

- **Word of mouth can do wonders:** Good word of mouth can spread through the whole network from friend to friend, increasing your exposure exponentially.

- **Great advertising opportunities:** Many online social network sites offer their own marketing options, giving you freedom to pick and choose if you want to advertise on them.

Things to watch out for when you consider social networking include

- **Friendship limitations:** Be careful not to overuse your friend network and abuse the friend card — no one likes a pushy sales pitch.

- **Time glut:** Social networking can take up time that could be spent focusing on selling or other marketing efforts.

- **Product boundaries:** Some products may fall flat when suggested through social networks. Use your network to test your market before sinking too much effort in.

- **Mindset:** Those partaking in the social network atmosphere may just be there for the gabbing opportunities, so they aren't always in the mindset of information research or product solutions; your marketing efforts may be in vain.

- **Word of mouth can sink:** Just as a good experience can spread through the whole network from friend to friend, so can a negative one.

If you're a participant in a social network, have created your own page, and post your own comments, major adaptations aren't needed for your landing page. Still, you may wish to run a version of your page that has a friendlier, more casual read to it — and offers direct selling. This could look something like, "For all my friends and friends of friends, I'm offering a great deal . . ."

If you're merely advertising on social networks with something, such as a banner ad, no landing page changes are required — except of course, making sure that your ad matches your content, which you should have already done.

Driving Traffic Traditionally

If blogging, twittering, and social networking takes you out of your comfort zone and you want a more traditional way to drive traffic to your landing page, you can find many options for this as well. Although optimizing your landing page for traditional traffic drivers is pretty straightforward, a few particulars exist that you need to be on the lookout for.

Using banner ads

Banner ads are one of the most original forms of online advertising ever introduced. Although still a mainstay in the online advertiser's arsenal, their popularity fluctuates with the times.

Since their inception, banner ads have seen the introduction of different ad sizes, the addition of animation ability, added sounds, and the *mouse over* feature, which caused the ad to grow larger.

Banner ads are a for-purchase option and can be bought as pay per click (PPC), pay per impression, or in really rare cases, a flat rate per month. The following list explains these options in further detail:

- ✔ **PPC** allows the advertiser to pay for a banner ad only when a visitor actually clicks the ad to visit her site.

- ✔ **Pay per impression** means an advertiser pays for his banner ad to be viewed a specific number of times, with no guarantee it'll be clicked.

- ✔ **Flat rate** doesn't take into account the number of views or how many times the ad is clicked. Small Web sites tend to offer this option for others to advertise with them.

Benefits of banner advertising include

- ✔ **Availability:** Banner ads are available on a large number of sites.

- ✔ **Size flexibility:** Different banner sizes are available to suit most advertising needs.

- ✔ **Multiple payment options:** Depending on your budget and goals, you can choose the pay per impression or the PPC model to meet your needs.

- ✔ **Easy placement:** Banner ads can be purchased either direct from independent sites that host this type of campaign or through online services that group together similarly themed sites.

- ✔ **Access to targeted markets:** Banner ads can be purchased on niche sites that offer information specifically on products like yours, thus focusing your ad exposure.

- ✔ **Variable costs:** Each site might charge different prices, so you can check around to find good deals.

Things to watch out for when you consider banner ads include

- ✔ **Be sure to know your demographics:** Do some research so that you know the visitor demographics to the Web site you're advertising on.

✔ **Be careful of cost overruns:** Keep an eye on how much your banner advertising costs you and be on the lookout for questionable results that might suggest click fraud. (See the section, "Driving traffic precautions," earlier in this chapter, for more on click fraud.)

✔ **Keep an eye on your return on investment (ROI):** Monitor your sales and always ask, "Are people buying as a result of the ad I'm running?"

✔ **Keep records:** Be sure the company or Web site you're using for your banner ads keeps good records that allow you to inspect the number of clicks/views you get compared to the amount they actually bill you for. Good record keeping helps you control your advertising ROI and overruns.

Banner ads are a very visual advertising choice, so you need the same visual on your landing page. Right from the start, you want the visitor to quickly connect your ad with your landing page, showing her that she's in the right place and will get the information that she expects.

We recommend that you change your header to include the image that you include in your banner ad, that you use similar (if not the same) keywords on both your ad and page, and that you repeat on your landing page any promotions your ad may have been advertising to reinforce to your visitor that he's at the right place.

Running classified ads

Classifieds are far from dead — especially the ones found online. A popular example is www.craigslist.com, where you get a traditional classified listing but with more options than newspaper versions could ever provide.

We're sure you've picked up a newspaper and flipped through the Help Wanted section now and again, but if you're not familiar with the online variety, we clue you in.

Online classified ads are identical in many ways to the print versions. You can choose pay-for or free listings, you can set how long you want the listing to be posted, and you can stipulate where you want it to be seen. The difference is the sheer volume of people that will potentially see your classified ad. By going online, you move beyond the subscription borders of the newspaper to literally worldwide exposure.

Benefits of online classified ads include

✔ **Cost-effectiveness:** Many sites don't charge anything to post a listing.

✔ **Access to unlimited target markets:** Online classifieds open your product or site to markets you might not otherwise have had access to.

- ✔ **Familiarity breeds trust:** Online classified sites look like the ads in traditional newspaper, providing viewers with a sense familiarity.

- ✔ **Great back-link opportunities:** Many classified sites allow direct links back to your site.

Things to watch out for when you consider online classifieds include

- ✔ **Indeterminate visitor quality:** You can't track or control the visitor quality.

- ✔ **Low buy threshold:** Classified users are often bargain hunters.

- ✔ **Inherent traffic restrictions:** Only sites that are really popular will give you much useful traffic.

Classifieds can work for you; however, you may not get the exact traffic that you're looking for. For this reason, you need to make sure you're using a targeted landing page different from your main landing page. Keep a close eye on your bounce rates and visitor time on your site.

Creating a good heading and tying it into your site is very important for the overall success of using classified ads. Make sure any offer or information you *say* will be there will in fact *be there*. If you run classifieds on different sites or in different cities, linking the ads to separate landing pages might be an advantage, so you can cater directly to the needs and expectations of specific site visitors.

E-mail marketing

E-mail marketing has been around just as long as banner ads, meaning they date back to almost the beginning of online marketing! Out of all the online marketing techniques, e-mail marketing has garnered the worst reviews. In addition, if not done properly, it can cost you big time in the way of fines or other penalties.

However, if used properly, e-mail marketing is still effective. E-mail marketing is nothing more than bulk direct mail, just through the computer instead of the post office. Although you can buy a list of e-mail addresses or gather them yourself, be very careful of where the addresses come from. Most countries have their version of the CAN-SPAM Act of 2003, passed by the U.S. Congress and enforced by the U.S. Federal Trade Commission, which sets out in some detail the guidelines for bulk direct mail done over the Internet. Be sure to look through the applicable publication to stay within the online rules of conduct devised for your country.

Benefits of e-mail marketing include

- **The ability to focus on a targeted audience:** With a highly targeted list of people, you have access to an open market.

- **Quite effective (in some contexts):** It may be the only way to find the people you want to find.

Things to watch out for when you consider e-mail marketing include

- **A boxcar full of regulations:** Make sure you that your list of e-mail addresses is made up of folks that really signed up to hear your message. The U.S., for example, can fine site owners as much as $11,000 for sending unsolicited spam. Ouch!

- **Know your product:** Not all product types work well through e-mail. If your product isn't getting results, change gears and either market a different way or change the sales message you're sending.

- **The ethical aspect:** If you're not a fan of spam and you're sending messages to others, well, you've become what you don't like! A fine balance exists between getting news about your product out there and irritating people.

The content you place in e-mails and the content you place on your landing pages must match very closely. When you run an e-mail campaign, always use a page not connected to your main sales landing page. A page connected or linked to your site can get indexed in the search engines, which means even after the campaign is over, visitors may still see it in their search results.

Two advantages of an isolated page are easy deletion and e-mail specific disclaimers. If you find your campaign just falls flat or gets a bad reception, you can simply delete the page. No fuss, no muss! As for disclaimers, your landing page for your e-mail campaign should have an "unsubscribe" option so folks can take themselves off your e-mailing list as well as an easy-to-find link to your Privacy Policy to set visitors' minds at ease. From personal experience, every time we've used e-mail marketing, even when people choose or opt-in to our mailings, some e-mail recipients still complain because they don't want the information, or forgot they signed up for the information in the first place.

Although e-mail marketing works for many marketers, over time we've personally gone away from this type of campaign. At this point, we only tell others it exists and briefly explain how it works. When faced with a client who wishes to run e-mail marketing campaigns, we warn them of the potential problems (spam rules, disgruntled customers, and so on) and don't actively assist in their campaigns.

PPC advertising and contextual ads

Pay per click (PPC) marketing is one of the biggest marketing techniques out there today. Powerhouses like Google and Yahoo! use it and have created their own brand to capitalize on its potential. Google AdWords and Yahoo! Search Marketing (SM) often go head to head with their PPC programs to provide the most cutting-edge alternatives.

PPC is just how it sounds; you pay for the action of someone clicking the ad you create. PPC marketing, although important in the context of driving traffic, holds enough information to be a chapter in itself. So we made one!

In Chapter 16, we go into greater detail about PPC campaigns and how they work, so rather than repeat ourselves, here's a quick overview of the benefits and cautions to tide you over.

Benefits of PPC marketing include

- **Control:** You control your daily budget and the ad locations.
- **Cost-effectiveness:** PPC campaigns fit almost any budget.
- **Market testing:** PPC campaigns can be used to test or sell into untapped markets.
- **Great functionality:** You have lots of tools available to assist you.
- **Easy accounting:** It's easy to figure out whether you're actually making a positive ROI.
- **Great customization options:** You can tweak the look and feel of your ad campaigns with text and images.

Things to watch out for when you consider PPC marketing campaigns include

- **A steep learning curve:** Depending on your skill level and ability to pick up new concepts, some find it a challenge to implement a PPC campaign.
- **Constant change:** Program elements and guidelines tend to change constantly, which can affect your costs and approach — in other words, you can't simply set up a campaign once and leave it alone.
- **Be sure to do the math:** PPC marketing is an involved process. We highly recommend that you regularly calculate what your ROI is, so you know whether your campaign is effective.
- **Make monitoring a priority:** Watch your daily costs compared to sales because it's easier than you think to spend a lot of money and have no sales to show for it!

✔ **Click fraud:** Remember that not all traffic is real traffic — believe it or not, some folks don't play by the rules. Click fraud is here to stay as a part of PPC, but you can monitor it so that it doesn't bite you too badly.

There's just too much to cover on PPC as part of an overview chapters, so we dedicate Chapter 16 to it. See you there!

Driving Traffic in Ways You May Not Have Thought Of

The Internet has taken run-of-the-mill advertising methods to a whole new level. Not only have print ads, commercials, and radio spots experienced a complete overhaul, the technological advertising opportunities are often a whole new ball of wax compared to what you're used to.

Videos and rich media is everywhere

You may not remember, but in 1979,"Video Killed the Radio Star" by British group The Buggles was released. You might wonder what this has to do with landing pages, but the song talks about how the shift in the music industry from radio to TV music videos was changing the world. In 2005, YouTube and similar sites that use interactive technology — the hip term for that being *rich media* — started another new trend known as social videos.

Just like TV overtook radio in The Buggles' song, video and rich media sites are starting to take over TV. Sites like www.hulu.com allow you to watch your favorite TV programs online at any time. This new rich media opens doors for even more ways to drive traffic to your site.

Take YouTube, for example: It allows the average person to post almost any video as long as it falls within their terms of use. Now, instead of paying thousands of dollars for a local TV spot that relatively few people see, you have access to millions of potential viewers at a fraction of the cost.

Benefits of rich media sites include

✔ **Mass exposure potential:** Successful videos can become an effective viral marketing tool. *Viral marketing* occurs when the video is passed from person to person because of its humor or appeal.

✔ **Message control:** The video posted is the one you create, so you know that what gets viewed is exactly what you wanted people to see.

✔ **Repeat visitors:** Many video sites offer systems to allow viewers to group or bookmark your video for watching later.

- ✔ **Distribution:** Some video sites allow for embedding, meaning you can put your video on sites all over the Web.

Things to watch out for when you consider rich media sites include

- ✔ **Not reaching the right people:** Most people want to be entertained, so if your video is on the dry side, it may get passed over more often than not.

- ✔ **The Needle in the Haystack syndrome:** With literally millions of videos, yours may get lost unless you're willing to keep it fresh and change it now and again or create a series of videos.

- ✔ **Amateurism is an acquired taste:** Amateur video isn't for everyone, whereas a professional-looking piece tends to win over a larger slice of the viewing public. Try to make your video as professional as you can.

- ✔ **No control:** You may find that sites you don't want anything to do with may be embedding your video as content — and there's not much you can do about it.

When you develop a landing page stemming from a video, you need to have a specific lead-in or call to action that ties the video into your page. A big bold lead-in, such as "Did you see our video? Here's how we made the soda explode" may be necessary to get them to visit a targeted sales pitch page.

The most powerful video use is when it becomes viral. *Viral* videos have been picked up by the news or spread like wildfire by word of mouth. You've probably experienced them in the form of an e-mail that everyone forwards to their whole address book because "you just have to see this." The purpose of a viral video is to get your brand in front of the customer and compel her to come to your site.

A perfect example of a viral video is the *Diet Coke and Mentos Eruption.* You may have seen it, or if not, will probably Google it. This video of what happens when Mentos candy is dropped into Diet Coke was viewed more than 10 million times since its release in September 2007. Imagine, 10 million people that see your brand!

Cross-linking

With conversions (and therefore sales) as your main goal and increased traffic helping you to reach that goal, *cross-linking* — reciprocal links from your site to other people's and theirs to yours — are a natural fit. Cross-linking to drive traffic comes in many forms, but can be broken into two categories: situations in which you pay sites for links, and situations in which you ask sites for links.

Paying for links is usually done through link exchange sites that are dedicated to finding Web sites that would benefit you. They have tons of companies, broken into categories that can link to your site. Payment for this service is often a *pay for link* format — you pay a flat rate for every link placed on someone else's site.

Although you can simply search for "link exchange" on your favorite search engine, they're a wonderful resource and often cost-effective, take great caution with this method. A sudden increase of links to your site on the Web can result in penalties from search engines, including in very drastic cases, removing your site from their searches. Search engines look to provide relevant, non-duplicate content, and too many links result in just that — too much of (the same) nothing!

The other option you have is to ask other site owners directly for reciprocal links. Similar to exchanging business cards, two companies or individuals place links on each other's site to exchange traffic. Reciprocal links are the safer way to go as you can control how many sites you set up links with, who they are and what they offer. Just asking is always a much simpler approach!

Benefits of cross-linking include

- ✔ **Increased traffic:** When sites are chosen effectively, you can gain a high volume of targeted traffic.

- ✔ **Domain recognition:** Can increase your Web presence and domain recognition in search engines (all part of *search engine optimization, SEO*).

- ✔ **Time:** Because setting up a cross-link is nothing more than a simple link, the linking process can be completed fairly quickly.

Things to watch out for when you consider cross-linking include

- ✔ **Relevancy (or lack thereof):** Your site needs to be relevant to the people visiting; if they arrive from a site that's completely off your topic, you may not appeal to them.

- ✔ **Violation risks:** Being too aggressive in cross-linking can get you moved way down the search list or even kicked out of the search engines.

The best thing you can do when utilizing cross links is to make sure the Web sites you link from and to are relevant to your visitors. If you have a site dedicated to fishing, you can cross-link with one dedicated to boats or fishing expeditions; however, sharing traffic with composting techniques — worms and bait being the connection here — might be pushing it.

Affiliate networks

We find *affiliates* thrown around a lot online. Affiliate programs are an agreement between you and another site owner in which you pay him a percentage or fixed rate — much like a finder's fee or commission — for every product of yours he sells.

Affiliate programs are relatively simple to become involved with, and you can even run your own. All you need is a clear agreement of the terms (such as payment amount, payment schedule, and rules of conduct), a product to sell, and people willing to sell it! Okay, that may be oversimplifying the process a bit, but aside from program management, that's an affiliate program in a nutshell.

You have two ways you can take advantage of affiliate programs. You can sign up for other people's programs to make money for yourself, or because we're talking about ways to drive traffic, create your own with the purpose of bringing people to your site. You can start from scratch and figure out how to create and manage your own program, or you can call on businesses that specialize in this field.

Benefits of affiliate programs include

- ✔ **Increased traffic:** Other sites driving traffic to your site relieves you of the burden of being the sole traffic generator.
- ✔ **Fast expansion:** Depending on the marketplace, if you have a hot product, you can literally explode and expand your business in a short period of time.
- ✔ **Services available:** With affiliate tracking software and other programs designed for this task, setting up your own program is rather easy.

Things to watch out for when you consider affiliate programs include

- ✔ **Costs:** Every sale made via the affiliate lead results in a cost to you. Be sure you calculate your ROI, so you don't lose money.
- ✔ **Questionable effectiveness:** Not every person that signs up to your affiliate program is effective at driving traffic. When 100 people sign up and only 1 is actually doing anything for your business, that can be discouraging.

When your personal efforts are used to drive traffic, the landing page the visitors come to has to take over the sale. The same is true when the efforts of others are what's driving visitors to your page. You can't just get them there; you have to convert them too! Focus on the above the fold area, bold headings, and for goodness sake, make sure what you offer is what the affiliate said you are! Meet your visitor's expectations in content, look, and promotional offer.

Picking up where others left off

Every day, companies online either let their Web addresses or domain names expire, change their focus, or move on. These companies have often invested time, money, and energy into marketing their sites to drive traffic.

When the site is no longer active, their traffic has nowhere to go. Here is where your opportunity presents itself. Just as a Great Horned Owl will make an abandoned nest his new home, you can purchase an abandoned domain and use the residual traffic to your advantage! You can either point the new domain at your current site so when folks visit the new-to-you domain, they're directed to your site, or you can build a small independent site at the new domain and then link over to your main Web site.

You are not targeting the Web addresses of thriving businesses, but keeping an eye out for a marketing opportunity. Benefits of picking up domains include

- ✔ **Increased traffic:** The original site owner has already done work to drive people to her site, or has already search engine ranking. If they don't want the traffic — don't let it go to waste!
- ✔ **Inexpensive:** Domains can often be picked up cheap.

Things to watch out for when you consider buying domains include

- ✔ **Past life:** Be sure the domain names you pick up are "clean" — no pornographic past life or association with controversial topics, are not contrary to what you sell, and don't have a bad reputation.
- ✔ **Traffic quality:** Well, you *are* taking over someone else's traffic. Your visitors expect to see what was there before, not you, so the level of traffic actually interested in what *you* have to offer is less.
- ✔ **Trademarks:** Avoid domains that belong to trademarked companies.

Because the traffic coming to your site isn't focused traffic, a generic landing page in most cases will do. To increase effectiveness, you can use a separate landing page for every domain. By researching the former marketing efforts of the company and what product it sold, you can fine-tune your landing page to that demographic.

Ever heard of the WayBack Machine at www.archive.org? If not, it's a fun and extremely helpful Web site. Just type in the Web address you're interested in, and the WayBack Machine, as shown in Figure 15-2, displays links to the Web site for how it used to look from a few months to years ago. This tool is great for seeing what type of site used to be on the domain before you buy it, what they did, and how it looked.

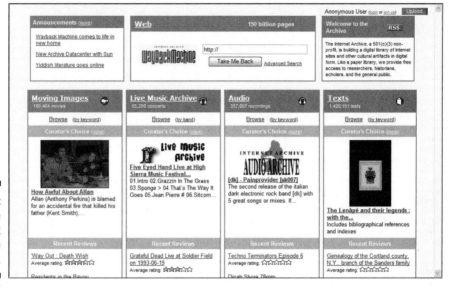

Figure 15-2:
The
WayBack
Machine
search box.

Chapter 16

Paying for Your Clicks

· ·

· ·

*O*ptimization of your landing page is simpler when you have control of the circumstances and you know who's coming to your site. Like a science experiment, you need to control the variables to see whether you can achieve the same results time and again. In the case of landing pages, the result you're trying to duplicate is often the number of sales made.

This is when *pay per click (PPC)* really shines. In simple terms, PPC marketing is when you pay an advertiser a fee whenever someone clicks an ad you create. Because you can control many of the factors that drive people to your Web site, you can quickly correct and optimize your landing page for better results.

Not only is PPC one of the easiest and quickest ways to test the effectiveness of your landing pages, for some products, PPC marketing is a sound, long-term strategy and a great way to fine-tune your sales pitch.

In this chapter, we discuss everything surrounding PPC marketing, including the nuts and bolts of how it works, who the biggest players are, what it takes to run a PPC campaign, and the cautions you need to consider before you use PPC.

Introduction to the Inner Workings of PPC

Like direct marketing of old, PPC is a more dynamic, traceable system to improve your marketing efforts. When used with a landing page, PPC can deliver a very trackable and successful one-two punch.

You may have heard conflicting things about PPC marketing; perhaps you're harboring some negative impressions of it, or you may have even tried it in the past, been given bad advice, and have given up on it. We're here to help you overcome that bit of negativity by not only talking about what PPC is and how to do it, but by also shedding light on potential pitfalls and what you can do to avoid them.

Using PPC isn't marketing hype or some quick money-making scheme, but a process. If you're serious about making money online as a business and can objectively look at what you're doing, you can be successful with PPC marketing. For all you left-brain thinkers out there, this one's for you.

We told you we'd tell you about the pitfalls, so we might as well get the bad stuff out in the open right now: With PPC, you're going to have a pretty steep learning curve at the beginning. On the positive side, you'll soon find a rhythm and a system that's going to work for you; eventually, running your PPC campaign will become second nature. That being said, don't be surprised if you're frustrated when you first start out; just keep uppermost in your mind that soon you'll see the fruits of your labor and be tracking conversions on your landing page.

Changing forever how marketing is done

PPC marketing got its start back in 1998, with a little Goto.com startup company. The concept of paying advertisers only when your ad is clicked was different than any other blanket marketing approach of the time. Newspapers, magazines, radio, and television all require payment regardless whether people read the ad. PPC costs you only when folks read your ad, get intrigued, and then click it.

When it comes to marketing online, PPC leveled the playing field between small and large businesses by providing the tools needed to track the actual value received compared to advertising costs going out. Eleven years after its inception, even with large companies like eBay marketing in the PPC arena, plenty of opportunities for small companies still exist if they can cut their own niche in this field of marketing.

By providing a marketing system that fits any budget or company size, PPC marketing has revolutionized the industry, but its transformation doesn't stop there. Just like in the past, advancement is inevitable.

Although you'll find a ton of PPC companies on the Internet, the three big players are Google AdWords, Yahoo! Search Marketing, and Microsoft adCenter (MSN Bing). Each of these Big Three tackles the PPC marketing program a bit differently, offering a different range of services, costs, and tools. This is great because every small, medium, or large business owner can find a niche where they can attract traffic at a good price so they can sell their wares.

Putting together the pieces

PPC systems are part of a symbiotic relationship among the Web sites displaying the ad, seekers of information, and advertisers offering services or products. Each part of this relationship brings together ample opportunities for all businesses to participate.

For those familiar with running traditional ad campaigns involving newspapers, classifieds, or direct mail, the similarity between such campaigns and PPC won't be lost on you. However, unlike a newspaper, you get to find out exactly how many people actually viewed your ad compared to how many responded to it, making the fine-tuning process that much easier.

Understanding the flow of events for a basic PPC campaign helps you wrap your mind around how a successful campaign works. As we discuss each step individually, see Figure 16-1 as often as you need to as a guide.

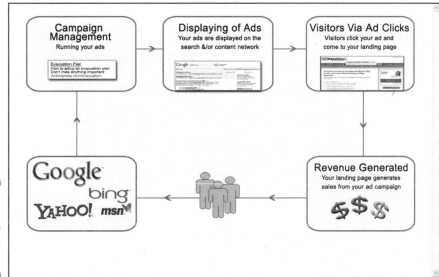

Figure 16-1:
An illustrated flow of PPC marketing.

Here's how we break down the steps involved in running a PPC campaign:

- ✔ **Choosing a PPC provider:** Google, Yahoo!, and MSN Bing each have their own rules, guidelines, payment schedules, and the like, and you have to figure out which provider meshes most effectively with your own marketing strategies. Officially, we can't sway you one way or another, but throughout this chapter, we give you the tools you need to make a choice that best suits your needs.

- ✔ **Managing your campaign:** After you choose a provider, set up your campaign and manage it. The business of writing ads, setting up your marketing demographics, determining run times, choosing countries for targeting, and your hopefully ongoing keyword research is all part of managing your campaign — and the work never stops.

- ✔ **Displaying of ads:** Your campaign is up and running with your ads showing on the search and/or content network for people to see. (The *search network* is when ads are displayed on the search engine results pages, whereas the *content network* has your ads displayed on other Web sites.) Both networks are effective but attract a different type of visitor.

- ✔ **Visitors via ad clicks:** As people cruise the Web — running their searches for specific topics and visiting various Web sites — they have the potential of seeing your ad, clicking it, and as a result, visiting your Web site. The page they're directed to is the landing page you designed with the sole purpose of encouraging them to perform the action you tell them to. This action can involve a purchase, filling out a sign-up form, or any number of things that will benefit your business.

- ✔ **Revenue generated:** Visitor conversion successful! Those visitors that turn into sales are the reason you're running a PPC campaign in the first place. For every sale generated or sign-up completed, you have an equal opportunity for repeat business if the customer leaves satisfied and tells his friends. As you perfect your campaign, you increase the likelihood of producing and increasing your revenue.

Spotting PPC ads online

Do PPC ads stand out over other ads online? Well, not really, but we can give you some easy examples of where you can find them online for reference. By understanding what the ads look like and where they're located, you can start to imagine how your ads will appear to potential visitors and customers.

Because we're discussing the major PPC players, Table 16-1 concentrates on some of the specs surrounding the ads offered to advertisers by Google, Yahoo!, and MSN Bing. The information here will probably change — that's just the nature of the online world — but at least you get a chance to see how similar, yet different, the three major programs are.

Always check things out before you jump into any project!

Now, with that little warning out of the way, check out Table 16-1 to see what's included in popular PPC ads.

Table 16-1	Overview of PPC Ads		
Ad Type	**Google**	**Yahoo!**	**MSN Bing**
Text ads	*Limited character counts:*	*Limited character counts:*	*Limited character counts:*
	Title 25 characters	Title 40 characters	Title 25 characters
	Two descriptive lines	Short description 70 characters	Descriptive text 70 characters
	URL 35 characters each	Long Description 190 characters	URL 35 characters
		URL (not specified)	Title and description must have at least six words each
Image ads	A variety of sizes	A variety of sizes	A variety of sizes
	JPEG, PNG, or GIF format	GIF, JPEG, or Flash format	GIF or JPG format
	Maximum file size of 50KB	Maximum file size of 30KB for Images or 40KB for Flash	Maximum file size of 40KB
Mobile ads	*Limited character counts:*	A variety of sizes, ranging from 1.0KB–5.0KB, 8–24 characters	A variety of everything, including ad sizes, styles, file sizes, and file types
	Title 18 characters		
	Four descriptive lines of 18 characters each		
	URL 20 characters		
Expandable ads (ads that get larger once rolled over or clicked)	Content network only	Wide variety of sizes	Wide variety of sizes
	Expand to double its size depending on screen space	Set direction of ad expansion	Set direction of ad expansion
	Can include streaming video or interactive features*	Can include streaming video or interactive features	Can include streaming video or interactive features
			Maximum 40KB file size

USA Beta version only. March 4, 2009

The ad information in Table 16-1 gives you the bare bones; needless to say, double-check the program rules of who you're running ads with. Table 16-1 also makes it clear that you have a wide variety of options available to you, depending on your advertising needs. Character counts, file size, and even what is and isn't allowed vary for every PPC company. So do your research!

When running a PPC campaign, your end goal — next to making money — is designing an ad that will be seen by many. If you're using the content network, your best chance is ad placement on very high traffic or niche sites. If you're using the search network, you're looking for your ad to appear above the fold, in the top part on a search results page.

Take the Google search page in Figure 16-2, for example. A *mouse trap* search generates ads on the topic down the right side of the search page. Ideally, you want to be above the results page fold to increase your chance of catching a visitor's eye.

With all PPC programs, people bid on keywords for the most advantageous ad position. Google, for example, determines ad placement with its ad ranking system. This ranking system takes into account your cost per click (CPC) and your quality score. (Your *quality score* is based on text, keyword, and landing page relevance. Because we go into greater detail on quality scores and their role in running a Google AdWords campaign in Chapter 17, we leave it at that for now.)

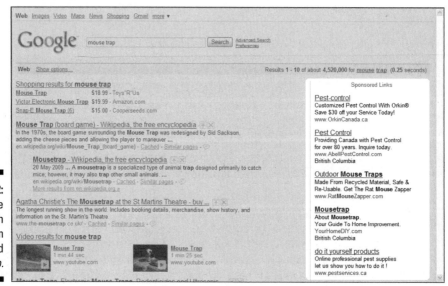

Figure 16-2:
Google
search
results from
the keyword
mouse trap.

With PPC ads everywhere, the largest network of PPC marketing currently belongs to Google. Google displays its ads on two different networks: search and content. The search network is, you guessed it, the ads that appear when a user performs a search, and the content network is a large group of individual Web sites that participate with Google to display ads. Web sites that participate have the phrase "Ads by Google" next to the ads. The site owners, or *publishers,* are paid a small portion of the PPC fee if someone clicks the ad displayed on their site.

Just as a wide variety of ad types and sizes are available, your ad can be worked an untold number of ways into someone's Web site — with a few spots being more popular than others, it goes without saying. The text block ad, as shown in Figure 16-3, for example, is the 300 x 250px size, which tucked quite nicely into the right-hand sidebar. This particular location is ideal placement to catch the visitor's eye because it's obviously not part of the article and yet provides relevant information that the visitor might be interested in.

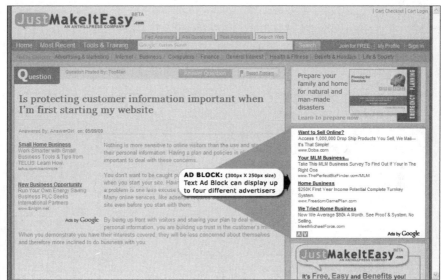

Figure 16-3:
A text ad for the right sidebar.

Compare the ad shown in Figure 16-3 to the one you see in Figure 16-4. You see the same ad size — 300 x 250px — but with an image ad, the whole look of the page is different. Not only can image ads make an impact, but an image ad is a great way to grab the attention of the visitor. Unlike a text ad, image ads also have the advantage that the information displayed is yours and yours alone.

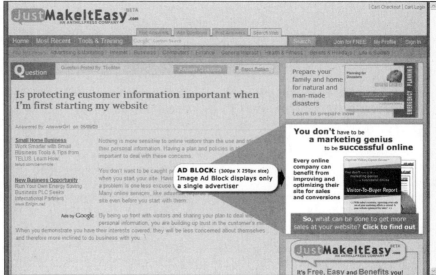

Figure 16-4:
An image ad
for the right
sidebar.

Keep your image ad bold, with a clear message and crisp graphics, but don't be over the top. You want visitors to be able to respond to your ad and not be distracted by outlandish colors or a confusing message. Your image ad also needs to tie in to the look and feel of the landing page it's directed to.

Wrapping Your Mind around PPC Marketing Campaigns

The opportunities in the PPC world are endless. We've found that, for our clients, wrapping their minds around all the options available to them is often easier said than done. You're probably no different from our regular clients, so we thought it we'd take a closer look at the inner workings of a PPC campaign as a way to help you see the forest for the trees.

Stepping through the process

Although the concept behind PPC advertising is relatively straightforward — you provide an ad, someone displays your ad, you get visitors, and those certain someones get paid for having sent you those visitors — how everything fits together is a lot more involved.

We use dry erase boards so much in our office when we explain ideas and strategies to our clients that we've looked at investing in dry erase board marker companies, but because we don't have that option with you, check out Figure 16-5, which is similar to what we'd scribble on a board for you if we could. An active PPC campaign typically has five levels of involvement:

- **The advertiser:** That's you
- **The PPC campaign provider:** Google, MSN Bing, Yahoo!, and so on
- **Strategy development:** Competitor analysis, keyword research, and goal setting
- **Management:** Assessment, testing, and fine-tuning
- **Tracking and reporting:** Analytics, conversions, and goal checking

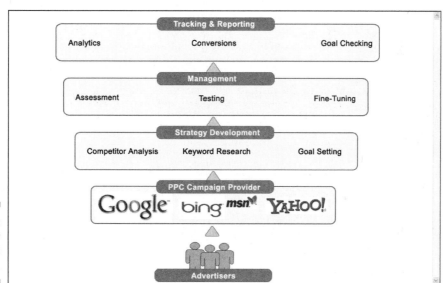

Figure 16-5:
An overview of a PPC campaign.

The following sections give you a tour of some of the major highlights in Figure 16-5.

PPC campaign provider

The campaign provider you choose to work with is ultimately a personal choice and, as with any choice you make in life, each option has pros and cons you must weigh. Here are some points to consider when you make your decision:

✔ **Google AdWords:** The largest PPC provider and holding the lead nicely, thank you very much, Google AdWords is currently the program of choice for many. AdWords offers many tools to help with ad creation, campaign management, and conversion tracking. No minimum monthly costs and daily spending maximums make sticking to your budget easy.

✔ **Yahoo! Search Marketing:** Yahoo! Search Marketing is the second largest PPC provider, with quite a wide reach in the marketplace. Similar to Google AdWords in look and feel, Search Marketing also offers search and content network ad placement. More hands on, Search Marketing has a longer delay between the ad review process and posting the ads online; it also offers many tools to help with ads, management, and tracking.

✔ **MSN Bing:** Newer to the PPC game, Microsoft has recently re-branded its search marketing program into Bing. Not venturing too far from the tried and true, Bing ads look similar to Yahoo! ads, which look similar to Google ads. In addition to the basic keyword, tracking and management tools, Bing has one trick up its sleeve in the form of a tool for copying your campaign from Google or Yahoo! over to it. Bing also offers budgeting controls to help keep your cash flow manageable.

Strategy development

PPC campaigns don't arise out of thin air; you have to plan for them. Here's a list detailing the kinds of things you're going to need to do to get your PPC campaign up and running:

✔ **Competitor analysis:** Snooping! Competitor analysis is checking out who's selling a similar product, at what price point, and what her ads look like. Making a list of the sites that show up in the top of the search engine for a product like yours provided you with an idea of what you're up against.

✔ **Keyword research:** We always begin by brainstorming the popular words (keywords) customers might search for when they are looking to describe our product. By writing down as many words as you can think of that describe your product, what people would search for, what benefits your product offers, or problems it solves, you're arming a strong keyword starting point.

When you consider you are paying for every keyword you want to use and the more popular the word is the more you have to pay, having a jumble of words doesn't do you much good. This is when the keyword tool of your PPC advertiser of choice comes in. Look up the words to see how much they cost, how many people are actually looking for these words, and what kind of competition you have. A penny-per-click ad with 10 searches a month is just as bad as a $100-per-click ad for 10,000 searches. Both are unrealistic for landing page results, unless you have a product price point that matches.

✔ **Goal developing:** Putting pen to paper is the best way to establish goals. If you don't write down how much traffic you want to see, what kind of conversion rate you want to hit, and how many sales you want to generate, how will you know whether you're succeeding in your campaign? These numbers can be adjusted and need to be realistic, but you need a goal to strive for.

Management

A PPC campaigner's work is never done. After you've done your initial setup, you need to test and retest that setup to make sure it's working for you, and you need to be able to institute changes if you're not meeting your expectations. Here are a few points to consider:

✔ **Assessment:** Pull out that piece of paper with your goals. Have you hit your numbers? Are some parts of your game plan working and other parts not so much? Why? Look at each piece and determine whether it's been a success for you or a flop. Fine-tune the successes and test or remove the flops to achieve your goals.

✔ **Testing:** Testing is nothing more than comparing one element against another. Take headings for example. If Heading A gets twice the conversion rate as Heading B, you'd be foolish not to dump Heading B. At that point, you'd fine-tune Heading A for maximum visitor response and move on to the next element to test. *Note:* Test elements above the fold first because they have the most impact on visitor reaction.

Some tests results are clear — it's easy to see which element is more successful — but if some test results are too close to call, you can extend the testing period so you have more data to compare or depending on what you're testing, it could be an element that just doesn't affect your visitors enough to make much of a difference.

✔ **Fine-tuning:** Small adjustments to your PPC campaign can lead to increased and consistent sales. Take the earlier headings example: If you know Heading A has the best conversion rate, you can adjust a word here and there to squeeze every last conversion out that you can.

Changing even one word in a heading or call to action can be the difference between a visitor converting or bouncing. Don't forget to mirror even the smallest change in ad formatting back on your landing page so that you can maintain ad-to-landing page relevancy for your visitor.

Tracking and reporting

Going hand-in-hand with all the management tasks you need to carry out to keep your PPC campaign running smoothly is all the tracking you need to keep an eye on and all the reports you need to generate. Keep the following in mind while you keep all the balls in the air:

✔ **Analytics:** Using software to keep track of traffic is by far the most used part of our PPC campaign tools. When you know your traffic patterns — when they come, from where, what pages they visit, and so on — you can focus all your marketing energy on what's relevant in terms of increasing your conversion rate, thereby, reaching your goals.

✔ **Conversions:** Conversions can be sales, sign-ups, or any other action your visitor takes as a direct response to your call to action. The number of people who visit your site and actually do what you tell them to is how you determine whether you have a high or a low conversion rate. The conversion rate depends on a number of variables — relevance, site design, and a clear call to action being just three within your control.

✔ **Goal checking:** Are you succeeding? With all the testing, fine-tuning, and tracking you're doing, are you actually reaching your goals? If so, be sure to set the bar higher for yourself so you don't become complacent. In our experience, when a site owner becomes comfortable where she is, the site becomes stagnant fairly quickly. The "I'm successful, why should I change things?" mentality is a danger to continued PPC success.

Being Realistic about PPC Marketing

PPC marketing wouldn't be around if it didn't have success stories. You've probably heard a story or two about how this teen or that grandma made a killing by running a PPC campaign, and those stories might even have been true but don't get your hopes up. Such wildly successful campaigns tend to be short-lived and hold a very narrow window of opportunity. As such, they're not a real good standard to hold your own campaign results up against. If you're looking for real results, don't look at the one-shot deals but rather look at your campaign in terms of its ability to sustain earnings for you for a longer period of time.

To maximize your PPC success, you need to be flexible and be prepared to change your campaign at any time. Not only will you increase the success of your PPC campaigns, but will also help you avoid common mistakes that often lead to poor results.

PPC isn't a magic path to unlimited riches, but it can be used to your advantage. With a little — okay, a lot — of planning and the knowledge to back it up, you can meet or even exceed your expectations. All it takes is a little effort.

Seeing whether PPC really is an option for you

Many want you to believe that PPC marketing is a no-brainer for anyone and everyone who owns a Web site. From firsthand experience, that just isn't the case. With the right product and the right PPC campaign, you're going to love the increase you'll experience in your pocketbook, but if either part of the equation falls flat, you'll be left wondering what happened.

So how do you know whether a PPC campaign is the right choice for you and your product? Consider the following:

- **Price point:** You have to be competitive in the marketplace but you can't price yourself into the poor house, either. Like any sale, too high of a product price makes a tough sell, but that isn't what you need to worry about when we talk price point. You need to consider how much profit you'll make on each sale compared to how much your PPC campaign cost you to get that one sale. If lots of people click your ad but you're getting only a handful of sales, the PPC cost may not make a PPC marketing campaign worthwhile for you.

- **Type of visitor:** Each product is going to attract a different interest level. Some products are great for attracting attention but not buyers. Lookie loo's are great for your ego when you see people have taken an interest in your product and have visited your page, but they don't help your pocketbook. With so much choice online, some products are naturally harder to get people to take an interest in. A test campaign tells you quickly what type of visitor you attract, and in effect, whether PPC is for you.

- **PPC competition:** You aren't alone in your PPC endeavor. Not only are you competing against other company's products, you're competing with them for the keywords. The more companies interested in the same keywords as you, the more the costs per click (CPC) are going to rise. You can be creative and find a niche that others haven't or you can cough up over $100/click if you absolutely must use the same word! (In Chapter 13, we give you some keyword strategy pointers. Check it out to see whether PPC is your best marketing choice.)

- **Traffic volume:** For people to click your ad, they have to be looking for what you offer. Without a moderate-to-high level of Internet traffic searching for your keywords, you can't reach the daily sales you want to achieve. You may have to face facts and realize that just not enough people looking are for the words you chose or the product you have. You then have to decide whether to expand your marketing efforts (increasing the number of keywords or researching high traffic words) or possibly abandoning the PPC campaign and taking a different approach.

✔ **Campaign management:** PPC campaigns are most effective with proactive management. This includes tracking conversions, testing new ad variations, expanding marketing options, or breaking campaigns into smaller, more manageable campaigns. All this attention takes time, so if you're expecting PPC campaigning to be a one-time setup with continued results, PPC probably isn't for you.

✔ **Ad restrictions:** Just as your keyword selection and target market need to be researched, so do the PPC company policies. All PPC companies have a Terms of Service (TOS). These terms often restrict the types of ads that can be shown or brand names that can be used in the ads. Save yourself the grief and read the TOS closely before you pour your creative heart and soul into something you're positive will work . . . but isn't allowed. If you discover that your ad design or product is going to be rejected under the TOS — unless you can come up with something different — PPC may not be your best choice.

Examining the pros and cons to PPC

Regardless of the PPC marketing option you choose, you're going be faced with a whole series of pros and cons. Time to just lay them out for you. Here are the things we've found that work for and against running a PPC campaign:

✔ **Tracking ability: Definite Pro:** Nothing helps marketing better than being able to track results. PPC offers you your own tracking software and allows you to track every sale and transaction so you can narrow down what's working and what's wrong.

✔ **Cost control: Pro:** Most PPC campaigns work off set budgets. You have the power to control how much you spend and when you spend it. This is most important in the infancy of your campaigns, when you're just establishing what works and what doesn't. No sense spending a month's worth of budget on the first day!

✔ **Profit math: Definite Pro:** You have hard facts to compare what you're paying in clicks to how many people are visiting your site to how many people are buying your product. Being armed with this information means you can calculate how much profit you're earning compared to costs going out.

✔ **Testing capability: Pro:** Testing goes hand-in-hand with tracking. Without one, there's no point in doing the other. PPC has matured greatly over the years as you can now test right down to the nitty-gritty of a visitor's location, time of day, and even in some cases, his personal demographic, such as age and gender.

✔ **Web adaptability/mutability: Pro and Con:** Although how quickly the Internet can change to keep up with trends and new technologies is a definite pro, these same changes can wreak havoc when it comes to staying current with the laws and guidelines of the industry — a con in anyone's book.

We've already lost count how many times the ad management software or the TOS for the program we're using has changed this year alone. However, after the changes are introduced, whether through legislation or legal origins, *you* are the one responsible for keeping on top of any and all changes in the industry that could affect your sales.

✔ **Learning curve: Definite Con:** The biggest contributing factor to PPC failure is not taking the time to fully understand the program and what's involved. (The second biggest contributing factor comes from not setting up a campaign effectively.) We're not going to lie to you; PPC requires a decent amount of learning, research, and tenacity to achieve success.

✔ **Click fraud: Very serious Con:** As with anything, you're always going to find someone trying to bend the rules. People cheating the system by clicking your ads to make money is certainly not a reason to disregard PPC as an option, but if you choose a passive campaign management approach and don't keep track of what's going on and where, you may be faced with high costs for false results.

✔ **Unsavory sites: Definite Con:** These sites — we're sure you've seen them in your online travels — are nothing more than cheap excuses for wall-to-wall ads. Not considered click fraud because they provide a service, they offer little value to you or your visitors and may even step right up to (and perhaps over?) the line of deceptive click methods. Once again, we return to tracking: You need to know where your visitors come from if you hope to avoid the unsavory side of the Web.

Watching your costs — a cautionary tale

If ever a subject needed more focus in school, math is the one. Everything from running a business to determining profits to meeting your home budget is based on math. So why, when people decide to market online, do they forget about the math? We have our theories, but we won't discuss them here!

Knowing what you're really spending is the only true way to know whether you're making a profit or a loss, or for that matter, if you even have money to grow your company bigger. Although PPC math isn't overly complicated, it's crucial that you master it if you really want to succeed. The bottom line here is simple: If you don't know the ins and outs of your marketing budget, you can't participate successfully in a PPC campaign.

You might read this and think, "Of course I know how much money I have and whether I'm in the black. I run the business, don't I?" Well, the following example shows how that might not be the case.

A company recently approached us with the request, "If you have some spare time, could you look at our page and give us some ideas on how best to convert even more visitors?"

This sounded like a reasonable request. They — we'll call them Energy Co. — took the initiative to sign up for a PPC program, began their marketing efforts, and made sales right out the gate. Great start!

Then we asked the golden question, "Are you making any money?" The obvious answer Energy Co. gave was, "We're selling products, so yes, we are." Unfortunately, that wasn't the case. Sure, Energy Co. made sales, but they didn't factor all the costs involved.

In fact, Energy Co. was losing money on every sale because its product price point and the market competition drove the cost of each click higher than anticipated. Did that mean that all their hard work was for nothing? Not at all! But it did mean that optimizing Energy Co.'s site to increase the click-to-sale ratio was essential.

So how can a business owner's impression of sales success be so far off the mark? If Energy Co. sells batteries for $9.95/package; take the values in Table 16-2 to figure out how much they really should charge to make a profit:

Table 16-2	Determining Profit Threshold
Variable	*Value*
Keyword selected	*Battery*
Number of clicks	*116*
Number of impressions	*2,262*
Click-through rate (CTR)	*5.1 percent*
Average cost per click (CPC)	*$0.98*
Cost	*$113.68*
Conversion rate	*7.8 percent*
Cost/conversion	*$12.63*

The scenario in Table 16-2 means that for every $9.95 sale, Energy Co. is actually losing $2.68! (Keep reading this section to get a further breakdown of the math involved.) The good news is almost all the variables in the table can be adjusted to create a more favorable outcome. That's what landing page optimization is all about — converting a marketing weakness, such as a low conversion rate, into better results.

How much you spend per click, whether $0.05 or $5.00, is inconsequential if you're making a profit! You need to understand the math behind the campaign to succeed.

You're probably wondering how we got the numbers in Table 16-2 and whether you can get a hold of the numbers you'll need to make an informed decision about whether to take the PPC marketing plunge. Don't worry. We're not accountants or math wizards, and getting the numbers you need is easier than it looks. Just to prove it, we walk you through the PPC math to help you out.

The PPC program you choose is going to have a reporting system to provide you with many of the variables you see in Table 16-2. The system keeps track of the number of clicks, number of *impressions* — how many times your ad appears on a page — and the CPC for you, so apply PPC math to those numbers so you can use them. The math stuff is concentrated in four distinct areas, which the following list makes clear (we use the numbers from Table 16-2 for this example):

- ✔ **Cost per click (CPC):** Unless someone clicks your ad, you don't pay a cent. Pretty straightforward. If someone clicks an ad to come to your page, it costs you. How much? That's determined by the keyword popularity and the Terms of Service (TOS) of your PPC provider. In the example, the costs are as follows

    $0.98 per click × 116 clicks = $113.68 for that traffic

- ✔ **Click-through rate (CTR):** Your CTR is the amount of people that click your ad compared to the amount of times your ad is shown on a page — the number of impressions, in other words:

    116 clicks ÷ 2,262 impressions × 100 = 5.1 percent

- ✔ **Conversion rate:** For all the people that come to your page, some are going to leave right away — giving you your bounce rate — whereas others are going to buy your product. The ratio of those that end up buying your product compared to all the people who visit and do nothing, make up your conversion rate:

    9 sales ÷ 116 visits × 100 = 7.8 percent conversion

- ✔ **Cost-per-sale:** For PPC to be successful, all your costs must balance to a positive number. The cost for your campaign compared with your conversion rate tell you whether you're making or losing money:

    $113.68 campaign cost ÷ 9 sales = $12.63 per sale

After the math is done, you can see that if it costs Energy Co. $12.63 to make one sale, $9.95 for that sale just doesn't cut it. Also important to note, these calculations don't take into account product returns, operating costs, shipping . . . the list goes on and on, and for an accurate business model, all these need to be taken into account.

For any PPC campaign to succeed, you need to start with a sound mathematical foundation. Take the time to review the factors here to ensure you know the maximum amount per click you can spend and the minimum product price to charge before it becomes a detriment.

Using PPC for Testing Purposes

PPC is one of the best ways to test concepts and product ideas before you spend a fortune on your marketing efforts. Having the answers to questions like what image has the greatest impact, which heading draws people into reading more, and which call to action actually gets results saves you time and money, while providing the information you need to make an informed PPC decision.

PPC testing strategies

Before you spend your whole marketing budget on a PPC campaign, we recommend testing your theories of what you think visitors will respond to by running small campaigns. In the planning phase of your core PPC campaign, you can test specific elements independently so that your final campaign has the best combination of factors.

You could use a low-key PPC campaign to test the following:

- ✔ **Ideas or concepts:** Do you have an idea but aren't sure whether others will like it? Make the desired action of your PPC campaign a sign-up page. This type of campaign is often used for newsletter sign-up sites or as audience testing for new books or workshops.

- ✔ **Price points:** Not sure what price to put your product at? A PPC split-test can tell you without a doubt. To run a split-test campaign, use two identical ads but have their URLs go to two different pages — identical in look but with a different price. This allows price to be the only factor tested.

- ✔ **Deals and special offers:** How do you know the best offer to match with your product? Just like testing your price point, use two identical ads that go to two identical pages, except for the special offer. This quickly shows you which deal or offer your visitors prefer.

✔ **Visitor demographics:** Want to know who's going to buy from you more often? Carry out your demographic testing with targeted campaigns. You always have the option (as part of the PPC program you sign up for) of specifying geographically where your ads are seen, at what time of day, and other demographic-related variables.

✔ **Product and page designs:** Do you have a couple different designs for your product packaging and just can't choose which one to go with? Back to split-testing! Two identical ads — except for the product presentation — going to two identical pages solves your dilemma. This can also be applied to images, text, headings, and every other page element you can think of.

The five biggest mistakes with PPC testing

As with any endeavor in life, you might just make a few mistakes now and then. When it comes to PPC testing, we guarantee you'll make at least a couple along the way. To help you avoid the major false steps, we bring the most common mistakes to your attention:

✔ **Going in blind:** When new PPC participants just throw together some keywords, put together an ad, and hope for great sales, they're just asking for disappointment. Not only do you need to know what keywords are effective, but you also need to run them against each other so you can refine your ads to the most effective combination possible. By planning ahead, you save campaign money in the long run by not wasting money on ineffective clicks.

✔ **Forgetting to track conversions:** Back to the math — a program that keeps track of your PPC variables is essential to keeping all your data current and accurate. Guessing just isn't an option here.

✔ **Testing beyond your budget:** Testing is only as good as its results. With too few statistics, you can't determine which test was a success, but if it takes more marketing budget than you have to gather the data, you need to rethink your approach.

An acceptable test campaign is 100+ clicks per ad, and in a split-test campaign, that equals 200 people that need to click your ads. If each click is $1, your test costs $200, so you need to make sure the keywords you use are within your budget for adequate data collection.

✔ **Excessive testing:** Testing is essential to gather usable data, but it can't be considered your PPC campaign. You begin with testing to develop your core campaign, but as you determine what works and what doesn't, those items become your control factor, and your ads and your pages start to solidify into a successful PPC approach.

For example, after you know what heading gets the best response, don't test it anymore, at least for a while. The same is true when it comes to the image you use; after you know what works, leave it alone. Use testing to weed out the underperforming elements — those that just don't get a response — not as a way of creating ever-changing ads and landing pages.

✔ **Not designing a landing page:** You can test all the ads you want but if you send your visitors to an untargeted home page, you're wasting your time and theirs. The idea here isn't merely to test the elements of your ads for effectiveness; you also need to establish what gets them to act after they arrive from your ad. This can be accomplished only with a highly targeted, keyword- and message-focused landing page.

Where Can You Find Out More about PPC?

Just like anything online, PPC adapts to the current trends and as such can change without notice. The best way to stay on top of the most current developments is to go to the source.

To sign up for a PPC program, visit

✔ **Google AdWords:** `http://adwords.google.com`

✔ **Yahoo! Search Marketing:** `http://searchmarketing.yahoo.`

✔ **MSN Bing:** `https://adcenter.microsoft.com/`

To find more information, visit

✔ **Google official blog:** `http://adwords.blogspot.com`

✔ **Yahoo! Search Official Blog:** `www.ysearchblog.com`

✔ **Microsoft official advertising blog:** `http://community.` `microsoftadvertising.com/Default.aspx`

To ask questions on our community site, visit

✔ **Just Make It Easy:** `www.justmakeiteasy.com`

Not only do these sites provide you with current developments, by going to the source of the programs, but you're also sure to receive quality information and have a better chance at side-stepping scams and false information.

Chapter 17

Running a Google PPC Campaign

*I*f you're ready for this chapter, that means your landing page is ready to go, you're fired up, and you're all set to invite visitors to your site. You've already put a lot of hard work into your page, so without further delay, get down to the next step: Actually setting up your own a campaign to get those visitors — or should we say buyers? — to your site.

To help you take your first baby steps in pay per click (PPC) marketing, this chapter is dedicated to setting up and running a simple Google AdWords campaign. We chose Google because AdWords is currently the largest PPC opportunity on the Web. We guide you through the how-to's of signing up, writing effective ads, and managing a campaign from start to finish as well as explore many of the other tools and options Google offers its advertisers.

Starting with Google AdWords

AdWords, like any other marketing campaign, takes some time to figure out. Having worked with AdWords for many years, with the benefit of large and small marketing budgets, we're always astonished at how much more can always be learned and tried. We don't mention this to overwhelm you, but rather as a reminder to open your mind to the limitless possibilities you have if you so desire.

Before you jump into your limitless possibilities, though, we start with the campaign basics. A small-scale campaign is the best way to get your feet wet. Although you can set up a large campaign all at once and test many factors at the same time, that approach falls under your Limitless Possibilities category and must wait for another day.

Laying the groundwork

As much as we both want you to jump into your first campaign, by doing a little advance prep work, you'll save yourself setup time and frustration, allowing you to get your ads up and running all the faster.

The easiest way we can think of for you to do the spade work for your campaign is to grab a pen and paper and answer some simple questions. You probably know some of the answers from when you designed your landing page, but having all the information in one spot is helpful:

- ✔ **Who's your target audience?** The more specific answers you can come up with here, the better. Think about where they're located, what they have in common, and what their occupations, ages, hobbies, and so on are.

   You're going to need this information to write your ads and choose where you want your ads to appear.

- ✔ **What's your language and currency of choice?** This relates to your target market and where you plan to market your products. If your business is based in Canada, but your target is the U.S., offer your product in U.S. currency. Or, you can choose to market in Canada and the U.S. and create separate campaigns that you've tailored for each region.

   The same goes for language. If your target market has a language different than yours, be sure to know this in advance.

- ✔ **Where will your ad link take your visitors?** Your ad is going to be clicked by people browsing online, so you need to know where you're sending them to. Remember, this isn't your home page, but a landing page designed for this ad campaign.

- ✔ **What keywords are you planning to use?** What words will your target market be looking for? You want your ads to show up when they search for things related to your product, so not only do your keywords have to relate to your product and your landing page, but they also need to be reflected directly in your ad. (See Chapter 13 for more on keywords.)

   Although developing a keyword list in advance will probably save you time during your campaign setup process, you can do the keyword research during your setup stage. For your first test campaign, you want only a few words — say, fewer than ten — in your ad group to test the success of your ad and landing page combination.

✔ **What do you want your ad to say?** Jot down some ideas of your own or do a search on Google for products similar to yours to see what others are writing. Take note of the phrases you like and if you're still stuck for ideas, you can also check out `www.justmakeiteasy.com` and ask its community.

As tempting as it might be to just come up with an ad and enter it during the setup process, we're far from sure that writing ads on the fly is necessarily the best way to go about it. By researching and preparing some examples in advance, you can quickly get through this step, though.

✔ **How much can you spend per month?** You can set the maximum amount per day that you spend on your AdWords campaign. If you know your monthly marketing budget, whip out the calculator, do a quick divide-by-30 calculation, and you know how much you can dedicate to each day. The more you have to spend — or the better the keyword price you get — the more often your ad may be shown and potentially clicked. Money that isn't spent that day simply rolls over to the next day, at no loss to you.

We recommend using a spiral notebook at first to keep your notes for future reference. As you perfect your keywords and ad design, you can refer back to what has and hasn't worked. As your campaigns develop and your expertise grows, you'll need a more elaborate tracking system, such as a spreadsheet.

Without answers to the earlier questions, you can't complete some areas that follow. You can return to these areas in your campaign at a later date, but that seems like more work that you need to do!

Choosing between the Starter or Standard Edition

We walk you through the Standard Edition AdWords account. A Starter Edition, while also available, is rather limited. The good news is, if you choose to begin with the Starter Edition, you can still apply many of the concepts we discuss here and, after you exceed its limitations, you can graduate to the Standard Edition at any time.

To help you make the decision that suits you and your business, take a look at Table 17-1. By comparing the Starter and the Standard Editions, you can make an informed business decision.

Table 17-1	Starter versus Standard AdWord Edition	
Option	**Starter**	**Standard**
Sign-up process	Simple	Complex
Number of products	One	Many
Ad types	Text only	All available
Analytics	Basic overview	Advanced reports with custom options
Location targeting	One region	Multiple locations
Cost controls	N/A	Bidding options
Planning tools	N/A	Conversion tracking, traffic estimator, and more
Placement targeting	N/A	Target specific publisher Web sites

The first step with taking part in any program is signing up, and AdWords is no different. Visit https://adwords.google.com and you arrive at a page similar to Figure 17-1. After you're there, click the Start Now button to get the sign-up process started. (We say *similar* here because we can't control how often Google changes the look of its sign-up page.)

Figure 17-1:
The sign-up and login page for AdWords.

We recommend you choose the Standard Edition, but the final decision is up to you. Review Table 17-1 to make the decision that best suits your needs. After you sign up or choose to graduate to the Standard Edition, you can't revert to the Starter Edition, so weigh your decision carefully.

After you sign up to Google AdWords, expect an e-mail from the Google AdWords Team welcoming you to the program. To make things easy, they include a link for you to sign in for the first time.

The Standard Edition account structure

As the organization chart in Figure 17-2 demonstrates, the Standard Edition AdWords account is broken into three main levels, with the end result being the ads you create. During setup, until you have an active campaign, you're not going to see the Ad Group level, but we feel it's important for you to understand how the entire organizational structure works together.

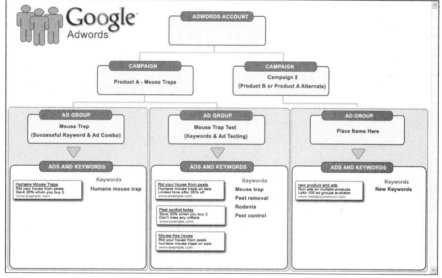

Figure 17-2: An overview of the Google account organization structure.

✔ **The account:** The first level of an AdWords campaign is the account. The account you open to join the program can hold more than one campaign. The account, although the beginning of your whole AdWords experience, is a relatively uncomplicated part of the process. Your account contains what you'd expect — your billing information, e-mail address, and the campaigns you run.

✔ **The campaign:** At the campaign level, AdWords is comparable to any other campaign you may have heard about. An everyday example is a political campaign. Although political campaigns are designed for a specific election and AdWords campaigns are geared toward a specific product, both can run on for years.

When you set up your first campaign, you will jump right in to creating an ad without the option of level three, ad groups. Although ad groups are optional in that you can run one or more ads under a campaign, you can use ad groups to your advantage.

✔ **The ad group:** Every campaign can have multiple *ad groups* — the third level of the account structure. The idea here is to create more than one campaign focus for your product, such as one for Canada and one for the U.S.

The ad group level is where you separate or compartmentalize the ads you run based on the keywords you have researched. Ad groups also allow you to test which keyword and ad combinations create the highest click-through rate (CTR) by visitors. Ad groups enable you to break your main marketing campaign into smaller, manageable parts. Think of ad groups in terms of running an ad in the newspaper; just as you can select one or more newspapers to advertise in, ad groups would be the individual newspapers you wish to advertise in.

To see how this works, check out Figure 17-2, which shows two ad groups created for a campaign trying to sell the archetypal *better mousetrap.* One ad group is the *control,* where the keywords and ad combination with the highest CTR is located. (You determine the control group after you run tests on ad and keyword combinations.) The other ad group is the test group.

The test group holds a number of keywords and ads that run at the same time. As people search for the keywords chosen, such as *pest removal,* Google determines which ad to display. As the ads are shown to more people, you can compare the CTR of each ad. If the ad with the highest CTR in your test group is also higher than your ad and keyword combination in your control, the new ad becomes the control, and you keep testing until you have the best ad and keyword combination you can design.

New and seasoned AdWords users alike find that placing ads and single keywords (or a tight group of related keywords) into their own ad group and then monitoring which ad and keywords perform best is the way to go. As your testing progresses, if you notice keywords and ads that do really well, separate them right away for easier management. You can also name your ad group with the keyword used (*pest removal,* for example) so you can find the ad group easier.

The AdWords structure is based on versatility. The ability of the advertiser to run anything from a small campaign with an ad and a keyword or two right up to an immense campaign involving hundreds of ads and thousands of keywords also means AdWords is suitable for any business or budget size.

Working within the AdWords interface

The AdWords interface, although fairly user-friendly, is still a challenge until you become familiar with where tools are located and where to go to check your campaign.

To give you a head start, Figure 17-3 shows what you see after you sign in to your account. Basic navigation tabs along the top and within the page take you to each of the main areas, but also notice many additional action buttons throughout, so keep your eyes open for all the tools at your fingertips.

At the time we are writing this chapter, Google is rolling out their new interface. Although subtle changes may occur to the pages you see compared to the images we provide, the concepts and basic workings of Google AdWords will remain unchanged.

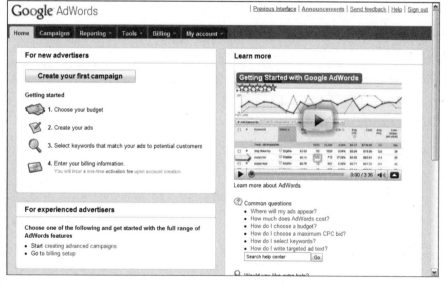

Figure 17-3: The first page new users are directed to in the Google AdWords interface.

Think of the main navigation tabs at the top as your toolbar. Each of the tabs, except for Home and Campaigns, is a drop-down list providing multiple selections. Tabs that you have access to include

✔ **Home:** An account snapshot, the Home tab gives you an overview of alerts, campaign performance, account status, keyword performance, and more. At a glance, you can see how your campaign is doing or be informed of crucial information, such as whether your account balance is running low.

On the Home tab, after you've set up your first campaign, you can customize the information presented by moving, adding, or removing informational boxes such as the campaign Watch List or Alerts.

✔ **Campaigns:** Jump right to your campaign management with this tab. Here you'll find a secondary (tabbed) navigation with campaign options, including Campaigns, Ad Groups, Settings, Ads, Keywords, and Networks.

✔ **Reporting:** Here you'll find everything to do with keeping track of your campaigns, including custom reports, Google Analytics, and the Website Optimizer.

✔ **Tools:** Home to more than ten tools for you to use, this tab offers the Keyword tool, conversion tracking, the Ads Diagnostic tool, the Ad Preview tool, and more.

✔ **Billing:** This tab lets you keep on top of your expenses with the Billing summary, set how you want to pay with Billing Preferences, and Make Payments to add more funds to your account.

✔ **My Account:** Manage your account with Account Preferences and Account Access drop-down options.

Also worth noting is the text menu in the top-right corner. This menu bar makes it easy to find current announcements, a help section, and even has a menu command to send feedback to the Google team.

When you're in any section of the AdWords interface, the Help link at the top-right corner provides you with help for that particular area. And this isn't just a blanket Help section; it actually tailors the help information to what you want to do at the time.

Getting off the ground with campaigns

Campaign is thrown around a lot today, from politics to marketing, but no matter what context it's used in, it generally means the same thing. When it comes to AdWords, *campaign* is a concentrated effort devoted to advertising your product to get sales.

You have two campaign options with AdWords: keyword and placement. We compare keyword-targeted and placement-targeted campaigns in Table 17-2.

Table 17-2	Campaign Options	
Characteristics	*Keyword-Targeted*	*Placement-Targeted*
Based on	Keywords	Specific Web sites
Appear on	Google.com, Google search partners, and all content sites in the Google network	Individual Google network sites you select or a specific set of sites you choose
Cost structure	Cost per click and cost per impression	Cost per click and cost per impression
Ads allowed	Text, expanded text, and image ads	Expanded text and image ads

Keyword-targeted campaigns are the most popular, so we walk you through this type. This type of campaign is based on an auction format, where the keywords chosen go to the highest bidder. The more popular a keyword is, the more advertisers pay each time their ad is clicked. The advertiser who is willing to pay the most will be placed higher in the search results than other advertisers.

Google rates the price of keywords on their own dynamic measurement called the *Quality Score*. The Quality Score is calculated every time a user searches for your keyword and takes into consideration a variety of factors, including the quality of your landing page and relevance of the keywords to the word or phrase searched, just to name a couple.

You are aiming for a high Quality Score for a number of reasons. In general, ads with a higher Quality Score receive more clicks, win a higher search page position and, because relevance is a factor, often get better conversion results as the people that click those ads get the results they're looking for.

You can improve your Quality Score by ensuring your ad matches your keywords, which in turn match your landing page. Google is trying its best to offer its users relevant information — if you can do that, you can improve your Quality Score.

A step-by-step process has been added recently to the Google AdWords program. By following its automated campaign set-up, you receive assistance every step of the way. Follow these steps to set up your first campaign.

1. **Sign in to your Google AdWords account at `http://adwords.google.com`.**

   These instructions are for first time users, if you have already set up an account or logged out, the procedure will be slightly different.

2. **Click the Create Your First Campaign button.**

   The page will reload and offer you the first step of setting up a campaign — your Campaign settings. Any of these settings can be changed at a later time, so don't worry that you're stuck with what you select today.

   Google has also provided a robust Help Center to answer many of your questions. At any time you can access this Help Center with the link in the top-right corner of the page or use the question mark button next to the different topics for guidance and explanations.

3. **Under the Campaign settings tab, enter your Campaign name.**

4. **Select the radial button for your audience Location.**

   The audience location allows you to decide how geographically targeted you want your campaign to be — from only your hometown to global.

   The language is English by default; click Edit next to 'English' to change the language choice.

5. **Skip the Demographic option and move on to the next section — the Networks, Devices, and Extensions section.**

   The radio button for All Available Sites and Devices is chosen by default.

   Selecting the demographics for your campaign is more advanced than you need to get into at this stage. Feel free to click the + sign to see the demographic option, but we don't recommend applying these settings until you are farther along in your AdWords learning.

6. **Click Let Me Choose.**

   We recommend only checking Google search and Search Partners boxes to start. Under Devices, check Desktop and Laptop Computers; otherwise, you get the warning shown in Figure 17-4.

   Selecting all options within this section is for more advanced users and therefore requires more ad management.

7. **Under Bidding and Budget, the radio button for Automatic Bidding is chosen by default.**

   The simplest bidding option, Automatic Bidding leaves the bid, or amount paid per click, up to Google. Its program will automatically adjust your cost per click (CPC) to get you the most bids possible within your monthly budget (determined next). You may want to put a maximum value of each bid, such as $0.50, so Google will not go over that amount for any single ad click.

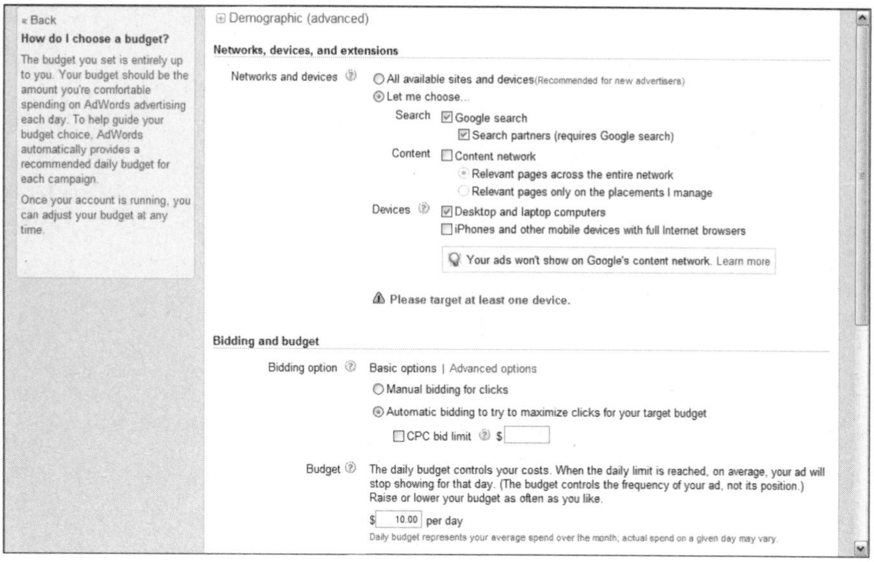

Figure 17-4:
Setting
your own
Networks
and
Devices.

8. **Enter your maximum budget per day in the text box provided.**

   Determining accurately how much per month you have to spend on your AdWords campaign is important. As we discuss in Chapter 16, doing the math behind your campaign ensures that you make money, not lose it per sale.

   Until you are more familiar with running your campaign, start with a low budget such as $10.00 or $20.00 per day. If you don't spend the daily budget, the funds simply stay in your ad account to be used at a later time.

9. **Review the remaining settings — Position Preference, Schedule and Ad Delivery.**

   Each of these settings is for advanced users. Click the + sign to become familiar, but at this stage, we don't recommend modifying them.

10. **Click the Save and Continue button.**

The first phase of setting up your campaign is complete. Now it's time to write your first ad.

Entering your first ad

If you've followed along so far, the next step in the campaign set-up process is to write your first text ad. You can change all ads at a later date or you can skip this step until you've outlined what you want to say, but it doesn't hurt to give it a try. (*Note:* Although the principles in this chapter relate to Google AdWords, the theories and strategies we discuss can be used for any PPC program.)

As part of managing any campaign, we recommend coming up with three or four text ads that you plan on running at the same time. As you determine which one of these ads has the higher conversion rate, put the under performers on ice and refine the one with the highest click-through-rate (CTR).

Don't delete old ads, simply pause them, or you lose the valuable stats collected.

All text ads have a very strict character count and a distinct look to them. To stick to the basics, we want to create a standard text ad. You can make life hard by counting the characters manually or making a template in a word processor, but Google has so many handy tools available to you as part of your AdWords account, you may as well let its Ad Preview tool do the work for you. Here's how.

1. **If you've been following along with the previous setting up a campaign section, you'll be in the Create an Ad area under the Ads tab. If not, log in to your account again and click the Campaign tab.**

2. **Enter your first text ad using the text boxes shown in Figure 17-5.**

   You can change the type of ad with the Choose Another Ad Type drop-down menu. For simplicity's sake, we'll be creating a text ad here.

3. **Enter your Heading (25 characters).**

   As you enter text, your ad is created on the fly in the Ad Preview box to the right. This is a great feature Google has added to let you see just how your ad will look and be laid out.

4. **Enter your two Description lines (35 characters each).**

   Notice as you type that there is a gray progress bar next to the text box, showing how close you are to using all your characters. Although it's not an accurate character count, it's a nice visual touch for keeping an eye on how much space you have left.

5. **Enter your Display URL (35 characters).**

   The Display URL is your Web address. This is the address you would have on business cards or in advertising. Short and often memorable, your display URL is the one a visitor will remember if they visit your site later or tell their friends about it.

6. **Enter your Destination URL (1,024 characters).**

   The Destination URL is the exact location within your Web site you want visitors to go to. This location is the landing page you have created for this particular advertisement.

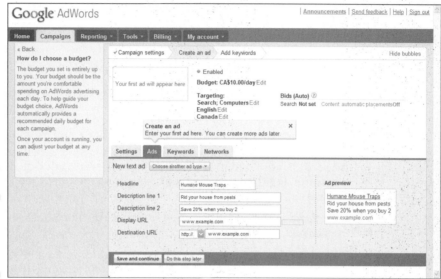

Figure 17-5:
Creating
an ad in
AdWords.

7. **Click the Save and Continue button.**

Once clicked, Google goes and reads the page it locates at your
Destination URL to provide you with keyword suggestions. A landing
page that's relevant to your topic and keywords is your saving grace
here. Seeing as you're faced with a computer that can't interpret your
page but takes every word and sentence literally, you have to ensure
that your landing page is very clear in its message.

Google knows that relevancy affects how the customer interprets your
landing page; therefore, it duly tests for relevancy and adjusts your keyword
costs accordingly. This grading system is in place for two reasons — to keep
the searcher happy by providing more relevant information and to stop or
reduce people from tricking visitors by using keywords not related to the
landing page.

Although ads are generally placed quickly on the network, staff often reviews
the ads before placement. Ads that don't follow the rules or have a problem
won't appear and you'll see an alert in your Account Snapshot on your
AdWords home page. Such rejections are a common problem and can happen
to every user, regardless of ad-writing ability, but at least you can review any
ads that don't meet the standard and correct them. To see exactly why the ad
was rejected so you know how to correct it, choose Tools➪More Tools➪
Disapproved Ads from the main navigational tabs.

Adding keywords

No way around it, your campaign success or failure is based on the keywords you choose. Google compiles a list of suggested keywords based on the destination URL you supply for your ad, but you don't have to accept all or even any of the keywords on the list. You have full control over the words you do and don't use. To pick and choose what keywords you want to use, follow these steps:

1. **If you've been following along with the previous Entering Your First Ad section, you'll be in the Add Keywords area under the Keywords tab. If not, log in to your account again and click the Campaign tab⇨ Keywords tab.**

2. **Scan through the list on the right of keywords that Google recommends for your ad.**

   Click the <<Add link next to the keywords you want to add to your list or, if you agree with all of them, click << Add All from this category link.

   As you add the Google suggested keywords, they will be removed from the list and appear in the large text box on the left, as shown in Figure 17-6.

3. **(Optional) Enter your own keywords into the list box on the left of the screen.**

   The Google scan of your landing page can be very informative when finalizing your keyword selection. This scan can give you great ideas you may not have thought of, or it can show you how far off base your landing page is! If the keyword suggestions are completely off the mark, revisit your landing page and figure out where it's falling short, or it might be necessary to create another landing page for that keyword group.

4. **Click the Estimate Search Traffic button located under the keyword list box.**

   You're provided with the average CPC — clicks per day — and cost per day you can then decide whether your keywords are worth your effort or whether you need to keep looking for better or additional keywords.

5. **(Optional) Below the Save and Continue to Billing button, click the + sign next to Negative Keywords and a new section will appear.**

   Negative keywords are words you want Google to omit when analyzing the search queries they receive from visitors. For example, if the negative keyword you enter is **free**, your ad doesn't appear when someone looks for *free mouse traps.*

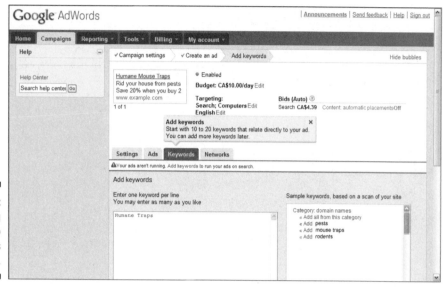

Figure 17-6:
Adding
keywords to
an AdWords
campaign.

6. **(Optional) Click the + Add button and enter any negative keywords you want to specify in the new text box that appears.**

A good list of negative keywords helps weed out people who are looking for other things, whether it be freebies or information. Popular negative keywords include: free, sample, definition, what are, bargain, cheap, discount, how to, and so on.

7. **Click the Save and Continue to Billing button and you will be directed to the Account Setup screen.**

Taking care of billing

Google AdWords is a for pay service, meaning they require — you guessed it — payment. In addition to the advertising costs, you are charged a non-refundable one-time activation fee of $10.00 US. The Billing tab, located in the top navigation, is the last step before your campaign is up and running live.

The AdWords program offers you the following two payment choices and accepts American Express, MasterCard, Visa, and debit cards with a MasterCard or Visa logo:

✔ **Postpay Billing:** Google will bill you after you accumulate advertising costs. You will be billed every 30 days or when your account reaches the *Billing threshold* of $50.00US. Google sets this billing threshold.

✔ **Prepay Billing:** Rather than billing you at the end of the month for services rendered, you keep a running balance in your account that enables Google to deduct your advertising costs daily. You can add more funds to your account balance at any time and if you run low, you will see an alert in your Account Snapshot on your AdWords Home page. In addition to the credit and debit card payment choices, prepay also permits bank transfers.

You cannot change from Postpay to Prepay, so choose carefully! For a full understanding of your choices, we recommend visiting the AdWords Help section at `http://adwords.google.com/support/` and searching for "Payment Options."

Use these steps to set up your billing information.

1. **If you've been following along with the previous Adding Your Keywords section, you'll be in the Account Setup area under the Billing tab.**

2. **Using the drop-down menu, choose your country and time zone on the Account Setup page.**

   The country your billing address is located and its currency determines payment options available.

3. **Click the Continue button.**

4. **Using the radio buttons, choose your form of payment.**

5. **Click the Continue button.**

6. **Click the Yes, I Agree to the Above Terms and Conditions check box and click the Continue button.**

   You are agreeing to a legal contract at this time. Responsibility falls on you to read and know the rules, including what ads are allowed, billing practices and your privacy rights. Always read the terms of any agreement before you click an Agree button.

7. **Enter your billing information.**

   The screen you see will vary depending on the payment type chosen. To complete this step, simply follow the instructions on the page you are directed to.

8. **Click the Save and Activate button.**

Managing your campaign with AdGroups

Okay, we assume you've now set up your very own basic AdWords campaign. If all is well, it'll soon be live on the Web where you'll see impressions or how many times your ad is displayed. Anytime you want to see how your campaigns are going, visit your Home tab for an overview in the form of the Account Snapshot.

You specify your campaign budget and parameters when you set up your campaign, which we spell out in the preceding section. After that's behind you, you can create ad groups within your campaign to capitalize on multiple keywords, ad variations, and ad placement. Google limits the number of campaigns you can run to 25 at any one time, but each campaign can have up to 100 ad groups.

Think of your campaign as an apartment building owner. The campaign sets the rules and guidelines its tenants must follow. Your ad groups are the tenants within that apartment building. Although all are under the main rules of the owner, they can bring in their own furniture and make the space uniquely theirs, so long as they stay within the rules.

To set up an Ad Group, follow these steps:

1. **Sign into your AdWords account and click the Campaigns tab.**

2. **Click the Create a New Campaign button in the top left-hand side.**

   While this button choice may seem odd, once clicked you are given the option to add a new ad group or add a new campaign.

   Note: After you have set up an ad group, an Ad Group tab (see Figure 17-7) will be available for easy navigation.

3. **Click the + New ad group button.**

4. **Type the group's name into the Ad Group Name text box.**

5. **Enter a new ad in the text boxes provided, as shown in Figure 17-8.**

   Creating this ad is the same process as any other ad you'd create. You are provided with an on-the-fly preview box and Google will automatically limit your character count to:

   - *Heading:* 25 characters
   - *Description line 1:* 35 characters
   - *Description line 2:* 35 characters
   - *Display URL:* 35 characters
   - *Destination URL:* 1,024 characters

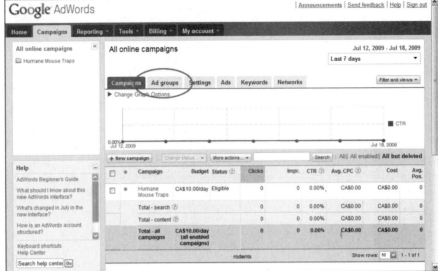

Figure 17-7:
Ad group
tab is added
to your
navigation.

6. **Enter your own keywords into the list box on the screen.**

7. **Click the Estimate Search Traffic button located under the keyword list box.**

8. **Skip the Placements option and click the Save and Continue button.**

   Managed placements are for more advanced AdWords users, as they are available only on the content network, require you to enter specific Web sites that you want your ad to appear as well as give you the option of adjusting your keyword bid for each of these specific placements.

Using Google Analytics

Even though analytics isn't really part of the campaign setup process, it does fall under the management heading. Google recognizes that a big part of a successful campaign is tracking its results and performance, so it created a free analytics program that ties into the AdWords program. To sign up, visit the Google Analytics home page at www.google.com/analytics or choose Reporting⇨Google Analytics and follow the instructions.

Google Analytics is software that compiles lots of different information about your site traffic — how people found your site, which areas they have visited, how many page views your site has, just to name a few — into tidy charts and tables for you to refer to. For best results, you need to have Google Analytics in place and reporting before you start running your campaigns. Without proper tracking from the beginning, you're not going to benefit from modifying and tracking your conversions.

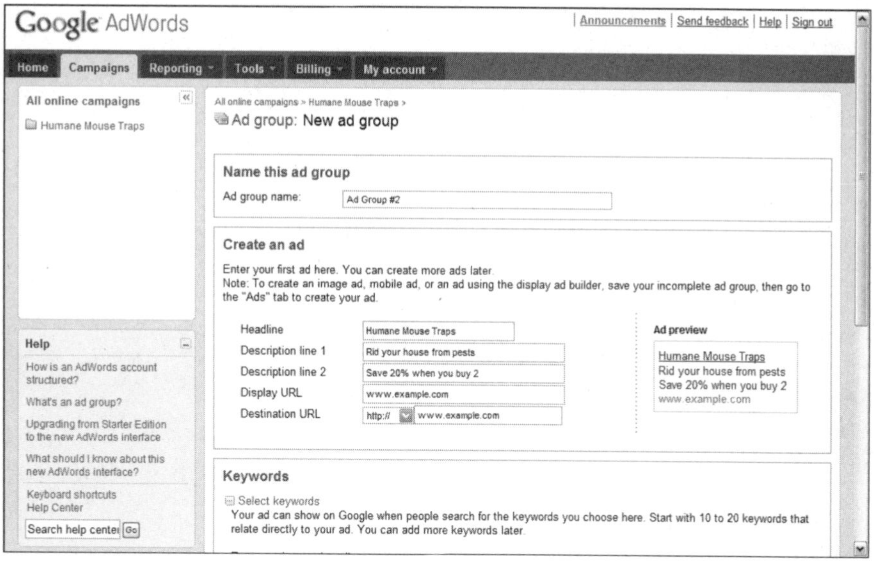

Figure 17-8:
Entering
a new ad
group.

You're looking for patterns of behavior from your visitors. If ten people visit your site and all leave from the same page, something at that point made folks lose interest. If eight out of ten people click the FAQ link from your shopping cart, some vital piece of information is missing on your order page. Armed with this information, you can analyze your page compared to visitor behavior to improve your conversion rate.

For clean results, set up Google Analytics (or any tracking software you may be using) to remove your IP address or computer from being part of the data collection. As a Web site owner, you're sure to visit your page numerous times, so taking this step ensures that your own visits aren't counted as standard visitor behavior. To filter out your IP address or computer so that Google Analytics doesn't pay it any mind, follow these steps:

1. **Sign into your AdWords account and click the Reporting tab ⇨Google.**

2. **Click the Analytics Settings link in the top-left corner.**

3. **In the bottom right-hand corner, click the Filter Manager link.**

   A new page loads, displaying a filter manager that allows you to be in charge of what information actually becomes part of your account statistics.

4. **Click the + Add Filter link on the right-hand side of the gray Existing Filters bar shown in Figure 17-9.**

5. **In the Add Filter dialog box that appears, enter a filter name (such as "My Computer") in the text box.**

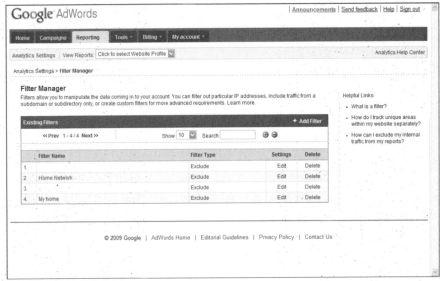

Figure 17-9:
Add Filters
to refine
your data.

6. **From the Filter Type drop-down list, choose Exclude All Traffic from an IP Address.**

7. **Type in your IP address.**

8. **Select the profile in the Available Website Profiles box that you want this filter to apply to.**

   There may only be one Web site in the Available Website Profiles box.

9. **Click the Add button to move the profile to the Selected Websites Profiles box.**

10. **Click the Save Changes button to save the filter.**

By removing your own IP address as well as those of your staff and family, you get a more accurate idea of how many people are visiting your landing page, how many of them are visiting for the first time and how many are repeat visitors. Without accurate data, you can't make informed choices as to what elements are working and which ones aren't.

Using Google's Free Advertiser Tools

Not only does Google provide its advertisers with the tools necessary to streamline the marketing aspect of the PPC, but it also provides many tracking and research tools you need — for free. In this section, we talk about just a few of the tools available with a brief explanation of how each can be used to your advantage.

To get started, sign in to your AdWords account, then click Tools⇨More Tools. This tab offers over ten different tools for you to use. Some tools you'll become intimately familiar with and use almost daily, while others you may never use. Just as you will, we have our favorites and discuss them briefly below.

Website Optimizer, a split-testing tool

We're big fans of split-testing, where you run two campaigns with one item that is different. The item can be anything from the heading, the product price point or an image. To increase the conversion rate on your page, you need to know what works and what doesn't. To make finding out what works and what doesn't easier, use Google's own split-testing tool, the Website Optimizer, instead of going to the trouble of testing each landing page separately.

The Website Optimizer allows you to choose a specific element of your landing page, such as the heading or the call to action, and run an experiment on which one is more effective at converting visitors to customers. At the end of the experiment, you're given a report with the results.

Google's Website Optimizer does all the split-testing work for you because it automatically selects which version of the page to show customers. For the software to work, however, you need to follow the instructions carefully because you need to make a few technical changes to your landing pages.

You can choose from two versions of the Website Optimizer — one simple and one more complex — with the only real difference being the number of separate items you can test. Keep in mind that the more complex version does require more technical expertise when you add code to your site.

Using the AdWords Keyword tool

Coming up with keywords can be a fun exercise in creativity, but it can also be frustrating when you run out of ideas. To get things started or stimulate the imagination if you're stuck, Google offers a Keyword tool. We find it similar to using a thesaurus because you simply type a word or phrase you're thinking into a text box and Google gets keyword ideas for you. Google cannot guarantee the keywords it suggests will improve your campaign, but they can certainly help you come up with more word associations than you realized.

Keywords are single a word or groups of words you believe your ideal customer would search for online. The more you can come up with, the more you have to work with and narrow down to the best results.

Using the Ad Preview tool (and checking on your competition)

You'll probably wonder now and then, "Are my ads really showing?" Your first impulse is to search Google for your keywords and look for your ad. Don't do this for two reasons: your impression-to-click ratio and the sheer size of Google.

Every time you use a regular search to find your keywords, you change the impression-to-click ratio. When you view your ad with a normal search, it counts as an impression, which skews your data. Second, if you run ads and want to check their placement, you need to look at different search results, be it Canada, the U.S., or Australia. Google runs separate engines with different ad search results.

To solve this problem, Google offers the Ad Preview tool. Not only can you search for your keyword without fear of having the impression *count,* but you can specify which search engine you want to use. The Ad Preview tool even lets you choose your location down to the coordinates you want to search.

Another advantage of using this tool is that you don't have any accidental clicks. Because you can't click any of the ads shown by mistake, it saves both you and other advertisers from paying for an invalid click.

As there are many tools, advantages, and uses for those tools, we could write a whole chapter just on the tools themselves. Google AdWords has a robust Help section you can visit at `https://adwords.google.com/support` to learn how to use them, as well as a whole slew of tips and tricks for your greater success.

Part VI
The Part of Tens

"Before the Internet, we were only bustin' chops locally. But now, with our Web site, we're bustin' chops all over the world."

In this part . . .

No *For Dummies* book would be complete without a Part of Tens section. This section gives you one final punch in the right direction toward creating your landing page. In Chapter 18, we provide you with a ten-point inspection list for your landing page and discuss how this list can be used if your landing page isn't performing as well as you want.

Chapter 19 then goes on to present ten surefire ways to increase your conversion rates. If your conversions are suffering, take a quick look through our list to find a solution to your landing page troubles.

Chapter 18

Ten-Point Landing Page Inspection

*F*rom creating our own landing pages and working with others to develop theirs, we've identified several factors that commonly hinder conversions. In no particular order, we include ten questions you can ask about your page to identify potential trouble areas on your site.

Keep in mind that we base our advice and tips on personal experience. You don't have to spend a long time online to find experts that give different advice than you find here. Why? Because a lot of landing pages are a bit of a gray area — more art than science, in other words — and the marketing strategies used for one demographic don't necessarily transfer to another. The best-case scenario is that you combine all the advice you see and then make your own ten-point inspection list.

To get you started, the following sections describe our ten-point inspection list.

Are You Effectively Using Audio Greetings and Background Music?

More and more landing page developers opt to use some form of audio greeting and background music. Are these effective? Well, that depends. Background music and sounds can be used effectively on some sites to get more feeling into it. This music can be an appeal to emotion; for example, using rock guitar riffs for a landing page selling snowboards or the sounds of ocean waves and seagulls when selling seaside condos. You can also use audio greetings as an appeal to trust by familiarizing yourself to the visitor.

All audio content really can go either way, though. Some demographics typically don't warm up to audio content like others do. Repetitive content you're forced to listen to every time you go to a landing page can be disastrous. If you use audio content, test whether it helps or hinders your conversions. One way to test whether your audio content works is to set up a focus group and get honest feedback. Another way is to split-test — use one landing page with sounds and music and leave the other without. Use your tracking software to determine the impact the audio content has.

With that, if you're running a landing page and want return customers and visitors, audio content can grow tiresome fast. Visitors can get sick of your catchy tunes or peppy greeting if they have to listen to it over and over. If you want that return business, be careful with redundant audio.

The More Testimonials, the Better, Right?

No doubt testimonials can have a huge impact on making visitors feel more secure about you and your product. However, split-testing on some client sites shows that there may be a limit to the number of testimonials that can be used effectively. (We review split-testing in Chapter 12.) Believe it or not, adding too many testimonials may actually decrease conversions. Who knows why this is — online shoppers are a fickle bunch. Assuming some testimonials help, just how many are too many? The only way to know for sure is to perform a split-test.

To make things even more complicated, you also have to consider the type of testimonial. The language used in the testimonial needs to appeal to your demographic. The best way is usually collecting many testimonials and then testing them. Sometimes a strategy of keeping a catalog of testimonials and then rotating them to make the site appear fresh works best.

One last thing on testimonials: Are they believable? Getting your mom to write a glowing review of your product may not carry the sale or build trust, not to mention fake testimonials raise some serious ethical questions. Testimonials need to be genuine and accurately reflect your demographic. As much as possible, make them specific; for example, include a picture, a full name, and a general location of the person in the testimonial — not just the initials or other minimal content. You don't want to appear as if you've been creating your own testimonials.

Have You Verified That Your Trust Elements Are in Place?

Conversion rates suffer if your trust elements aren't in place. *Trust elements* are those features used on a landing page that let the visitors know that you're on the up and up. This may include logos from professional affiliations, testimonials, and even a clear Return Policy. Trust elements make all the difference. Would you buy products or services online if you weren't sure that the site was legit and associated with established secure sites? Not convinced? Run a split-test that features one landing page with trust elements and one without. You may be surprised. (See Chapter 12 for more information on split-testing.)

Are Your Headings Crafted Carefully?

We spend countless hours researching, testing, writing, and rewriting headings because they're the first thing most visitors read when they arrive at your site. If the heading isn't working, the rest doesn't matter. When you inspect your landing page for trouble spots, pay close attention to those headings. The good news is that you can go to plenty of places to get inspiration for your headings. Many Web sites, such as Yahoo.com or CNN.com, use great teaser headings to get visitors to click. Read through a few of their news of the day headings. These headings encourage you to click and read the entire article. Check them out.

If you use a pay per click (PPC) campaign, consider matching the language of your ad to the language of your headings. This goes a long way in ensuring visitors that they've landed on the right page. For instance, if your ad includes World's Best Cat Litter, you may find that having *cat litter* in the heading really helps. Visitors know that they've found the site they wanted right away.

Have You Removed or Explained Any Jargon?

Landing pages and technology have a language all their own. We've seen headings, such as You're at This Page because of PPC Advertising. What? If you use a term in your writing, you need to explain the term, and if you have to explain a term, you're likely not speaking your demographics' language. Some developers lose track of their audience and speak in technical terms and jargon, which decreases your conversions.

Do You Have Any Urgent Language on Your Page?

A little bit of urgency goes a long way, such as Buy Now and Get a Second Free, or Order Now and Receive Free Shipping. Creating a realistic sense of urgency really helps the conversions. When you inspect your landing page, make sure you use urgent elements.

However, you need to walk a fine line here. If visitors feel rushed to the sale or sense that your calls for urgency aren't genuine, this urgent language can reduce conversions. For example, Order before Midnight, or the Price Goes Up and Buy Now, Only Two Left may cause visitors to leave your site without a conversion. Keep your calls to urgency genuine, because if not, they can actually decrease conversions.

Is the Price Right?

Price is a big one when you inspect your site. Many landing page developers simply pull a price out of the air and stick with it. Maybe your conversion problems can be traced directly to your listed price. For instance, should your price be $29.95 or $39.95?

Pricing is never random; test to see where customers are comfortable. If your price is too low, your visitors may not perceive value; but if your price is too high, they'll drift to another site. Two methods to price a product effectively include feedback from focus groups and split-testing.

Have You Conducted a Focus Group?

Inspecting your page is one thing, but having others inspect your page is quite another. Focus groups provide feedback that you may not otherwise get. Focus groups don't need to be elaborate, simply get 8–15 people together in the same room and listen to their feedback. We can't stress enough the benefits of using a focus group. Ideally, you get together a focus group before you release your landing page to work out the kinks and then again after your site's been up and running for some time.

Does Your Landing Page Look Like a Home Page?

You may be tempted to make your landing page more like a home page. Keep clear the distinction between the differences between a landing page and the home page. A *home* page is the introductory page to an entire Web site and typically has many elements and many pages from which you can navigate. A *landing* page doesn't have to be (and shouldn't be) all things to all people; it's more focused and dedicated to the purpose of conversions. With your landing page, remove all distracting or unneeded elements because distractions kill conversions. Remember, streamline your landing page to make conversions; remove elements that don't flow logically to the conversion page. Keep your message focused with the conversion goal always in mind.

Is Critical Information above the Fold?

Last but not least is fold talk (which we cover in even more detail in Chapter 4). Conversions are lost when critical information is below the *fold,* which is the area visitors are most likely going to read and explore. Every landing page developer needs to get the information in the fold right. Every area in the fold is prime real estate, the heading and the content chunks are all critical to keep your visitors on the page. You can find more information on writing content for the fold in Chapter 6.

You may want to test many other elements, such as checkouts, image placements, language used, colors, fonts, and more, when you inspect your landing page. All these elements need to be tested by you but also with split-testing and focus groups. Inspecting and updating your landing page often relies on the quality of the testing procedures you use.

Chapter 19

Ten Surefire Ways to Increase Conversion Rates

*T*his entire book is peppered with hints, tips, and tricks to get your landing page operational and make conversions. In this chapter, we condense all the info in this book to ten surefire ways to increase your conversions. If you were studying for an exam, this chapter would be your cram.

Keywords, Keywords, and Keywords

Your conversions ultimately suffer if your keywords aren't researched and tested. We dive deeper into keywords in Chapter 13, but remember, keywords provide the framework from which your advertising campaign is built. Choose the wrong keywords, and the game could be over before you begin. We recommend the following when it comes to keywords and the tools to use:

✔ **Research keywords and create a comprehensive keyword index.** A *keyword index* is a researched and documented list of associated keywords. Your keyword index needs to include your original keyword extrapolated to include related and associated keywords. From this index comes the language you use on your page. Use an online keyword tool, such as the Google AdWords Keyword Tool, as shown in Figure 19-1, or Wordtracker (at `www.wordtracker.com`). Coming up with the right keywords is all about the research.

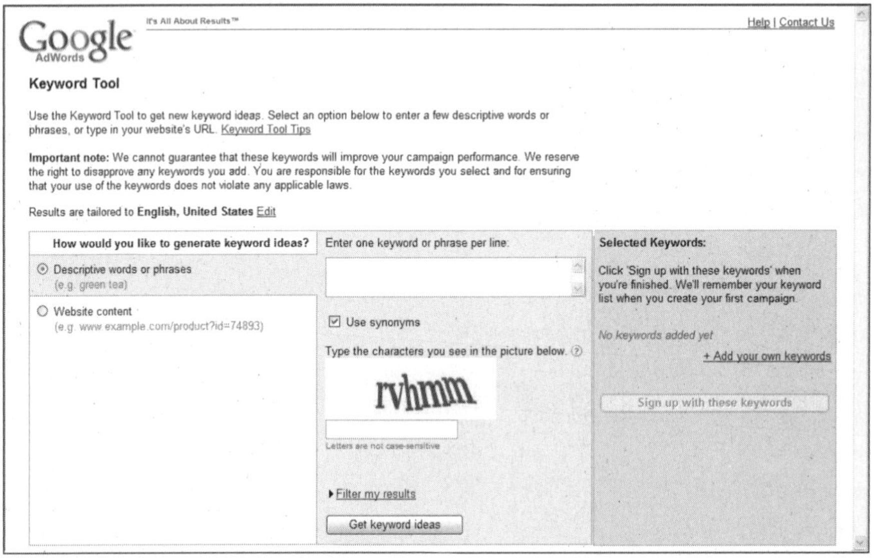

Figure 19-1:
The Google
AdWords
Keyword
Tool.

✔ **Think outside the keyword box.** Is the keyword *sight* or *site, shoe* or *shoes, long tail* or *short tail?* When choosing keywords, you need to broaden your scope. Look for common misspellings of words to incorporate, and research singular and plural uses of words and phrases. Synonyms are great to use; many tools, such as the Google AdWords Keyword Tool, allow you to search for these synonyms. Also, research the short-tail and long-tail keywords to use on your site. Short-tail keywords and long-tail keywords represent keyword phrases or more than a single keyword. We discuss these various types of keywords in Chapter 13.

✔ **Place keywords where they belong.** Placing keywords correctly on your landing page is very important, but where do they belong? Keywords in the URL are ideal, and keywords in the heading and first paragraph of your landing page are critical. Don't saturate your landing page with keywords to appeal to the search engines, though. This strategy makes the site search engine friendly but not easy to read for your visitors.

Remember that your site has to be reader-friendly. The amount of keywords on a page is referred to as *keyword density.* You can choose from many online utilities to test the keyword density of your page, including the SEO Chat Keyword Density Tool, as shown in Figure 19-2, at www.seochat.com/seo-tools/keyword-density.

Figure 19-2:
The
Keyword
Density Tool.

Be Up Front

Things that are hidden make your visitors suspicious. Everything on your site needs to be open and easy to find. This includes all pricing information, such as shipping, handling, product cost, and more.

Never hide fees. Don't spring any unpleasant surprises on your customers. Those that really want your product will be willing to pay that little extra in shipping — if they know about it in advance. Also important is to keep your shipping charges in line with your purchase price. Very few will pay a $12 shipping fee for a $10 product.

Place your Return Policy where it can be seen, often in the footer. By offering your Return Policy, guarantees, and other terms or conditions at the beginning of the purchase process, you show customers you have nothing to hide and that their purchase choice is safe with you. Don't forget a link to your Privacy Policy to help them feel safe ordering from you. Your customers want to see

- A clearly visible and friendly Return Policy.

- Product fees with no additional hidden costs.

- A detailed Privacy Policy that outlines what you do with personal information.

- An outlined Terms of Use Policy and a Terms of Sale Policy.

- A secure online transaction with HTTPS. Regular Web pages use *HTTP (HyperText Transfer Protocol).* Pages that require secure transactions use *HTTPS* in which *S* stands for *Secure.* This protocol adds security to the regular HTTP protocol.

Use the Fold Wisely

The fold, which we discuss in Chapter 4, is a critical part of your landing page's success. You ability to capture your visitor's attention in the fold can dictate your conversion success. Many elements can be in the fold, such as the heading, descriptive content, pictures, branding information, and more. Your fold has to entice your reader and keep her interested. This doesn't mean filling your fold area with graphics or Flash. Some things to remember when you create your fold are

- **Write for readers who just skim text.** The text in the fold area should be in *chunks* — text that's easy to read quickly but still gets across the message. Short, well-crafted paragraphs often work the best.

- **Watch out for page load times.** Keep images small and avoid Flash. A page that's slow to load sends visitors packing.

- **Write a catchy heading.** Headings are very important in the fold. They need to catch the reader's attention and at the same time, reflect the keywords you choose. They don't need to be flashy or use multiple colors. A simple black and white scheme with well thought-out text works well.

Develop Persuasive Content for Body Text

When it comes to writing the text for the body of your landing page, you need to be persuasive. Here are the three approaches you can incorporate into your main text to gather the reader's attention:

- ✔ **The ethical appeal:** A writer must first gain the audience's trust, and anything that contributes to this is an appeal to *ethos* (ethics). To achieve this trust, let your audience know that you have personal experience with the subject matter (such as, "I loved this product so much, I bought the company"). Also, cite the experts and use methodologically sound and recent statistics to gain your audience's respect.

- ✔ **The rational appeal:** While gaining the audience's trust, you need to engage them rationally. An appeal to *logos* (reason) is anything that requires the brain to engage. Any statement that uses cause-and-effect reasoning or any other logical reasoning device, such as a syllogism, is processed logically. Facts and statistics, for example, function as rational appeals. The bulk of a landing page's message uses rational appeals, not only to make the sale in the short-term, but also to maintain the customer's loyalty over the long-term.

- ✔ **The emotional appeal:** An appeal to *pathos* (emotion) is anything that plays upon the audience's emotions. This can be the text used and other elements, such as pictures or audio content. Be aware of the ethical considerations of the emotional appeals if you plan to appeal to emotion; be sincere.

Focus Your Efforts on the Customer

Okay, admittedly focusing your efforts on the customer sounds obvious, but it's often overlooked. Many developers impress with Flash and other elements that are neat but actually may get in the way of conversions. Make your landing page specific to your customer and then write for him. To do this, make a complete customer profile. The *customer profile* is a representation of your ideal visitor: what she's like, where she lives, what she has for breakfast, and so on. The more you understand about your ideal customer, the better you can create a landing page just for her.

You may think this sounds ridiculous, but you may be able to focus on your demographic better if you create a specific persona of your ideal visitor. Create a one page summary of his characteristics, likes, dislikes, geographical location, number of children, education, and so on. Give the person a name and create your landing page with him in mind. Doing so gives your marketing efforts a focus.

User-Friendly Layout

Your landing page needs to be as simple and as professional as possible. We include several strategies you can use to keep your landing page uncluttered while still providing the necessary information. Some of these strategies include

- **Using bulleted lists:** These are great for grabbing attention because
  - They're short.
  - They're easy to read.
  - The eyes are drawn to them when skimming a page.
  - They can get across your point quickly.
- **Using bold to emphasize certain words:** Eyes are drawn to the bold text unless it's used too often. If that happens, bold can be distracting and annoying.
- **Correcting grammatical and spelling errors:** Nothing is more distracting for readers than an overload of grammar errors and spelling misteaks.
- **Using short sentences and paragraphs:** Many online readers simply scan content. Lengthy text can turn off visitors. Plan for lazy readers.

Spend Time on Your Headings

Your headings, particularly the main heading in your fold, is the best chance you have to capture your visitor as soon as she hits your landing page. The heading needs to contain your keywords but also needs to engage your readers right way. We suggest taking the time to develop your skills at writing quality headings. Work and rework that heading until your get it right. Here are some suggestions:

- New Hair Loss Remedy
- Get the Latest Music Now
- How to Travel to Europe for Less Than $400
- Five Ways to Ease Back Pain
- Buy Now and Save
- 75 Percent Off Ladies Shoes
- Buy One Knife, Get a Second Free

Entice and Focus

Everyone likes a freebie! Attract your visitors into purchasing by sweetening the pot with free shipping, a free gift, or an unexpected discount. Your visitors will think twice about leaving if you offer a limited-time offer or a free gift they'd love. The following list features some examples:

- ✔ Buy Now, and Get a Second Free
- ✔ Free Shipping for the First 100 Customers
- ✔ Free Newsletter Just for Signing Up

You get the point: Enticing your visitors is all about the value add.

Be Visible

Can your visitors contact you? Do they know where your business is located? Placing your contact information on your landing page can have a significant impact on your conversion rates. Believe it or not, some unscrupulous people are on the Internet, and nobody wants to be tricked by one of these folks. Therefore, you need to distinguish your company as a legitimate business. Your contact information goes a long way to accomplishing this: Include your business address, e-mail address, fax number, phone number, and so on.

Focus on Gaining Visitor Trust

If visitors don't trust you, they won't buy from you. That's hardly a newsflash, but it's important to keep in mind. Don't give any reason to make visitors think you're a fly-by-night operation. To gain visitor trust, use your trust elements, which includes phrases like

- ✔ 100-Percent Guaranteed
- ✔ Your Privacy Is Our Concern
- ✔ We're Here 24/7 to Help You

Trust elements aren't just *your* words. One great trust element to include would be testimonials from other satisfied customers who trust *you*. Other trust elements to include are

- ✔ Professional registrations and affiliations
- ✔ Privacy policies
- ✔ Money back guarantees
- ✔ Secure transaction technologies
- ✔ Trust logos

Index

● **G** ●

● **H** ●

● T ●

Notes

Business/Accounting & Bookkeeping

Bookkeeping For Dummies
978-0-7645-9848-7

eBay Business
All-in-One For Dummies,
2nd Edition
978-0-470-38536-4

Job Interviews
For Dummies,
3rd Edition
978-0-470-17748-8

Resumes For Dummies,
5th Edition
978-0-470-08037-5

Stock Investing
For Dummies,
3rd Edition
978-0-470-40114-9

Successful Time
Management
For Dummies
978-0-470-29034-7

Computer Hardware

BlackBerry For Dummies,
3rd Edition
978-0-470-45762-7

Computers For Seniors
For Dummies
978-0-470-24055-7

iPhone For Dummies,
2nd Edition
978-0-470-42342-4

Laptops For Dummies,
3rd Edition
978-0-470-27759-1

Macs For Dummies,
10th Edition
978-0-470-27817-8

Cooking & Entertaining

Cooking Basics
For Dummies,
3rd Edition
978-0-7645-7206-7

Wine For Dummies,
4th Edition
978-0-470-04579-4

Diet & Nutrition

Dieting For Dummies,
2nd Edition
978-0-7645-4149-0

Nutrition For Dummies,
4th Edition
978-0-471-79868-2

Weight Training
For Dummies,
3rd Edition
978-0-471-76845-6

Digital Photography

Digital Photography
For Dummies,
6th Edition
978-0-470-25074-7

Photoshop Elements 7
For Dummies
978-0-470-39700-8

Gardening

Gardening Basics
For Dummies
978-0-470-03749-2

Organic Gardening
For Dummies,
2nd Edition
978-0-470-43067-5

Green/Sustainable

Green Building
& Remodeling
For Dummies
978-0-4710-17559-0

Green Cleaning
For Dummies
978-0-470-39106-8

Green IT For Dummies
978-0-470-38688-0

Health

Diabetes For Dummies,
3rd Edition
978-0-470-27086-8

Food Allergies
For Dummies
978-0-470-09584-3

Living Gluten-Free
For Dummies
978-0-471-77383-2

Hobbies/General

Chess For Dummies,
2nd Edition
978-0-7645-8404-6

Drawing For Dummies
978-0-7645-5476-6

Knitting For Dummies,
2nd Edition
978-0-470-28747-7

Organizing For Dummies
978-0-7645-5300-4

SuDoku For Dummies
978-0-470-01892-7

Home Improvement

Energy Efficient Homes
For Dummies
978-0-470-37602-7

Home Theater
For Dummies,
3rd Edition
978-0-470-41189-6

Living the Country Lifestyle
All-in-One For Dummies
978-0-470-43061-3

Solar Power Your Home
For Dummies
978-0-470-17569-9

Internet
Blogging For Dummies,
2nd Edition
978-0-470-23017-6

eBay For Dummies,
6th Edition
978-0-470-49741-8

Facebook For Dummies
978-0-470-26273-3

Google Blogger
For Dummies
978-0-470-40742-4

Web Marketing
For Dummies,
2nd Edition
978-0-470-37181-7

WordPress For Dummies,
2nd Edition
978-0-470-40296-2

Language & Foreign Language
French For Dummies
978-0-7645-5193-2

Italian Phrases
For Dummies
978-0-7645-7203-6

Spanish For Dummies
978-0-7645-5194-9

Spanish For Dummies,
Audio Set
978-0-470-09585-0

Macintosh
Mac OS X Snow Leopard
For Dummies
978-0-470-43543-4

Math & Science
Algebra I For Dummies
978-0-7645-5325-7

Biology For Dummies
978-0-7645-5326-4

Calculus For Dummies
978-0-7645-2498-1

Chemistry For Dummies
978-0-7645-5430-8

Microsoft Office
Excel 2007 For Dummies
978-0-470-03737-9

Office 2007 All-in-One
Desk Reference
For Dummies
978-0-471-78279-7

Music
Guitar For Dummies,
2nd Edition
978-0-7645-9904-0

iPod & iTunes
For Dummies,
6th Edition
978-0-470-39062-7

Piano Exercises
For Dummies
978-0-470-38765-8

Parenting & Education
Parenting For Dummies,
2nd Edition
978-0-7645-5418-6

Type 1 Diabetes
For Dummies
978-0-470-17811-9

Pets
Cats For Dummies,
2nd Edition
978-0-7645-5275-5

Dog Training For Dummies,
2nd Edition
978-0-7645-8418-3

Puppies For Dummies,
2nd Edition
978-0-470-03717-1

Religion & Inspiration
The Bible For Dummies
978-0-7645-5296-0

Catholicism For Dummies
978-0-7645-5391-2

Women in the Bible
For Dummies
978-0-7645-8475-6

Self-Help & Relationship
Anger Management
For Dummies
978-0-470-03715-7

Overcoming Anxiety
For Dummies
978-0-7645-5447-6

Sports
Baseball For Dummies,
3rd Edition
978-0-7645-7537-2

Basketball For Dummies,
2nd Edition
978-0-7645-5248-9

Golf For Dummies,
3rd Edition
978-0-471-76871-5

Web Development
Web Design All-in-One
For Dummies
978-0-470-41796-6

Windows Vista
Windows Vista
For Dummies
978-0-471-75421-3

Available wherever books are sold. For more information or to order direct: U.S. customers visit www.dummies.com or call 1-877-762-2974.
U.K. customers visit www.wileyeurope.com or call (0) 1243 843291. Canadian customers visit www.wiley.ca or call 1-800-567-4797.

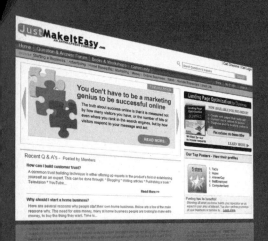

How $50 can make you an online success story

$50 may not sound like much, but the truth is, it could be the difference between being an online success or failure.
The secret is in how you use it.

Writing your own success story starts by learning the secrets of successful people and applying that knowledge to your own business. At JustMakeItEasy we understand what it takes to be an online success and are dedicated to bringing you that knowledge.

This is why, when you activate your exclusive Discount Offer at JustMakeItEasy.com, you will receive $50 in savings towards your continued education and access to other visitors through our Question and Answer forum.

AN ANTHILLPRESS COMPANY